THE

LIFE, CHARACTER, AND ACTS

OF

JOHN THE BAPTIST;

AND THE RELATION OF HIS

MINISTRY TO THE CHRISTIAN DISPENSATION.

BASED UPON THE JOHANNES DER TÄUFER OF L. VON ROHDEN

BY

WILLIAM C. DUNCAN, D. D.,

AUTHOR OF THE "HISTORY OF THE EARLY BAPTISTS," "PULPIT GIFT BOOK," "TEARS OF JESUS OF NAZARETH," ETC.

FIFTH EDITION: CORRECTED AND ENLARGED.

NEW YORK:
SHELDON & COMPANY, 115 NASSAU STREET.
NEW ORLEANS: WILLIAM DUNCAN.

1860.

Stereotyped by VINCENT DILL,
29 & 31 Beekman St., N. Y.

PREFACE.

The basis of the present treatise is a German monography written by L. Von Rohden, of Lübeck, and published by him in 1838, under the title "Johannes der Täufer in seinem Leben und Wirken, dargestellt nach den Zeugnissen der heiligen Schrift." The book is commended by Neander, in his Life of Christ, as "the production of a promising young theologian of Lübeck, and a work well fitted for general circulation."

The whole of the treatise of Von Rohden has been translated and is presented in this volume. Carefully elaborated additional matter, however, amounting to from one-third to one-half as much as the original work, has been incorporated into the body of the monography; and much has been given in the form of critical and explanatory notes, of which only a few, and those of little value, are found in Von Rohden. In this way the treatise has not only been adapted more completely to the wants of the general reader, but has also been converted into a convenient manual of reference for the use of such as are interested in biblical studies, on all points relating to the history and labors of John the Baptist.

In preparing the material which has been added, the

author has had constant reference to those critical authorities which treat most fundamentally of the various topics which have come under consideration. Among the writers to whom he is most indebted, whom indeed he has carefully consulted on every point of importance, he would mention J. G. E. Leopold, monography on John the Baptist, entitled "Johannes der Täufer, eine biblische Untersuchung" (published in 1825); Dr. A. Neander, Leben Jesu (Life of Jesus); Dr. G. B. Winer, Biblisches Realwörterbuch; Prof. J. L. Jacobi, in Kitto's Cyclop. of Bib. Literature; Drs. A. Tholuck and F. Lücke, Commentaries on the Gospel of John; and, in their New Testament Commentaries, Dr. S. T. Bloomfield, Henry Alford, M. A., and Drs. H. Olshausen, W. M. L. De Wette and H. A. W. Meyer.

This is the first book devoted exclusively to the treatment of the life and ministry of John the Baptist which has ever appeared in the English language. The subjects which it considers the author has attempted to discuss with thoroughness and with impartiality. If his treatise shall be found to fill a place hitherto untenanted in English religious literature, he will be abundantly rewarded for his labors.

W. C. D.

New Orleans, Sept. 15., 1852.

PREFACE TO THE FIFTH EDITION.

THE difficulty of treating, in a satisfactory manner, subjects which admit of so much discussion, and so much fair difference of opinion, as the Life, Character, and Acts of John the Baptist, can be known only to those who have attempted a similar kind of composition. No two candid writers, even of a like theological training, could, by any possibility, harmonize in all points in composing a complete Life of the Forerunner; if they should attempt, as is done in this volume, to determine the nature of his mission, and to describe his character, upon the basis of an exegetical examination of all the passages which are found relating to him in the New Testament. A general and not a minute correspondence of views, is all that can, in such a case, be properly expected. Those, then, of any system of religious belief, who hope to find all their own ideas of the Forerunner reproduced and reflected in this Treatise, will find their expectations disappointed. The book is the result of an independent, and, it is believed, thorough, examination of the topics discussed in its pages; and it was written with no other object or hope, than the discovery and disclosure of the truth as far as it relates to the Ministry of John the Baptist.

The Author is gratified by the distinguished marks of favor with which his work has been very generally received. Its popularity is sufficiently evinced by the fact that, within less than a year from its first publication, it has passed through four editions. The fifth edition now makes its appearance. In this, a number of typographical errors which found their way into the first and subsequent editions, has been corrected; and alterations have been made in portions of the book, where the original text was liable to be misconceived.

New pages of interesting and pertinent matter have been added, in several parts of the Treatise, particularly in the concluding chapter; and such changes and improvements have been made, as could be affected in a stereotyped work.

Since the publication of the first edition, there has appeared, in Germany, a work by Prof. Gams, of Hildesheim, on "John the Baptist in Prison," which discusses its subject in a space of 296 pages; and also a treatise of 41 pages, by B. Gademann of Münchberg, on the "Relation of John the Baptist to the Lord, according to the Evangelical Accounts"; published in the last number of Rudlebach and Guericke's "Zeitschift" for 1852.—From England, besides Huxtable on the "Ministry of S. John the Baptist," a thorough treatise, but reaching only to 67 pages (published in 1848),—the Author has received Dr. Wm. Bell's "Enquiry into the Divine Missions of John the Baptist and Jesus Christ,"—a work of 345 pages, published in the last century, which is wholly occupied with proving from the connection of John and Jesus with each other, that the mission of each must have been divine. It is not, therefore, properly speaking, a treatise on "the life and ministry" of the Baptist. He has obtained, moreover, Dr. George Horne's "Considerations on the Life and Death of John the Baptist"; a work published first about 1769, the aim of which is "to deduce moral and religious reflections from the circumstances and conduct of the Baptist." A "Portrait of John the Baptist," by Henry Belfrage, D.D.,—published in 1830 in Edinburgh, but unknown in 1852 to the Author of the present Treatise,—has also been received. The picture of the Forerunner presented in this neat duodecimo of 237 pages is a fine conception finely executed. A series of Articles on the Baptist, by Judge Joel Jones (of America), will be found in Vol. IV. of the "Jewish Chronicle."

October 1st, 1859.

TABLE OF CONTENTS.

PART FIRST: PRELIMINARY SKETCH.

Page

CHAPTER I: Condition of the Jewish People in a theocratic point of view at the time of the Birth of John, ... 9

CHAPTER II: Prophecies and Expectations regarding the Baptist, ... 22

PART SECOND: JOHN BEFORE HIS PUBLIC APPEARANCE.

CHAPTER I: Birth of the Baptist, ... 85

CHAPTER II: John's Family Relations, . . 52

CHAPTER III: Development of John and Preparation for his Public Ministry, ... 76

PART THIRD: MINISTRY OF JOHN BEFORE THE PUBLIC APPEARANCE OF CHRIST.

CHAPTER I: John's Preaching of Repentance, . . . 94

CHAPTER II: John's Baptism, ... 117

CHAPTER III: Effects of the Ministry of John among the People, ... 138

CHAPTER IV: The Baptism of Jesus, ... 150

PART FOURTH: JOHN AFTER THE PUBLIC APPEARANCE OF THE MESSIAH.

CHAPTER I: John's Testimony respecting Christ, . 172

CHAPTER II: The Disciples of the Baptist, . . . 191

Page

CHAPTER III: Reference of his Disciples to Christ, . 198

CHAPTER IV: Relation of the Baptism of John to that of the Disciples of Christ and to Christian Baptism, ... 205

PART FIFTH: CLOSE OF THE BAPTIST'S MINISTRY.

CHAPTER I: John's Imprisonment, ... 224

CHAPTER II: The Baptist's Doubts in Prison, and his Mission of Inquiry to Jesus, . 233

CHAPTER III: John's Death.—Glance at his Character and his Importance for the Development of the Kingdom of God, 253

PART FIRST.

'RELIMINARY SKETCH.

CHAPTER I.

CONDITION OF THE JEWISH PEOPLE IN A THEOCRATIC POINT OF VIEW, AT THE TIME OF THE BIRTH OF JOHN.

FOR four hundred years had the voice of the prophets been silent, when the man was born who was to uplift it for the last time, and who, as the closing point of the whole Old Testament theocracy, was to exhibit that theocracy in its highest brilliancy, ere it was extinguished forever. Only so long as they needed constant warning, correction and punishment, that they might not fall away from the worship of the true God, which had been enjoined upon them from of old, and engage in the enticing idol-worship of the surrounding nations, only so long had God conversed with his people by men specially inspired. When, however, the rigid punishment of the seventy years' exile had purified the nation, and had grounded them immovably in the faith on one God, Jehovah ceased to make known his will by special interpreters. The time had now come in which the Jewish nation was to atone for its great guilt by lasting repentance and by meek and trustful submission, and when it was, by means of an assiduous examination of its holy books, to prepare itself more and more for understanding the advent of him who should fulfill the law and the prophets ; when it should, through the agency of the numerous storms which shook the state politic, its grievous civil disorders and servile subjection to a foreign yoke, be aroused to an increasing attention to itself, to a knowledge of its sinfulness, and to a longing after a spiritual deliverer ; when, finally, a belief in the one God of the Jews should spread itself from that nation yet farther among other people, and constitute a firm connecting link for the later proclamation of the gospel among the heathen.

While, however, this last object was completely attained, by means of the varied connections formed by the Jews with heathen nations, by means of the partial subjection of Palestine to the Romans, and by means of the dispersion and settlement of a great number of Jews in heathen lands,—as was shown to be true, in particular, on the first proclamation of the gospel by the Apostles, when the proselytes who embraced the faith did so more readily not only than the heathen, but even more readily than the Jews themselves,—the fulfillment of the divine views respecting the agency of the Israelites themselves in proclaiming the gospel, was limited to a very small number of that people. A part of the nation, either reduced to despair at the sight of continued political troubles, and in view of the ignominious subjection of the holy people, surrendered by degrees their belief in a coming deliverer, or, on account of the long delay in his advent, doubted respecting the personality of the promised Messiah, and, spiritualizing the prophecies, referred them to the light and salvation which were to be spread abroad by the Jewish people, conceived as an individual, among all heathen nations. Others, on the contrary, held on with unshaken determination to the expectation of a personal Messiah who was soon to appear ; but, as their mind and thoughts were directed only to earthly happiness, to deliverance from the hard yoke under which they sighed, to riches and honor, there was formed among them a conception of the promised Redeemer corresponding to these expectations. They thought of him as a mighty theocratic king after the likeness of David, who would with conquering arm prostrate to the dust all the enemies of the holy people, and create for them a power and dominion over the whole earth such as had never before been known ; to whom every knee should bow after an earthly manner, and who should shower down upon his subjects all earthly goods without cessation and without measure.

While external political commotions, considered favorable to their views by the one class, but thought destructive of their expectations by the other, produced among the people either a stupid indifference to all promises, which they supposed they needed no longer, or gave birth to utter hopelessness or to distorted hopes,—the study of the sacred writings wrought out, among the majority, a knowledge opposed to that revealed from on high. One class of minds remained firm in their adherence to the letter of the Old Testament, without penetrating to its spiritual sense, busied themselves with trifling interpretations and with making onerous additions to the law, believing that they could obtain wisdom by means of insipid mystifications of its written characters, and so obscured the clear sense of holy writ by their peculiar conceits that they could no longer find their way out of the labyrinth of their own statutes to the simple words of the Lord. A second class, observing the indiscretion of the former, contended indeed for the written revelation, apart from all human additions or admixtures ; but they gave themselves little trouble, or they understood not how, to search into the inner meaning of what was written, and, through their indifference towards all religion, in particular to all of a higher character, passed by the prophets especially with indifference, if they did not reject them altogether; while they interpreted every part of Scripture according to its fleshly sense, and, adopting from one passage whatever was pleasing to their ears, endeavored to make the rest conform to their extorted interpretation. Naturally enough, neither mystic nor cabalistic speculations, united with the most absurd literal interpretations, nor yet an obstinate adherence to the written words in opposition to all human explanations, and its accompanying stupid ignorance of the meaning of all which went beyond ordinary earthly, nay, even animal, wants and enjoyments, could be made the means of leading the people to a knowledge of the true condition of their hearts, which was, in fact, the real cause of all the mournful calamities which, falling one after another upon the Jewish nation, were specially intended to break its hard-heartedness as with an iron hammer, and to bring the people to a consciousness of their own sinfulness and of the necessity of a deliverer from their internal enemy. External morality and propriety of conduct were, with most, the object of their strivings; on the attainment of which they imagined that they had performed their whole duty, and sufficiently assured themselves of the favor of God, especially if, in addition to the practice of outward morality, they recognized him with their mouths as the true and living Jehovah. Those, on the other hand, who looked with eagerness for the coming of their earthly Messiah, supposed, in accordance with their material conceptions respecting him and the divine intention regarding themselves, that they, as legitimate descendants of Abraham, had an inalienable right to share in his glorious dominion. It did not occur to them to doubt whether a fleshly descent from Abraham would be sufficient; for they scarcely imagined that a condition wholly different would be required for entrance into the Messianic kingdom.

The current opinion among the Jews at the birth of Christ, and for some time previous to his coming, was that the Messiah would be a mere temporal ruler, a king who would reign over not only the Israelites but the whole world. This opinion was held not merely by the common people, but by most of the Pharisees and lawyers of the nation. It was grounded upon such passages of the Old Testament as Ps. 2: 2., 6—8., Jer. 23: 5, 6., Zech. 9: 9, 10. This expectation is spoken of by Josephus, *Jewish War*, 6. 5. 4., where he says that his countrymen were chiefly induced to undertake the contest which ended in the destruction of Jerusalem, by "an ambiguous oracle which was found also in their sacred writings, that 'about that time one from their country should become ruler of the inhabitable earth.'" Suetonius, also, and Tacitus, both heathen writers, bear testimony to the prevalence of this expectation throughout the entire East; the former of whom says (*Vespas.* c. 4.): "There had been spread abroad throughout the entire East an ancient and fixed opinion that it was in accordance with the decrees of the Fates that the Jews should go forth at that time and take possession of the world;"* while the latter remarks (*Hist.* v. 13.): "Many were persuaded that there was contained in the ancient records of the priests a prediction that the East would at that very time acquire strength, and that proceeding forth from Judea they

* Percrebruerat Oriente toto vetus et constans opinio, esse in fatis ut eo tempore Judæi profecti rerum potirentur.

would take possession of the world."* We find accordingly that the less spiritual of those who acknowledged Jesus to be the Messiah desired, while he was yet living, to proclaim him king (Jno. 6 : 15. coll. Matt. 21 : 8, 9.). Yet together with this fundamental error they entertained other ideas of the Messiah, some of which were more correct ; as, for instance, that he would be born at Bethlehem, of the line of David, but of obscure parents (Jno. 7 : 42. coll. Is. 11 : 1., Jer. 23 : 5., Mic. 5 : 2.) ; that he would perform great miracles (Jno. 7 : 31.) ; and that he would never die (Jno. 12 : 34. coll. Ps. 110 : 4., Dan. 7 : 14.).

In this manner was the wilderness created in which a way was now to be built for the Lord by the preaching of the new-commissioned prophet ; but the quagmires of human error and corruption were here evidently too deep, and the ruins and rubbish of selfish and self-sufficient wisdom and justice heaped up too densely, to permit a way for the entrance of the Lord into the hearts of the people to be prepared very soon, and, in most cases, by any means whatsoever. Above all, that cold-hearted sect that is known under the name of Sadducees, which, carrying to the utmost extreme its opposition to the human arbitrary additions to holy writ which were in vogue among the sect of the Pharisees, either received the doctrine of Moses in dead orthodoxy, and would not recognize the representation of it given by God himself in the prophets, because it was foreign to their feelings and unintelligible, or, in general, they allowed what was written to remain written, and suffered it to have no further control over or influence upon their hearts ; and so, walled up within their own cold

* Pluribus persuasio inerat, antiquis sacerdotum litteris contineri, eo ipso tempore fore ut valesceret Oriens, profectique Judæa rerum potirentur.

intellectual wisdom, they could only laugh scornfully and shrug their shoulders at the intelligence and demands which John was to bring, and of which they had not the remotest conception.

Just as little could the Pharisees, with their fleshly expectations of the Messiah,—certain as they thought themselves to be of sharing in his kingdom,—with their external holiness constantly displayed before the eyes of the people, and with the punctilious conscientiousness with which they fulfilled, in public, the very letter of the divine law, and every commandment of their own or their forefathers' invention (for it is obvious that it is not difficult to fulfill the *letter* of the law externally), conceive how repentance and forgiveness of sin should be preached to *them;* and when, in addition to this, they were conscious, as the greater number of them was, of their endeavors to deceive God and men, their pride and their lust after sin were altogether too great to permit them to acknowledge their wickedness and their need of repentance and salvation; and, in consequence, hardening themselves with haughty contempt, and therefore hardened by God, they passed, unmoved, by the man who was sent to call their attention to their true condition, and to inform them what they needed in order to be made partakers of the coming salvation (cp. Luke 7: 30.).

Meanwhile, however, there were also some among the Pharisees, as we learn from the gospel history, who thought seriously within themselves of their sanctification, and who strove with uprightness to fulfill the law in every point, and hoped thereby to assure themselves of the divine favor. Even these recognized, at first, only the external side of the divine commandments, and had not yet penetrated to their internal and spiritual meaning; they too had not yet attained to a right understanding of the real condition of their own hearts, which was the root of their sinfulness; they also placed too much reliance upon the performance of external observances, ceremonies, and rites; but they still earnestly desired, while treading the wrong way, to discover the right; and they only needed to have their eyes gradually, or, as oftener happened, suddenly opened, and they would at once perceive, when undeceived respecting these external ceremonies and made acquainted with their own high destiny, the folly of such outward observances, and would be brought to a knowledge of the Saviour. From among these the voice of the forerunner might and afterwards did win many to the Lord.

There was still another sect among the Jews of that time; but they pertained less to the sphere of the labors of the Baptist, on account of their seclusion and wide removal from the theatre of religious and political events then occurring. These were the Essenes, a company of men who, having actually reached a consciousness of their great spiritual necessities, had withdrawn from the vortex of the world and its false hypocritical strivings, and established themselves in the region beyond the Red Sea; where they passed a life devoted to God in quiet contemplation, and, like the nobler mystics of all times, sought to be wholly absorbed in God and in his revelation. Among these pious people, one might suppose, would John's proclamation of the true salvation which was about to appear, have been followed by the most important consequences; and, in point of fact, their former mode of life proved for many of them a transition step towards Christianity; but others again were so much occupied with their theosophic speculations, expected so confidently to find in these their highest happiness, were so proud of their virtue, and so contemptuous in their treatment of those who, in their estimation, were far inferior to them in morality as well as in knowledge, that they were unable to tear themselves away from their imaginary felicity, in order to place themselves on a level with the despised populace, and were unwilling to strive anew with the severest self-denial to obtain nothing better than what they were also to receive. This overvaluation, therefore, of their own peculiar maxims and of their own piety, led them away from rather than towards the Redeemer.

Since by far the greatest portion of those whose tendencies have just been described came to the preaching of John with dumb ears and hardened hearts, one might conclude that neither he nor his more distinguished successor could have produced any considerable change in the religious condition of the Jewish people. And such in truth would have been the result, had there not been found, besides those hearts which were entangled in unbelief or bigotry, in indifference or anxiety, yet others, confessedly a small number, who received with trust and so much the more joyfully the word of God, believed his prophecies, and were led from a right understanding of their own character to a very nearly correct knowledge of the predictions respecting the Messiah which are recorded in the Old Testament. We speak not here of the mass of the common people, who, lending themselves to every impression, as they heard gladly all that was new, listened with pleasure also to the discourses and exhortations of the Baptist, acknowledged him as a prophet and spread abroad his fame, but, for the most part, without suffering his words to find a deep entrance into their minds, and without doing what he commanded. Even if, at times, they were struck for the moment with the truth of his preaching, even if they were filled for a season with good resolutions, they permitted not what they had received with half a heart, if not with half an ear, to take deep root in their soul ; for the next new impression would scatter the building, yet scarcely begun, in total ruin ; the next new temptation would summon all their sinful desires and passions once more from their fresh-made grave. These were not they out of whom the exhortations and announcements of the Baptist could prepare a susceptible and fertile soil from which the seed he sowed would joyfully spring forth and produce abundant fruit.

We refer rather to another smaller circle of souls whose names were written in the book of life, who did actually, in accordance with the will of God, let the great sufferings of their time serve as a means of making them more attentive to their own personal condition, of leading them to seek in themselves for the causes of those troubles which they at least so patiently endured, and of causing them, in consequence, to begin rooting out the evil that was within them before they busied themselves with the improvement of their political condition. These must soon have come to the conviction that evil was far too deeply rooted in their hearts, its poison had diffused itself far too widely in their veins, for them to stifle it by their own strength, or for anything external to be able to cast it out ; and thus had they been led by their feeling of necessity to a longing for a Messiah who could, first and before all, free them from their spiritual misery, and lead them back to peace with themselves and with God. Guided by their own necessities and by the knowledge obtained from their own condition, and enlightened by the divine Spirit, obtained in answer to their prayers, they came now with altogether different sentiments to an examination of the holy Scriptures, especially of the books of the prophets. They soon discovered, in promises given before, long before, just such a Messiah announced as they desired to behold; and, though ideas of the earthly greatness and royalty of him that was expected mingled with more correct conceptions in their but partially enlightened minds, redemption from the guilt of their sins remained always the main subject of their thoughts and expectations. Right well, therefore, did they understand John; and right gladly did they receive the embassy which proclaimed to them the true and longed-for Messiah. At a later period, it could not have been difficult for them to become better acquainted with the true end of Christ's existence, and to yield, one after another, as they did, their erroneous opinions respecting his earthly domination, without surrendering in any degree their faith in him as the only true Redeemer.

The number of this class was small, only such belonging to it whose minds were most deeply impressed with a feeling of their religious necessities; and even these entertained among their more correct ideas the additional false expectation that Christ would be a temporal sovereign. The disciples of Jesus themselves, in despite of all the instruction which they had received to the contrary during their intercourse with their divine teacher, did not give up their hopes of his restoring Israel to earthly grandeur, until after the resurrection (Acts 1 : 6. coll. Matt. 20 : 20, 21., Luke 24 : 21.). It cannot be expected, therefore, that the other pious worthies of the nation who also cherished comparatively true views respecting the Messiah, should have been able to divest themselves of their incorrect conceptions, and have looked for a prince whose reign should be wholly spiritual. It is a singular fact, however, and one worthy of being noted, that the Samaritans, a people of heathen origin intermixed with Hebrews, who received the Pentateuch (or, Five Books of Moses), entertained ideas respecting the Messiah which were more consonant with the truth than those of the Jews themselves. The political element was not at all mingled with their expectations ; for they looked merely for a prophet who should inculcate religious truth, and convert the people from their sins unto holiness. Their conceptions of the Messiah, whom they appear to have expected under the name *Shaheb*, or *Taheb* (*Conversor*, i. e. *Converter)*, were probably based upon Deut. 18 : 15., with reference also, perhaps, to such passages as Gen. 12 : 3., 18 : 18., 22 : 18., 26 : 4., 28 : 14. ; but though they seem to have been correct as far as they went, they were, of course, quite meagre and imperfect (Jno. 4 : 25. ff.). This expectation of theirs served as a preparation for their reception of the doctrines of Christianity, both as taught by Jesus himself (Jno. 4 : 39, 40.), and as proclaimed by the Apostles (Acts 8 : 5. ff., 9 : 31., 15 : 3.).*

Of these elements, which existed in about the same proportions, with greater or less gradations and shades of difference, in general among the whole Jewish people (and, perhaps, every-

* There exists at this day a remnant of the Samaritan people. They are reduced to a few families, dwelling in Nablus, the ancient Shechem, whence they go three times a year to worship, as did their ancestors, on Mount Gerizim. They yet retain and make use of the Mosaic law, in the form known as the Samaritan Pentateuch ; but the language which they employ in their ordinary transactions is the Arabic. They still adhere to the Mosaic institutions ; they rigidly observe the Sabbath ; celebrate only the Mosaic feasts ; observe the year of jubilee ; believe firmly in the unity of God ; allow no image of Jehovah ; practice circumcision and holy lustrations ; believe in angels and the resurrection, and annul marriage only according to the prescriptions of the Mosaic law. (Winer, *Realwörterbuch*, Art. Samaritaner). For further information regarding these modern Samaritans, see Robinson, *Bibl. Researches*, vol. 3. p. 96–136, and the account of Mr. Fisk in the *Amer. Miss. Herald* for 1824.

where, and at all times), was the multitude composed to which John was to proclaim the approaching Saviour. For all was his appearance alike necessary ; the slothful and sleeping were to be aroused from their dreaming ; self-blinded religionists and hypocrites were to be exposed in their true colors ; those who were running to no purpose in pursuit of a false object were to have their fruitless and hasty endeavors exhibited before their eyes ; the proud in their self-made justice were to be made weak in their confidence ; while those who were hoping in quiet and struggling on in the path of rectitude, were to be filled with joy and introduced to him who should prove to them their all in all. Thus, in the sending of John, God gave unto all an opportunity to gain clear information respecting themselves and the coming Messiah ; and those who were deaf to his word and hardened their hearts, had, therefore, no valid excuse for their guilt. This work of God's was one of divine mercy ; but, as is always the case in the dealings of his providence, it proved a curse and a witness against those who proudly turned their backs upon the invitation, and let it pass them with indifference.

CHAPTER II.

PROPHECIES AND EXPECTATIONS REGARDING THE BAPTIST.

As the last great prophet of the old covenant exhibits to us many other peculiarities in the circumstances of his appearance which differ widely from those of the other prophets, so also is he the only one among them all who was announced to the people by a special pre-nunciatory prophecy, by which he was, as it were, legitimated. Since the prophets had been silent during so long a period, the expectation of such an one as John and the remembrance of what was to be his peculiar character, had, it may easily be imagined, almost entirely disappeared from among the nation. The olden time had passed away, and the new was not qualified to estimate at their full value the honors and rights of the prophets; and on this account it was quite necessary that a special divine declaration should indicate the appearance of the last of the prophets, who was to be separated by so great a lapse of time from his predecessors, and should keep alive among the people an expectation of his coming. Independently of this, the fulfillment of the prophecy respecting the Baptist was intended to be, on account of the close connection of this event of national interest with the coming of the Messiah, a sign and a proof (*Heb.* אוֹת) of the approaching fulfillment of those other important Messianic promises; in order that, by means of this notable occurrence, the unbelieving might be convinced of the truth of God's word, and that believers, having their attention drawn to the significance of the times, might prepare themselves to receive the Lord in a becoming manner. On this account, it would seem, then, must Malachi, with whom the brilliant series of the prophets was brought to a close, have made mention, at the end of his prophecy (4 : 5, 6.), of the forerunner who was to prepare the way of the Lord.

It may, indeed, be doubted, at first thought, whether that prophecy really refers to John ; for the forerunner there mentioned is to precede the great and terrible day of the Lord, and to arouse the people to repentance (of which repentance, it may be remarked, only a single individualizing lineament is there drawn, namely, the re-establishment of unity in families, which, naturally, cannot exist apart from other happy influences, but is mentioned in that connection as one only among the blessings which were to flow from the universal re-establishment of love and friendship, and, therefore, of an entirely new spirit among men), in order that the Lord might not be compelled, on his coming, to destroy the whole land as one accursed and obnoxious to condemnation. Now the first appearance of Christ was by no means a coming to judgment, and, in particular, it was not a grand and fear-inspiring advent. The reference in this passage of Malachi appears, therefore, to pertain rather to the second, yet future, advent of the Messiah, and to the precursor then to be expected. It is to be noted, however, on the one hand, that there is no precise distinction to be recognized in any part of the Old Testament between these two appearances of Christ. Events which to the spiritual eye appear perspectively near to the view, are conceived and represented as actually connected ; and hence we find the Messiah described in the prophets, now as a powerful and fear-inspiring king, now as a lowly and despised servant of God ; and his appearance spoken of, now as a day of terror and revolu tion, now as drawing near amid a calm and cheerful peace. What can only be spiritually understood of his first coming, and is literally perceptible externally in his second, is conceived of as unfolding itself in a single and undivided appearance. It must be observed, on the other hand, that there actually exists so intimate a connection between the first and the second advent of Christ, with respect to the judgment, that the two might have been very suitably united and treated as one by Malachi. Whoever does not believe upon the coming Saviour, is already condemned by him, and receives his punishment without delay; he who hails him with joy, is justified, and his reward tarries not. The judgment begins with the first appearance of Christ, though it may be not at all visible to the bodily eye; and, so far, this first appearance may with justice be called the great and terrible day of the Lord. One must here, as everywhere in the prophets, understand well how to separate the moral drapery and ornament in which they are clothed, from the spiritual contents of the prophetic representations.

Even after this difficulty in the prophecy of Malachi has been removed, there yet remains another; for the promised forerunner is called Elijah (without doubt, because he, like the great Tishbite Elijah, should arouse a race which had become perverted and had fallen away from God, to repentance, and should work in the spirit and with the power of Elijah, Luke 1 : 17.); and yet John denies expressly that he is the promised Elias (Jno. 1 : 21.). This passage would in truth be very difficult to understand, did we not possess in other parts of the New Testament a complete explanation, according to which John is really intended in this prophecy of Malachi's; from which circumstance we are obliged to conclude that John answered his interrogators in the negative in an altogether peculiar sense.

In the very announcement of the birth of the Baptist by the angel (Luke 1 : 17.), we find a most pointed reference to the passage in Malachi, and one which throws light upon the question now under consideration. He is here spoken of as one who shall go before the Lord "in the spirit and power of Elias ;" from which we are allowed, if we feel so inclined, to draw the conclusion that Malachi in his prophecy means that a man *like* Elias, and not Elias in person, should be the precursor of the Messiah. According to this entirely legitimate explanation, the forerunner is called Elias in this passage of Malachi just as in other prophecies the Messiah is called David, in which there is evidently no thought of the personal re-appearance of that monarch (Jer. 30 : 9., Ezek. 34 : 23., Hos. 3 : 5.). In this sense may Christ's declaration that John was the expected Elias (Matt. 11 : 14., 17 : 12.) be understood ;* though, it may be, as we shall see further on, that it is to be taken in a somewhat different and higher acceptation. Furthermore, Mark introduces the passage as a proof that John's appearance was made in accordance with the intention of God (1 : 2.) ; he cites it, indeed, as if it stood in Isaiah, but this inexactness arose probably from the fact that the passage of a similar bearing which follows in Mark, was borrowed from Isaiah, and the evangelist wished to make use of the former, whether conscious at the time or not of its different connection, as an introduction to and commentary upon the latter. Be this as it may, no difference results in the main point under consideration.

Finally, we have the positive explanation of Christ himself (Matt. 11 : 10.), that John is the one to whom the passage

* Such is the view of Tholuck, *Com. on John*, Kaufman's Eng. trans. 2d N. Y. ed. p. 79.

refers ; and, in Matt. 17 : 10. ff., and Mark 9 : 11. ff., he speaks in such a way of the promised Elias, that, as Matthew says, his disciples understood him to designate John as that individual. After the brilliant transfiguration which took place upon the mount, the glorification of Jesus, his disciples,—who, relying on the passage in Malachi, supposed that now, since Elias had again appeared, the glory of the Lord of which Malachi speaks, must openly reveal itself,—asked him, in substance, the following question : "How stands the case now with that prophetic declaration which the scribes have ever in their mouths, that the proof that Jesus cannot be the true Messiah is the fact that Elias must first precede the royal advent ?" They expected that Jesus would answer them : "Yes, now have you seen Elias, and now too will be revealed the fullness of the glory of the Son of God." Our Lord, however, whose object it was to show them more and more the necessity of his sufferings and death, of which he had already spoken, replied to the following effect : "It is true that Elias shall come first and bring all into readiness for the reign of Christ, but how can you reconcile with this view yet other expressions of Scripture which declare that Christ must suffer and be treated with contumely ? If these expressions are consonant with the truth, as cannot be denied, and if Christ must undergo many sufferings, another Elias different from him whom you expect as the precursor of his royalty, must appear, or rather, Elias must appear in different form from what you anticipate ; and, in fact, he *has* already actually appeared, and has suffered and died as the type of his master." In giving this representation, Jesus evidently had reference to the imprisonment and death of John the Baptist.

On examining the words of Christ, it cannot escape our notice that he does not expressly assert that John is the Elias promised in Malachi ; but, on the contrary, he appears to admit some difference between the two, notwithstanding their general resemblance. This difference he expresses yet more distinctly in another passage (Matt. 11 : 14.), where he declares indeed that John is Elias, but adds the limitation, "if ye will receive it." The identity of the two persons, therefore, is not here unconditionally asserted, but only in a certain aspect of the case ; so that we are not constrained to believe that they were one and the same, but may admit it or not, as may seem to us more probable. The question now presents itself, how are we to explain the circumstance that, though the passage in Malachi has an evident reference to John, as Christ himself acknowledged, he does not, nevertheless, declare in express terms that John was Elias, and the additional circumstance that John, for his part, altogether denies the reference.

We must here revert to what has been already remarked respecting the character of prophecy in general, and of this prophecy in particular. Malachi did not distinguish between the two appearances of Christ ; but conceiving of the two as one, he has represented it as being preceded by the forerunner. The question then arises, whether, if the two advents be united, the prophecy alludes only to a precursor of the first, or also to one of the second appearance. We have, in fact, no ground to deny the latter supposition ; nay, since the first coming of Christ is in a certain sense only a type of his second and yet future coming, we have rather reason to expect that a forerunner will in like manner usher in the future advent, under circumstances more remarkable, it is probable, than those amid which the first precursor appeared. In accordance with this view, John the Baptist constituted only a partial and typical fulfillment of this prophecy regarding Elias ; but it must be left undecided whether this Elias shall be really the Tishbite raised again to life, or only a prophet *like* him. If this hypothesis be received as the truth, we can easily explain why Christ referred to John as Elias only in a limited sense,—because, in fact, a yet more perfect Elias was to be expected ; and why John himself replied so pointedly in the negative when he was asked whether he was Elias,—because he knew full well that this prophecy was fulfilled in him, though really, only partially, and that he was by no means the true Elias ; though we are not to conclude from this, what cannot be true, that John thought of Christ's second coming. The Baptist, however, gave no additional explanation of the sense in which he responded to the question in the negative ; because it would have been, on the one hand, something altogether foreign from his earnest straight-forward prophetic character, to which a brief yes and no were appropriate, to enter upon expositions of this kind ; and because, on the other hand, such was the object which they sought who put the interrogatory, that he deemed them unworthy of any further explanation.

The Pharisees evidently intended to assure themselves, as soon as possible, of the forerunner of a Messiah accommodated to their fleshly way of thinking, to draw him over to their side, that he might secretly play into their hands ; and hoped by means of this examination to win him over to their interest. In order to prevent them from instituting such a formal examination of his claims as a prophet, John must have abruptly responded in the negative. But he had also an altogether special reason for giving them a distinct denial ; and this was the fact that an expectation was probably entertained by the people, as seems to be proved also by the questions put to

Christ by his disciples,—an expectation based on the passage in Malachi, which they understood in its most literal sense,—that the Tishbite would actually appear in person as one who had arisen from the dead (cp. Sirach 48 : 5. ff.). If the question were put to him in this sense, he must likewise have responded, as he did, in the negative. Those who had been impelled to him from a feeling of their internal necessities, did not on their part suffer themselves to be dispirited by this denial, since the positive explanation of his calling, by the Baptist, in accordance with another passage of the Old Testament, which we have yet to examine more closely, knit them more firmly into his companionship. In any event, the following truths are firmly established by our examination of the passage in Malachi : It really refers to John, and is fulfilled, though not completely, in him ; and the forerunner must be conceived of as preceding the first advent of Christ, not only because the mention of his coming in the prophecy is general, but because, in particular, the passage is unquestionably referred to John in the New Testament, and the name Elias is conferred upon him, with, however, as has been seen, a not insignificant limitation. We have, accordingly, in these verses of Malachi, a direct prophecy, if not of the person of John, at least of his office as the precursor of Christ ; and in the comparison between him and the Tishbite Elijah we have an indication of his personal character and of the relation in which he stood to his time.

We have, moreover, a positive explanation of John's respecting himself and his calling (Jno. 1 : 23.), which, in like manner, refers us back to a prophetic passage in the old Testament. The same passage, Isa. 40 : 3–5, is employed by the three evangelists, in the beginning of their respective narrativès (Matt. 3 : 3., Luke 3 : 4–6., Mark 1 : 3.), as a proof not only of the propriety, but also of the necessity, of the Baptist's appearance. In the place in question the subject is the deliverance of Israel from great trouble : Jehovah announces to his people an end of sufferings, and sends a messenger before him in order to prepare a way for him who was soon to appear as a deliverer, and to make ready for his advent. Without doubt, the prophet, in this passage, speaks of himself as this ambassador and messenger, who is, in this and the following discourses, to proclaim and prepare a way for the coming of the Lord. Neither the Baptist nor the evangelists mean to assert that the forerunner there alluded to is actually identical with John ; though Matthew seems to declare it when he says : "this is he that was spoken of by the prophet Esaias," etc. ; while Mark ("as it is written in the prophets,") and Luke ("as it is written in the book of the words of Esaias,") would evidently only indicate by the citation the necessity of the advent of John. Matthew, however, only intends to say that this John is the complete realization of that forerunner spoken of in Isaiah, which latter can only be regarded as the type of the former, just as the advent of the Lord in Israel, there described, is only an image of his advent in the flesh. So conceived as a type, this passage is peculiarly applicable in the connection in which it stands in the evangelists. As the coming of the Lord spoken of in the prophet, was now realized in its highest sense, so must the coming of the forerunner be also realized in its relative highest sense ; and, therefore, John could with entire correctness declare that in him was fulfilled the prophecy contained in the passage under consideration. The passage, therefore, must be classed among those to which a double application may be assigned, primarily to events near at hand, but secondarily to others yet, at the time of the prophecy, far removed in the latter,—the former being, so to speak, typical of the former. So must the citation be explained, unless we have recourse to the not very satisfactory expedient of "accommodation," and paraphrase with the "later Commentators" alluded to by Bloomfield (on Jno. 1: 23.), "What the prophet (namely, Isa. 40 : 3.) there says, *holds good of me;* you will find there, what will be a sufficient description of my person and office." The original historical reference is evidently such as has been stated.* Alford, however, remarks: "The primary and literal application of this prophecy to the return from captivity is very doubtful.. If it ever had such an application, we may safely say that its predictions were so imperfectly and sparingly fulfilled in that return, or anything which followed it, that we are necessarily directed onward to its greater fulfillment,—the announcement of the kingdom of Christ."

How it happened that all three evangelists made use of this citation, is easily explicable when we consider this evident connection between that prophecy and the appearance of the Baptist. It had, no doubt, become customary in the regular and almost stereotyped narratives of the life and acts of Christ while upon earth, which were circulated in the churches, to introduce the history of the ministry of John with this citation; and hence we find it in the same connection in all three evangelists. The evangelists, however, have only the third

* According to the evangelists, who follow the Septuagint, the words "in the wilderness" (*ἐν τῇ ἐρήμῳ*) belong to the participle "crying" (*βοῶντος*); but in the original Hebrew they are connected with "prepare ye" (*ἑτοιμάσατε*, instead of which we have in John *εὐθύνατε*, "make straight"); thus, "the voice of one crying, 'Prepare ye in the wilderness, etc.'"

verse from Isaiah in common, while John also refers only this one to himself; and it is clear that this indicates most strikingly and most concisely the relation of the Baptist to Christ. Luke alone adds the fourth and the fifth verse (the last only in part), which contain a further description of the office of the forerunner, and a promise of the approaching glory of God; and which are quite applicable to John's case, though not so much so as verse third. Luke, also, with spiritual freedom changes the citation, in order to make it suitable to the object for which he introduces it. He leaves out, for example, the words, "and the glory of the Lord shall be revealed;" without doubt, because Christ had as yet appeared only in humility, and not in glory. On the other hand, the following, "all flesh shall see the salvation of God," was with him the chief reason of introducing the citation; for the condition of beholding this salvation is that a road be broken up into the heart, in order to render easy and finally to allow, the entrance of the Lord into the soul. To open up just such a road had John the Baptist come as the forerunner of Christ. Upon this passage in Isaiah,—which, on account of its being typical, could have been, and was, recognized as prophetical only by its fulfillment,—the Jews appear not to have grounded any expectation of a forerunner; but only upon the altogether direct prophecy of Malachi. For this reason, those among the nation whose hearts were hardened to every holy impression, understood not what John meant when he referred to the passage, and were unequal to the task of finding out the drift of his words; while, on the contrary, those whose souls were susceptible, obtained, by means of the same explanation, a clear insight into the peculiar character and vocation of the Baptist.

Finally, we have yet to examine another expectation which, as it appears, many among the Jews entertained at the coming of John; and which they exhibited when they asked of him whether he was "*the prophet*" (ὁ προφήτης, Jno. 1 : 21.).* It will, perhaps, be difficult to ascertain at the present time, precisely who it was they supposed "the prophet" to be. The conjectures which are founded upon 2 Maccabees 15 : 13, 14; 2 : 1. ff. are evidently wholly unsatisfactory. The supposition that Jeremiah is there called simply "the prophet" and that from this circumstance he was afterwards so distinguished by the nation, is incapable of being proved; and, moreover, that Matthew appears to have had a conception of Jeremiah's returning alive among the people (16 : 14.), cannot be adduced in favor of the hypothesis, for such a return, according to the ideas of those whom Matthew introduces as the speakers, is possible also to the other prophets; and, to conclude the whole, it can be proved in no case that Jeremiah was ever actually spoken of among the people as simply "the prophet." We must, perhaps, go back in preference to the promise of Moses (Deut. 18 : 15.): "The Lord thy God will raise up to thee a prophet from the midst of thee, of thy brethren, like unto me." This promise, it is true, was referred by the Jews at a very early period to the Messiah (cp. Jno. 6 : 14., Acts 3 : 22., 7 : 37.), but interpreters were never entirely certain that a prophet different from the Messiah is not here meant (cp. Jno. 7 : 40.); at least, it seems to have been thought

* To render ὁ προφήτης as does the received version, by "*that* prophet" is erroneous, and is liable to lead the unpractised reader to suppose that we have here a repetition; for, as the words stand, "Art thou *that* prophet," the expression can only mean "Art thou Elias," which is an insignificant tautology. We should translate "Art thou *the* (expected) prophet?"

worth while by those who interrogated John, when he answered their query respecting his being the Messiah in the negative, to inquire of him, in a second question, whether another prophet than the Messiah is announced by Moses, and whether he was that particular prophet. Here also were they foiled in their object by John; and since they, under the influence of their perverted fleshly expectations regarding the Messiah, and, in a similar manner, regarding his precursor, knew not what to think of his reply, they requested him to give a positive explanation of his meaning. The explanation which they desired was given by the Baptist in words which, to their dull understandings, were as unintelligible as his former replies.

The conceptions, therefore, which John had respecting himself, his calling, and the position which had been assigned him by the express declaration of the Old Testament, were clear and decided, as we shall show hereafter when an appropriate opportunity presents itself; whilst, on the other hand, the ideas of the Jews respecting him vacillated in uncertainty, now to this side and now to that, according as their Messianic expectations and their insight into the Old Testament were more or less perverted.

PART SECOND.

JOHN BEFORE HIS PUBLIC APPEARANCE.

CHAPTER I.

Birth of the Baptist.

We find intelligence of the history of John's birth in Luke alone (1 : 5. ff.) ; but in him it is so much the more complete, probably because, for some reason or other, information which had not been circulated beyond the members of the Baptist's family, was fully accessible only to that evangelist. We are obliged, on this account, to follow Luke's authority solely ; for the apocryphal history which we have in the so-called Protevangelium Jacobi, is notoriously so much corrupted by the intermixture of fables, that it is entitled to none of our confidence.

Luke gives the time of John's birth with a great want of precision : "in the days of Herod, the king of Judea" (1 : 5.). Herod the Great is evidently here meant, who, according to the best calculation, exercised his dominion over Judea, as he had obtained it, by means of cunning and cruelty, from the year 40 to 4 B. C. of our era. From this general representation we can arrive at no certain conclusion with regard to the time of the birth of John. The most we can do is to refer back to the period of the birth of Christ, which, it is admitted, occurred in the last year of Herod's reign ; to which, therefore, the birth of John, who was six months older than Christ (1: 26. 36., coll. 56, 57.), must also be assigned. His parents were of the priestly caste. His father Zacharias performed his functions in the temple at the time of the birth of his son: he could have been, therefore, according to the Jewish law, not yet over fifty years old;* and, as himself as well as his wife Elisabeth did not expect to have any children, their union must have borne upon it the curse of childlessness. It may readily be supposed that both parents, who are represented to us as pious worshippers of Jehovah, were in the habit of praying earnestly to their God to remove from them this disgrace; and that Zacharias, when he, while presenting the daily incense-offering, prayed in the temple for the welfare of the people, offered up also in this holy place his own individual petition to the Most High (cp. v. 13.).

Accordingly, it happened, as we are informed, on a certain occasion, that, when it had again become his duty, in the course of office, to present the incense-offering to the Lord in the sanctuary, and when, perhaps, he repeated his customary prayer with redoubled earnestness, an angel appeared to him, and stood in full view before his eyes. Zacharias, not expecting such an apparition, was seized with fear and terror; just as the pious worthies of the old covenant, conscious of their own demerit and impotence, were wont, on the appearance of an angel, to utter on the instant an expression of terror and alarm. The angel, thereupon, addressed him, as was customary in such cases, with the words, "fear not." When his fears

* The *Levites*, it is true, became superannuated at the age of *fifty* (Num. 4: 3., 8: 24.); but it is not certain that this was the case with *priests*. Extracts from rabbinic writings quoted by Lightfoot (Hor. Heb.) would seem to indicate the contrary (cp. v. 18.).

were allayed, the angel announced the joyful tidings that his prayer had been heard, and that his wife Elisabeth should bear him a son. At the same time a name was bestowed upon the boy, indicative of the nature of his future dignity: *John*, that is, *God-sent*, given by God, created in an altogether peculiar manner by the gracious interposition of God, and therefore bound to him by altogether peculiar ties.*

With the announcement of the name is connected the prophecy of the angel respecting the duties of the son and the significance of his advent. The mention of his name and the pre-announcement of his birth were of themselves sufficient to produce the joy which his parents must have felt in the approaching birth of a son long-desired but no longer expected, and which many others must likewise have experienced on the appearance of a man who was to be so distinguished. Another reason is adduced for the pleasure which was felt in the expected birth of John: it constituted the condition of his ministry at a later period, as all must have perceived to whom the complete development of the kingdom of God was thought a matter of consequence, and who longed for the salvation of which John was to be the proclaimer; and it was grounded

* The name *John* comes from the Hebrew יהוחנן (*Jehochanan*), the contracted form of which is יוֹחָנָן (*Jochanan*), meaning, as usually explained, *Whom Jehovah has given*; but better, *God is gracious.* This is represented in the New Testament by Ἰωάννης, with which, as to meaning, the Greek Θεωδῶρος (*Theodorus*) is nearly identical.—The name of John's father, *Zacharias*, is the Hebrew זכריה (*Zekharyah*, *Zechariah* in the E. V. of the Old Testament), and means *Whom Jehovah remembers*.—His mother's name, *Elisabeth*, is the Hebrew אֱלִישֶׁבַע (*Elisheba'*), *Whose oath is God*. Aaron's wife was so called (Ex. 6: 23.).—The appellations given to children among the Orientals are always significant; and those in the Old Testament usually bear their meaning on their face.

in his personal disposition, in his relation to the Israelitish nation, and, finally, in his relation to the coming Messiah, all which three facts stand together in a necessary connection. He was to be "great in the sight of the Lord," in contradistinction from earthly greatness in the sight of men ; spiritually great in his office as the preparer of the advent of the kingdom of God. He was to possess externally the highest legal perfection in his character of Nazarite (Num. 6 : 3., Judges 13 : 14.), those bearing which name bound themselves by a vow to practise, for a short time or for their whole life, as the case might be, certain external ceremonies and observances. Such a person must he be, because he was to exhibit once more the highest moral perfection of the old covenant, and, at the same time, the unsatisfactory nature of that covenant as a means of attaining true salvation ; and, therefore, was he at his appearance to introduce to him who could free from the curse of sin and from the constraint of the law.

The most remarkable part of the angel's announcement, is that John "should be filled with the Holy Ghost even from his mother's womb" (i. e. while he was yet within the womb, and henceforth). That the Holy Ghost here spoken of is not the Holy Spirit specially so called in the Christian Church, which was first poured forth after the completion of the work of redemption (Jno. 7 : 39.), needs no proof. What is here meant is the divine Spirit in general, which operates in man before his redemption and leads him towards his salvation, the movements and workings of which every man can trace in him self, nay, which even coöperates in the development of unconscious children ; for it is certain that a man may be filled with the Spirit of God and yet be himself totally unconscious of the fact, while the Spirit is carrying on his development. The reception of the Spirit, however, independently and with our free consent, in the operation of the second birth, can obviously not occur except with our own full consciousness; and the passivity of the receiving soul must first have been freed from its imperfections and made complete by the activity of the Spirit's reception and by the commingling of the two elements, before we have truly become possessed of the Holy Spirit.

The resemblance between the narrative here given of the birth and external character of the Baptist and that which we find in the book of Judges (chap. 13.) respecting the Israelitish hero Samson (Heb. *Shimshon*), is remarkably striking in several important particulars. Samson's mother, like John's, had been previously barren (vs. 2, 3.); an angel announced unto her that she should bear a son (v. 3.); that son was to *begin* the work of delivering his people (v. 5.); he was to be "a Nazarite unto God" from his mother's womb; and, finally, the Spirit of God wrought upon him and within him (v. 25.). It is well to note with regard to this latter particular, that, though Samson is not said to have been *filled* with the Spirit of God as it was promised John should be, the operations of this Spirit upon him are represented as being of a peculiar character. It is said that "the Spirit of the Lord began *to move* him at times in the camp of Dan, etc."; where we are to understand the words *to move* in the sense of *to impel, to drive on* (לְפַעֲמוֹ, an expression occurring in the Old Testament only here); the idea being that the Spirit began to move him with irresistible power, in spite of himself as it were,—a stronger expression, in one point of view, than that used by the angel when speaking of the Spirit's connection with the Baptist (cp. 1 Kings 18: 12., 2 K. 2: 16., Is. 8: 11., Ezek. 3: 14.).—The narratives of the birth of Isaac and of that of Samuel are in some respects parallels to this of the birth of John (v. Gen. 18 : 10. ff., 1 Sam. 1 : 2., ff.), and should be considered in connection.

After this description of John's personality follows that of his employment among the people : "And many of the children of Israel shall he turn to the Lord their God." His office was limited to the preaching of repentance, and to pointing to him that was about to appear : he himself could bestow no new life, but could only prepare the way for its bestowment. That the sphere of his action should be restricted to Israel is grounded, perhaps, on the simple fact that Israel was, according to the counsel of God, the only people specially prepared for his labors ; and even Christ himself confined his ministry to this nation, while whatever else was necessary to the establishment of his kingdom on earth was left to be supplied by the apostles. John was to turn men to God, that is, to turn them away from their earthly and fleshly mode of life and conduct, and incline their minds again to God ; and in accomplishing this, a knowledge of sin was first to be awakened, and then an effort for self-improvement to be excited ; but the actual power of self-improvement was first to be bestowed by Christ.—John's office as precursor of the Messiah is represented in a manner quite peculiar in the announcement of the angel. He is to go before him, namely, before the Lord their God, who is the subject of the remark, before God, who is now about to appear personally in the flesh, and is to attack the depravity of the times in the spirit and power of Elias, to preach repentance, to punish, to administer discipline, to unite again by stronger links all the bonds of human society where the loosening of family ties had torn them asunder, to turn the godless to the leading of a more pious life, and to point the people to the Lord, that they may be made ready for his advent. In this promise, that John should here and there abate the corruption of the times, by means of his preliminary invitations to repentance, the angel refers, as has already been remarked, to Malachi 3 : 24 ; obviously only in order to render his announcement more comprehensible, more agreeable, and more credible to Zacharias, because he now proclaims to him the fulfillment of that promise in his son.

This whole occurrence bears, as has been noticed, a very striking resemblance to the birth of Israel from the decrepit Abraham and Sarah. The case was quite different with Mary, since the birth of her child was not to be brought about by the combined agency of the factors generally necessary in such an occurrence ; and hence her question, "*how* shall this be," is altogether in order, though she entertained no doubt as to the fact itself. Here, on the contrary, the natural relation of the ordinary organic conditions, which rendered such a creation as was promised to him in the highest degree improbable, were impressed in so lively a manner upon the mind of Zacharias, that he could not, for the moment, conceive of the truth of the announcement, or imagine in what way it could be fulfilled ; and, therefore, he demanded a proof, a miracle, by which the truth of the angel's assertion might be established. This requirement of a proof, this suggestion of the external improbability of what was promised, shows how very much Zacharias was inferior to Abraham and Sarah in a trustful confidence in God : he stood in the same relative position as Sarah, and besides this he recognized the angel as an undoubted messenger from God, while Sarah saw in him who spoke to her only an ordinary traveller.

Notwithstanding this general recognition, on the part of

Zacharias, of the angel as a divine messenger, the latter,—since in this expression of doubt respecting the truth of his promise there seemed to be likewise conveyed a doubt of his mission,—once more proclaims himself an authenticated herald of God, one sent from him to make the announcement which Zacharias appeared to discredit. In order to legitimate his claims the more completely, he calls himself by a name, designating thereby the near relation in which he stands to God. That he here gives himself a Hebrew name, is altogether in character, since he had to speak in Hebrew to a Hebrew. He does not declare how he is called among his equals and by God, for this a man could not have comprehended ; but he indicates to Zacharias, in a way intelligible to him, the characteristic of his individuality, expressed by means of a proper name,—a practice which we find so frequently followed in giving names, especially among the nations of the East. He is called and is *Gabriel*, i. e. a man of God ; a name which is further explained by the addition, "that stand in the presence of God." He is, therefore, one of the chief angels and messengers of God, who receive their commands immediately from him (cp. Tob. 12 : 15.). Whoever, then,—for such additional conclusion may we draw from the words of the angel,—does not believe in him as the chosen of God who is to make known his promise, does not believe in God, and transgresses by his unbelief. The proof which he requests, Zacharias shall indeed receive ; but it shall be a punitive proof. In order that he may be able for the future to restrain his tongue from sinning, by means of expressions of unbelief, against God and his ambassador, he shall "be dumb and not able to speak ;"* and therefore, also, shall

* This expression of the received rendering is tautological ; not so the Greek, however, in which we have the word σιωπῶν (*siopon*), *silent*, i. e.

he not be able to tell others of the promise made to him, and profane it, perhaps, by the repetition of his doubts.

This punishment was intended to school Zacharias, that he might be increased and perfected in his spiritual graces. A knowledge of the unbelief which dwelt in his heart, the punishment which ensued as its consequence, the fulfillment of a divine promise which appeared so improbable to him, all these must have wrought powerfully upon his heart and purified it from the dregs which it yet retained. This object must have been especially subserved by a condition such as his now was; when, dumb and deprived of his ordinary social intercourse, he was thrown back upon himself, and could enter upon a private self-examination in serious earnestness, in order by upright repentance and a change of disposition to prepare for the dwelling of the divine in his heart. Yet, on account of this anticipated change, the punishment was not to be of continued duration. Its termination is fixed; "until the day that these things shall be performed," that is, until, by the birth of his son, the fulfillment of the promises made to him shall begin. They shall be fulfilled, however, adds the angel yet again with firm and unhesitating confidence, each in its own time, neither too early, nor yet too late; his birth, as also his ministry, shall be made known and exhibited, each in its own appropriate hour.

There is no need of repeating here the observation that the angel must, if he wished to be understood, have conformed, in his outward appearance and language, to the ideas and conceptions of the man with whom he conversed. All doubts of the

not speaking (*mute*). In v. 20., therefore, we should read, "thou shalt be *silent*, and not able to speak"; the first member of the clause denoting the *fact*, and the second the *reason*.

truth of our narrative based upon this conversation on the angel's part after the manner of man, must, in consequence fall to the ground. But, more generally, the fact that an angel is represented as having appeared to Zacharias, has given rise to suspicions of the truth of the whole narrative. It is not our intention, as it would be quite foreign from our object, to enter here upon an examination of the question of the possibility and probability of such angelic appearances ; but we must at least say thus much, that the whole sacred history of the Old as well as of the New Testament contains so numerous descriptions of similar apparitions, which can be rejected only by the most marked exegetical arbitrariness, and that, still further, the existence of angels and their employment in securing the salvation of man have in their favor so much testimony from Christ and the Apostles, that it would be difficult to establish the contrary on grounds at all satisfactory. If no didactic value is assigned to all that the New Testament says respecting angels and their office,—since it is in fact true that the whole of this doctrine can have and will have no material influence upon Christian faith and Christian doctrine,—we must at least admit that the certainty of the existence of angels lies at the basis of all these expressions respecting them and their office among men. And, if the so much abused theory of accommodation is sought to be applied to the present case, there cannot surely be adduced as a powerful reason in favor of its application, the assertion that Christ and his disciples mentioned angels as frequently as they did without attaching any other meaning to what they said than we do when we speak of the apparition of fairies and spirits. Nay, is it at all probable that a man who was a lover of truth could by any possibility have intentionally expressed such ideas in his discourses, if he was convinced of their untruthfulness? Or is it likely, on the other hand, that Christ himself entertained ideas on the subject as incorrect as those which he expressed are declared to be? This, least of all, will be likely to be asserted, if one only observes how Christ by no means follows blindly the representations of others, but gives new and independent descriptions of the angelic office, as, for example, in Matt. 16 : 27, 18 : 10, 25 : 31, 26 : 53.

That angels do not now appear, can be no proof that they did not appear in those days; for we only read of their coming either when man in his weakness needs such immediate instruction from God, or when great world-formative epochs arrive in the development of the kingdom of God; and accordingly at the time of the ministry of Christ upon earth, we see all the powers of light and of darkness appearing in person, with all their weapons, upon the field of combat, for here was to accrue to each party either victory or destruction. And, after all, what is there so improbable in the supposition that God, who exerts his powers so variously, visibly and invisibly, in the operations of nature which are immediately known to us, since he makes use upon earth of so endlessly varied means and ways of carrying out his intentions, should possess also in a higher sphere instruments and organs who assist in accomplishing his will upon earth, and whom he sends when and where it may in his wisdom be necessary? With respect, then, to the appearance of the angel, and thus far generally in the account of the evangelist, we can find no reason to doubt the historical truth of the events there narrated; and we proceed accordingly to a further examination of the simple subject. We will return to a consideration of the dumbness of Zacharias at a later period in the narrative.

As the incense-offering was presented daily, the people who were tarrying meanwhile in the court of the temple, knew very nearly the precise time at which the priest would return from the sanctuary ; and it must, therefore, have seemed to them the more remarkable that he remained on this occasion so much longer than was usual. The conversation with the angel could not have been of long duration, but Zacharias consumed some time in recovering from the first shock of his alarm. When, at length, he came forth, it was plainly perceived by his confusion and his whole disturbed aspect that something extraordinary must have happened to him ; and when he now remained speechless, instead of pronouncing the blessing which the people expected, and gave them to understand that he could not speak, and therefore was able to confer the benediction upon them only by signs,* they could come to no other conclusion than that he must have had an ecstasy in the temple, or must have seen some strange sight, or some apparition in the flesh ; which conjecture, probably spoken out aloud by the bystanders, Zacharias confirmed by nodding his head and waving his hand, whilst he remained standing before them without the power of speech.—What reception he met with afterwards from the remaining priests and from his wife, we are not informed in the narrative. Without doubt, they looked upon him with special reverence as one honored by God with some important revelation, and made no further inquiries of him respecting the object of his vision. It is likely that even to his wife he communicated no more than the fact

* "It was not his office," says Alford, "*to pronounce the benediction*," as Von Rohden has here represented, "but that of the other incensing priest ; so that his 'not being able to speak,' must mean, *in answer to the inquiries* which his unusual appearance prompted."

that God had announced to him the birth of a son and assigned him a name. He continued to remain in the temple until the completion of the week in which he and his colleagues had to perform the priestly functions, without, it would seem, its having fallen to his lot to enter the sanctuary again. At the expiration of the week, he returned to his place of residence and to his wife.

The pregnancy of Elisabeth actually occurred, as had been announced; but not in such a way that we are compelled to regard the event as a special divine miracle, though it retained the character of a gift of divine favor. Elisabeth, who recognized it as such, concealed herself for the first five months, withdrew herself from social intercourse with her friends into loneliness, partly in order to become well assured of her pregnancy before she made her appearance in public, partly in order to be freed from every reproach,—which, however, did not originate with her husband,—on account of her having been so long unfruitful; praising God because he had taken away from her the disgrace which attached among the Jews to unfruitful women, because he had looked upon her with favor at his appointed time, and had thought her worthy of such a blessing.

At the period indicated, the promise was fulfilled in so far that the child to which Elisabeth gave birth, was actually a son. The whole town, as may readily be supposed, and the relatives and neighbors of the parents took the liveliest interest in this happy event. They saw indeed nothing particularly wonderful in the birth of the boy, but only a new proof of the greatness and mercy of God who had blessed Elisabeth with a child in her old age.—According to the Jewish law, the eighth day after the birth was the time appointed for the circumcision of children (Gen 17 : 12.). It was customary on this occasion for all the kindred and acquaintances of the parents to come together, in order to pass the day in festivities, and to be witnesses of the circumcision and the naming of the child. As it was usual for the child to receive its name from one of its relatives, the friends wished in this case to call him after his father Zacharias, in the confident expectation that the parents would urge no objection.—It is probable that previous to the institution of the rite of circumcision, children received a name immediately upon their birth.—Names were, as with us, usually bestowed by the parents ; but sometimes the relatives of the child had a voice in the matter, by the parents' consent (cp. Ruth 4 : 17.). There are several instances mentioned in the Old Testament in which, as here, the child receives its name expressly from the circumstances attending its birth, or from something note-worthy in its own or the history of its family (cp. Gen. 16 : 11., 19 : 37., 25 : 25, 26., Ex. 2 : 10., 18 : 3, 4.).

Elisabeth, informed by her husband of the occurrence in the temple, and knowing what, according to the will of God, her son was to be called, opposed the intention of her kindred, and bestowed upon him the name of John. Astonished at this procedure, the relatives could discover no reason for conferring upon the child a name so wholly unknown in the family. She remained, however, firm in her opinion ; and, in consequence, the father, who had perhaps been present as a dumb guest at this transaction, was referred to and requested to decide the question. They communicated their meaning to him by signs, because men are accustomed to act towards dumb persons as though they were deaf ; for that he was really also deaf it is not natural to conclude, else could he have known nothing of the whole controversy, and nothing, moreover, respecting that which they now required of him. Zacharias, therefore, asked by signs for a tablet, the only way in which he could in this case make himself understood, and wrote thereon the words, "His name is John."* All, thereupon, wondered much at this strange idea of both the parents.

At the same moment the punishment was removed which Zacharias had brought upon himself by his unbelief. He now saw and was convinced of the truth of the angelic message, which he had, no doubt, in all seriousness and full of repentance, long since believed in his heart. He had now completed the probation assigned him by the angel; now, therefore, was his mouth again opened and his tongue loosed; and the first use which he made of his recovered speech, was, as was proper, in singing a song of praise to the Lord. The presence of a divine power was so clearly evinced in this whole event that the assembled company and all the acquaintances of Zacharias, in view of these revelations of divine energy, were inspired with a holy fear and awe. In that entire region these occurrences were frequently related and much talked of; yet in such a way that a knowledge of them did not spread beyond that small mountain country in which Zacharias resided, and, on this account, it appears not to have reached as far as Jerusalem. Men spoke much respecting the child, and pondered in their hearts as to what were to be the future character and

* In the words "and wrote, *saying*, His name is John" (v. 63.), the word *saying* is used, as we often employ it, of what is merely written and not spoken (cp. 2 Kings 10: 6.). There is no likelihood of the words being misunderstood as they stand in English; but Luther's "schrieb *und sprach*" may be; and it has therefore been condemned as of ambiguous import (so by v. Rohden, p. 34, note).

fate of this priest's son whose birth had been attended by so much that was wonderful. Meanwhile the child itself was rapidly and vigorously developed under the protection and training of the Lord.

This whole event is so simple, so accordant with nature, and discovers so fully the hand of the Lord, that one wonders in what respect it is liable to exception. He who will believe in and acknowledge no miracle, although so much that is miraculous, and so much that is inexplicably enigmatic, is occurring before his eyes ; he who imagines that he can see with his human eye through all the divine arrangement of the world, and cannot be convinced that there are higher laws, by means of which, at times and in particular at such great turning-points of history, the order of things as known to us is interrupted, and yet without its being in the least destroyed : he, it must in general be admitted, would take exception to the miraculous dumbness of Zacharias, and it would be difficult, we grant, to convince such a one of the truth of the narrative. That this miracle could be explained after the order of natural causes, is certain ; but it is equally certain that, according to the view of the writer, not a natural occurrence, but an actual miracle, is here intended to be narrated.—He, on the contrary, who does not object to the credibility of miracles, will readily perceive how exactly, as has been already noticed, this divine treatment of Zacharias must have constituted the most suitable means for his moral improvement ; and he will acknowledge the divine wisdom which is manifested in the narrative, rather than deem it a fiction.

A fact very nearly analogous to this occurrence, we find in the conversion of St. Paul, who was made blind for several days in order that he might be led, during the lapse of this period, to an examination of himself; and in this way was the entire change which took place in his character produced. What is fable and what is not, one may very readily discover by reading, after the perusal of this simple and natural narrative, the history given in the so-called Protevangelion Jacobi (Cap. 22. ff.) of the deliverance of John and his mother from the massacre of the children at Bethlehem; in which it is said that a rock was divided and received within it the mother and her child, and that within this they were concealed during the time of the persecution. This would indeed be a monstrous miracle; and such as would militate against the divine wisdom and holiness. That a man should be preserved alive within a rock would be something repugnant to the course of nature; and by causing it to occur God would himself overthrow his own laws. In general when a miracle is not necessary, it is not permitted to take place; and it is clear that the deliverance of John and his mother might easily have been brought about in a natural way, just as that of the child Jesus occurred in a manner altogether in accordance with the laws of nature.

CHAPTER II.

JOHN'S FAMILY RELATIONS.

In order to obtain a clearer insight into the character of John and his peculiar development, it is necessary to become acquainted with the persons among whom he passed his childhood, and from whom he received his first impulses and impressions. It has already been mentioned that he was of priestly descent, since his father and mother belonged, according to Luke 1: 5., to the tribe of the Levites. His father, indeed, as we are further informed, belonged to the course of Abia, and, therefore, according to 1 Chron. 24: 10., to the eighth division of the twenty-four priestly classes who, in accordance with Solomon's arrangement, performed, eight days each in succession, the service of the temple. The character of the parents is given in general terms, briefly but distinctly: "they were both righteous before God," that is, in the eyes, in the estimation of God, and not merely before men. We are moreover informed in what this righteousness consisted: they walked "in all the commandments and ordinances of the Lord blameless," that is, they conducted themselves strictly as the law of Moses had prescribed. Since, however, this law is composed chiefly of requirements and interdictions relating to external actions, the righteousness which is attained by the fulfillment of these commandments can only be an external and legal righteousness, if there be not superadded thereto a change of the heart produced by the operation of the spirit of Christ. It is evident, then, that nothing else is meant by these expressions but a Jewish, and not a Christian, righteousness and blamelessness. They were called righteous among the Jews who strove zealously for a fulfillment of the law, in contradistinction from the godless, who sinned deliberately and of set purpose. Such righteous persons as strove with all diligence to perform the requirements of the law, must have come, by these means, so much the more certainly to a knowledge that it is indeed possible to live up to the letter of the law, but not to acquire the disposition of mind which such conduct pre-supposes ; and so must the parents of John, the more righteous they became, the more scrupulous they were in their fulfillment of the requirements of the law, have entertained so much the more eager longing after a deliverance, as well from the domination of the sin which was intrenched in their hearts, as from the yoke of the law itself, which, with all its painful injunctions and interdictions, and with its mass of inconvenient ceremonies, could have seemed to others only a burden too intolerable to be borne.

But how were those ideas and expectations obtained, which they fostered respecting this deliverance ; for, as we have seen in the preliminary sketch, expectations of a very various character had been formed among the Jewish people regarding the Messiah. The best explanation of this phenomenon is afforded in the song of praise which Zacharias raised after the use of his speech had been restored to him on the occasion of his son's circumcision. In this example of the unbelief of Zacharias,—we may remark in passing,—and of the punishment which it superinduced, we may perceive most clearly how little are just and blameless performers of the law of Moses to be regarded on that account as thoroughly holy men in their dispositions ; for in this case the issue of the trial did not depend upon the performance of a commandment, but upon the exhibition of a proper state of feeling, of a thorough and perfect confidence in God, and upon the unshaken recognition of the truth of God's promises and of his power to carry them into execution. Accordingly, we see the righteous and blameless priest Zacharias wavering in his faith towards God, but afterwards brought, by means of a severe discipline from God, to repentance for his transgression and to a change of disposition. In his song of praise he speaks, it must be admitted, in a state of elevated inspiration and with prophetic intuition; but it remains none the less certain that what he said was not merely something placed in his mouth by the Holy Spirit, so that he was, so to speak, only a machine of utterance, but that his words were an expression of his own inward consciousness and firm conviction,—which latter were urged onward, in this moment, by the powerful external excitation to which he was subjected, to such a degree of enthusiasm, that he regarded the deliverance as actually at hand, although only its preparation was involved in the birth of his son. This inspiration, or enthusiasm, is here characterized as a filling with the Holy Spirit, because it was a *divine* inspiration, excited by God and busying itself with divine revelations, though many of these revelations were not perfectly understood and were explained in an earthly manner by Zacharias.

According to his representations, he by no means thinks that the redemption is to be one of a merely political kind, a deliverance from the enemies of his people, but one also from sins; yet political freedom forms in his conception an important part of the hoped-for deliverance. He appears not to be well able to conceive of a perfect worship of God and freedom from the punishment of transgression, unconnected with a preceding deliverance of the nation from servitude ; and hence he represents both as being introduced by the Messiah. This is his view of the subject-matter of the oath which God swore to Abraham, and of the announcements of the prophets respecting the office of the Messiah. And yet it appears to be clear to him,—a conclusion which he had come to, perhaps, from the announcement of the angel,—that the son who had been born to him is not to prepare a way for the Messiah in so far as he is to introduce a political revolution, but only in so far as he is to bring the people to a knowledge of salvation, a salvation which consists in the forgiveness of sins. The object of John's ministry is "to give a *knowledge* of salvation" ; he is to arouse men to a feeling of its necessity. Salvation itself, however, is given by the Lord (v. 71.). Forgiveness of sins appears here as the great prerogative of the Messianic time ; which, however, the economy of the Old Testament could not confer. The sacrifices of the Old Testament could effect no internal and actual remission, but only a purification of the flesh (*καθαρότης τῆς σαρκός*, Heb. 9 : 13.) ; sin itself remained unpunished only on account of God's forbearance (Rom. 3 : 25.). Now, on the other hand, real and effectual forgiveness is to be sent, partly by the actual taking away of the consequences of sin, partly by the impartation of the new higher life to men.*—

* This part of Zacharias' song of praise is very often misinterpreted. The English Version reads "to give knowledge of salvation unto his people, *by* the remission of their sins" ; and this rendering of ἐν ἀφέσει (lit. *in remission*), which is based upon the incorrect translation *per remissionem* given by Beza, is followed by Bloomfield (Greek Test.) when he says, "this [knowledge of salvation] under the Law, was *by legal righteousness ;* under the Gospel, *by remission of sins.*" Now, ἐν ἀφέσει cannot here grammatically mean *by the remission ;* and, if it could, it ought not to be so rendered without absolute necessity, since it is not true that "a *knowledge of* [i. e an acquaintance with]

Hence we perceive that a moral redemption by means of the expected ministry of the Messiah, was the prominent idea of Zacharias. In his opinion, however, as it seems, the knowledge of the salvation which was now to ensue, is to be communicated to the people by John only in a general way, for he is merely to announce to them that the Messiah is about to come. The essential nature, therefore, of the repentance which John was to preach, although his attention had been called to it by the angel (v. 17.), he does not appear to have correctly conceived.

The bestowment of this salvation Zacharias refers to the

salvation" is given by means of the remission of sins, though it is true that salvation itself may be said to be so imparted.—There is another rendering of the phrase given by Grotius and followed by Kuinoel (3d ed. of New Testament) even more objectionable, viz.: "*for* the remission" (the *in remissionem* of the Vulgate); but this unquestionably would require the Greek to read εἰς ἄφεσιν. Besides, John could not confer forgiveness of iniquity; this could be done by Christ alone.—Luther adheres more closely to the meaning of this particular phrase, but his translation of the whole clause is erroneous. Following him the verse is properly rendered, "und Erkenntniss des Heils gebest seinem Volk, *die da ist* in Vergebung ihrer Sünden," i. e. *and givest to his people knowledge of salvation, which* [sc. knowledge, for *die* refers here to *Erkenntniss*] *consists in forgiveness of their sins.* According to this the forgiveness of sins is produced by a knowledge of (i. e. an acquaintance with) salvation; but it is evident that it is the *appropriation* of salvation, and not the *knowledge* of it, which effects such a remission.—There is only one rendering of the verse which will fully answer the demands of the Greek and of the facts of the case, viz. "to give unto his people a knowledge of the salvation *which consists in* forgiveness of their sins," or, more stiffly, "a knowledge of salvation, which salvation is forgiveness, etc." The phrase ἐν ἀφέσει connects in construction with σωτηρίας (*of salvation*), the article τῆς (which we might expect to find before ἐν ἀφέσει, thus, τῆς ἐν ἀφ., *that consists in*) being omitted as often elsewhere in such constructions in the New Testament (see Winer, *N. T. Gram.* § 19. 2.). So render and so explain all the best modern New Testament critics, as De Wette, Meyer, Olshausen, Kuinoel (4th ed. of New Testament.).

merciful love of God towards us (by which *us*, however, he means the Jews, for his words are stamped by the prevailing particularistic idea that salvation was to come only to that nation), by means of which and in consequence of which the uprising from on high, i. e. the star ascending on high in the heavens, the spiritual sun, has graciously appeared unto us,* in order to shine and to scatter light upon those who wander in darkness, and "to guide our feet into the way of (i. e. which leads to) peace" (v. 78.).—From these expressions of Zacharias we perceive quite clearly that he belonged to the number of those pious souls among the Jewish nation who prepared themselves in quietness for the great period of the development of God's kingdom, which had been promised them ; who searched the Scriptures and sought to confirm and strengthen thereby their Messianic expectations ; and who held fast, with

* Thus Von Rohden, but not very clearly or correctly. His *Aufgang aus der Höhe, uprising from on high* (which is also Luther's rendering) does, it is true, verbally represent the Greek words *ἀνατολὴ ἐξ ὕψους*, but it gives no fair idea of the meaning of the passage. 'Ανατολή is evidently equivalent here to *φῶς ἀνατέλλον*, its use being based, no doubt, upon those passages of the prophecies in which the Messiah is spoken of as a *Light* (Heb. אור, Greek *φῶς*), as Is. 9: 2., 49: 6., 60: 1–3. cp. Jno. 8: 12.: it signifies, therefore, *a rising light*. "*Day-spring*" i. e. *day-dawn*, the rendering of the received version, is, consequently, inadequate. It is better, moreover, to connect *ἐξ ὕψους* (*from on high*) with the verb *ἐπεσκέψατο* (*hath visited ; better, hath appeared unto*), and not, as is customary, with *ἀνατολή ;* and to translate the whole clause, "*a rising light hath visited* [or *hath appeared unto*] *us from on high.*" Cp. Robinson, *N. T. Lexicon*, sub verbo 'Ανατολή.—The word *ἀνατολή*, it should be remarked, has been thought by not a few commentators to be an application of the term as used in the Septuagint, as a translation of the Hebrew צמח (*tsemach*, i. e. *sprout, branch*), the Messiah being so called in Jer. 23: 5., Zech. 3: 8. ; but *ἐπιφᾶναι* (E. V. *to give light to ; better, to shine upon*) in the next verse, though not wholly conclusive, speaks strongly against such a construction, which is now unsupported by the leading biblical critics.

unwavering confidence in the truth of the divine promises, to the hope that the expected deliverer would very soon appear; in a word, that he pertained to the number of those who "looked for redemption" (Luke 2: 38.). Of none of these who so expected are we authorized to pre-suppose that they had an altogether pure conception of the merely spiritual dominion of the Messiah, and of his granting deliverance merely from sin and its consequences, but not from external bondage; for the long-continued and grievous oppression which they had endured, the national pride excited by the preference which they, the people of God, had enjoyed and expected still to enjoy over others, and the numerous prophetic announcements of the high dignity of the Messiah, were too nearly associated in their minds with the idea of ascribing to him, as they did, external power, and we find similar expectations cherished too long even by the disciples who received instruction from Christ in person, for us to expect that, before the appearance of the Saviour, any Jew could have of himself attained, by the study of the Scriptures, to the only true and worthy doctrine of the Messianic kingdom. It is true, we admit, that Simeon saw in advance the sufferings which the Messiah had to undergo; but this did not, even in his case, exclude the expectation of an earthly glory and authority which were to follow, just as we find in the Messianic prophecies these two aspects of the Saviour united. That in Zacharias especially expectations of the spiritual employment of the Messiah were connected with others of his earthly power and victorious dominion, is too evident to allow us to pre-suppose that he had a thoroughly clear insight into the character of the Christian theocracy.

Ideas similar to those of Zacharias were, no doubt, entertained by his wife Elisabeth; of which, however, we do not possess such express evidence in the Holy Scriptures. She also was pious, she also longed for the coming of the new and great epoch; but she must also have found it equally difficult with her husband to free herself wholly from earthly Messianic expectations. That she too hoped with her whole heart in the near advent of Christ, and now especially, since the promise had been made to her that she should give birth to his forerunner, and that she acknowledged, even before he was born, him that was about to come, as her Lord, though in what precise sense it may not be easy to determine, we have the proof in Luke 1: 39–45., where we find a narrative of the visit of Mary to Elisabeth, and, in particular, of the first meeting of the two women. Mary had already received the announcement that it was her destiny to become the mother of the Messiah, and she had been referred to her kinswoman Elisabeth as a proof and assurance of the possibility and of the real fulfillment of the promise, since she who for a long time had been supposed unfruitful, had now received through the divine agency an assurance that she would soon become a mother. As Mary commenced her journey to the residence of Elisabeth as soon as she received this information from the angel, Elisabeth could not possibly have had previous intelligence of what had happened to Mary; yet, as soon as she beheld her, she fell into a divine enthusiasm, and a voice within informed her that this was the maiden chosen by the Lord to give birth to the Saviour. Her violent excitement in feeling and her joy at this meeting and this divine revelation, are partaken of by the child in her womb, as often occurs in the last months of pregnancy. The child moves within the womb, and this she takes for a new proof of the correctness of her judgment, ascribing to the child itself an emotion of pleasure on account of the coming of its future master. Thus was the meeting a means to both the women of confirming and strengthening their faith in God's promises; for Elisabeth received an additional sure proof that he whose precursor her son was to be would not fail to make his appearance; while Mary was made the more certain, by this anticipatory recognition on the part of Elisabeth, that a heavenly favor, so super-abundant to a woman's heart as was that promised, was to be conferred upon her; and, partaking of the inspiration of her friend, she bursts forth in a song of praise to the Most High.

As we find no further traces of other family connections and of other relatives of John, we must discuss so much the more carefully the connection which had, without doubt, the most important influence upon his development,—that with Mary, and, therefore, with Jesus himself. In Luke 1: 36, the angel, when he refers Mary to Elisabeth, speaks of the latter as her *relative.* The two were probably sister's daughters; for, since Elisabeth was sprung from the tribe of Levi, according to Luke 1: 5., and Mary probably from the tribe of Judah, they could not well have been related in any way except as the daughters of sisters, of which sisters the one had married into the family of Levi, whence sprung Elisabeth, and the other into the family of Judah, whence the origin of Mary.* Kinswomen so nearly

* It is certainly making συγγενής (*a relative*) too definite to translate it "*cousin*" as in the received translation, if that term is to be taken in its restricted and now usual signification. The relationship between the two women was probably that of cousinship, but this idea is not obtained from the meaning of the Greek term which designates their connection. Mary may have been the *niece* of Elisabeth, as some think; an opinion which the difference between

related could not have remained long unacquainted with each other ; and the manner in which their meeting is narrated in Luke appears to intimate that they had been previously known to each other. They must have been still more closely united together in the bonds of friendship by the encouraging promises which they had each received ; and it is natural to expect that they often, at a later period, visited each other, in order to communicate the observations they had made during the growth and training of their sons and the hopes which had been thereby produced, that their mutual confidence in the divine announcement might be strengthened and confirmed.

It has appeared strange to certain critics that neither John nor Jesus is mentioned by any of the evangelists as alluding at any time to their relationship ; and some have supposed that they preserved silence upon this point for fear of being charged with working together upon a pre-concerted plan. Such a hypothesis, however, is totally unnecessary. Indeed, it is more likely that a declaration on their part of their relationship, would, in most respects, have been an advantage to their cause. Jesus, however, was averse from attempting to acquire influence by any such merely mechanical process ; he preferred to further his designs by appealing to a better and a higher kind of testimony (Jno. 5 : 32. ff.). Besides, it was his aim to propagate his principles and to bring men to a knowledge and confession of the truth not by means of external pomp and splendor, but by a power whose working was internal and spiritual.—But, after all, it cannot be positively decided whether John and Jesus did, or did not, speak of themselves publicly as

the ages of the two seems specially to favor. "Cousin," in its old sense, i. e. *blood-relation*, correctly represents the original term.

relatives. On this point the evangelists are silent ; and to the relationship itself Luke alone bears testimony. It may be, on the one hand, that they made no mention of it ; and did not, because they took it for granted that it was known, and because to have spoken of it would not in any way have assisted the end which they had in view. Or, it may be, on the other hand, that they did allude to it, but that the evangelists have not recorded the fact ; and that they have not done so, because they supposed it to be already known to their readers that such a recognition had been publicly made, or because they concluded that allusion to it was not consistent with their object in writing.*

From the very probable pre-supposition respecting the intimacy of Mary and Elisabeth, above considered, it has been by some further concluded that John and Jesus must have been also acquainted at an early period ; and with this certainty (we should perhaps rather say probability), it is asserted, the words of John, "and I knew him not" (Jno. 1: 31, 33.), conflict in an inexplicable contradiction. But this contradiction is not, in truth, so inexplicable. It may be removed by two distinct modes of explanation ; in the one mode, by giving to the words, "and I knew him not" a more limited application than to take it in the sense of "I was not acquainted with him" ; in the other, by contending for the possibility that the two youths were entirely unacquainted with each other. To decide, in accordance with the latter view, on the possibility or impossibility of an acquaintance between the two, is rendered the more difficult by our limited knowledge of the history

* See upon this point a more full discussion by Leopold in his *Johannes der Täufer*, p. 123–125.

of their boyhood. There is, nevertheless, one particular of this history to which it will be well to give attention.

According to Luke 1 : 26, and 2 : 4., the proper residence of Mary was Nazareth in Galilee ; but Zacharias and his wife dwelt in the "hill country" of Judea, i. e. in the eastern part of the tribe of Judah, on the Dead Sea (1 : 65.) ; and the city in which they lived was probably called Judah, or, according to another reading, Jutta or Juta, which is mentioned in Josh. 15 : 55, and 21 : 16., and must have been situated in the neighborhood of Hebron (1 : 39.).* The dwelling-places of

* In this verse we read εἰς πόλιν Ἰούδα, *into a city of Judah ;* nor can the Greek, supposing Ἰούδα to designate the geographical division *Judah,* have any other meaning. It has, however, been a subject of much debate *what* city is here meant. Some suppose that it is *Jerusalem ;* but this cannot be true, because a.) the article (τήν) would in that case have been used before πόλιν (*city*) ; b.) the region around Jerusalem was not called "the hill country" (v. 65.) ; c.) the birth-place of John was near the desert (v. 80.). Others think that Hebron is referred to, a sacerdotal city, which is spoken of in Josh. 21 : 11. as being in "the hill-country of Judah" ; and the supposition may be correct, as there is nothing in the text that militates against it. Another and at present the prevailing opinion (originating with R. Valesius, 1613), is that Ἰούδα is itself the name of a city, it being either a softened form of, or an error of the text for, Ἰούτα, a Greek form corresponding to the Hebrew יוּטָּה (E. V. *Juttah*), a sacerdotal city situated in the highlands a few miles south of Hebron (Josh. 15 : 55., 21 : 16.). This city still exists as a village, under the name *Yuttah* (Robinson, *Bib. Researches*, vol. II. pp. 190. 195. 628.). So think, among other authorities, Kuinoel, Meyer, Reland (*Palæst.* p. 870), Bloomfield, Robinson, Von Rohden (as above), and Leopold (*Johannes der T.* p. 24.).—It is very questionable, however, whether mere *conjecture* (for this is only conjecture, *all* the codices having Ἰούδα) is sufficient authority for changing a reading : it certainly is not, unless the necessity is urgent, which it surely is not in the present instance. De Wette, who is in a case like this no mean authority, declares against the conjecture that Ἰούδα stands here for Ἰούτα, speaking of it as "an error so much the more improbable, since, on account of the want of all traces of it in critical monuments, it must have been com-

the two families, therefore, were distant from each other, by the shortest route, at least from ten to twelve German, or from forty-five to fifty-four English, miles ; and, consequently, from the difficulties then existing in the way of travelling, the mutual visits of the two women could not have been so very frequent. At the time of the birth of Jesus, indeed, Mary was in Bethlehem, but she must have fled directly afterwards to Egypt (Matt. 2 : 14.) ; and, on returning from that country, she went back to Nazareth, and, therefore, continued widely separated from Elisabeth. The best opportunity at which they could see each other, occurred on the occasion of the yearly festival-journey to Jerusalem, which every Israelite was bound to perform ; but it does not appear to have been the general custom for sons of less than twelve years to make the pilgrimage to Jerusalem in company with their parents. At this age we find Jesus visiting the temple, for the first time, as it would seem (Luke 2: 41. ff.). This was the age at which children were expressly bound to the observance of the law, and attained, in a measure, the proper degree of maturity for acquiring citizenship in Israel. If now, as is in the highest degree probable, the two families met, at a subsequent period, on this festal occasion, it cannot, in all likelihood, have been otherwise than that the mothers, who had so much to communicate with each other, brought about also a mutual acquaintance between their two sons, who, the oftener they saw

mitted by Luke himself" ; to which he adds, "it militates, moreover, against the supposition, that Christian antiquity knows nothing of this birth-place" (on Luke 1 : 39.). The same critic says that the form of the Greek leaves it undetermined what city is intended ; and was probably meant to do so. Upon the whole, this latter seems the preferable view. The rabbins suppose that Hebron (as above) is referred to (Othon, *Lex. Rabb.* p. 324., Witsius, *Miscell Sac.* II. p. 380.).

each other and the riper the age at which they met, must have become the more intimate. How, then, could John say, "I knew him not"?

In drawing such a conclusion as that just noticed, one proceeds upon a pre-supposition which needs first to be proved. It is overlooked by him who takes such a view of the case, that the parents of John are mentioned no more in the whole subsequent period, and that, in consequence, nothing prevents us from supposing that they, at least the mother, died not long after the birth of their son, or perhaps ten or twelve years after, especially since, according to Luke 1 : 7., they were, even before the birth of John, "well stricken in years." If, then, the care and education of John were intrusted to strange people, who perchance knew nothing of the family of Mary, we may very well conjecture that the youthful Jesus continued, if not entirely unknown, at most only very superficially known to the Baptist; that, at least, the latter had heard nothing of the great expectations which his parents cherished respecting Jesus, for these indeed, they had not imparted indiscriminately to every person among their acquaintance. And if we recollect, also, that John, according to the representations of the evangelists, early withdrew, of his own accord, into solitude, and shunned the companionship of men, he might, in truth, have said with entire correctness, "I knew him not"; for, admitting that he had seen Jesus once, perhaps, as a boy or youth, we cannot expect that he should still recollect him, when he saw him again as a man in his thirtieth year.

On the grounds above-mentioned, therefore, it would be difficult to prove beyond a question, that there must necessarily have been, at an early period, an intimate acquaintance between John and Christ. Such an acquaintance, however, seems to be more strongly indicated by the words with which John accosted Jesus on the occasion of his baptism. It is upon this address in particular that the assertion of a contradiction between Matthew and the words of John, "I knew him not," has been founded.

When Jesus comes to the Jordan unto John, in order to be baptized by him, the Baptist attempts to restrain him with the words, "I have need to be baptized of thee, and comest thou to me?" These words pre-suppose, in any case, a knowledge of the perfect moral purity of Jesus, at least of a purity more perfect than that which John was conscious he possessed; nay, perhaps also a knowledge of the greatness of Jesus and of his elevation above him, though this latter sense is by no means the first suggested, and is not necessarily the first to be sought for, in the expression. Such a knowledge, it would seem, John could have obtained in no other manner than by a personal acquaintance with Jesus. Whether the Baptist may or may not have seen him for so long a time as has been found possible, or whether he was only informed generally of his purity and holiness by other people, it is clear that, in either case, he knew Jesus at once, when he came into his presence. How, now, are we to harmonize these words of John with his other expression, "I knew him not"?

One might say that John, in consequence of his possessing the prophetic spirit, had a presentiment, when he first glanced at the unknown Jesus, of his dignity, and would, on that account, have prevented him from being baptized, without, however, having a full assurance that the new candidate was the Messiah, of which fact he was first informed by the voice from heaven. But of such an impression made upon John by the appearance of Jesus, there is not the slightest indication given in the narrative. Had it really been produced, we should rather expect to be made acquainted with the fact, in some such words as these : " And when John saw him, he prevented him." On the contrary, however, the narrative as it stands, leaves every where the impression of a previous ordinary acquaintance between John and Jesus; while, moreover, the commencement of the recognition of Jesus by John is expressly referred to the voice from heaven.

This last remark leads us to the right explanation of the whole matter. We must look at that with which John became acquainted respecting Jesus on the occasion of this administration of baptism, in order to understand what that was respecting him of which he had never before been informed. We read that he, in his remarks regarding Jesus, recognized him as the Son of God, as he who was soon to baptize with the Holy Spirit, as the Lamb of God who taketh away the sin of the world, as he who was higher than himself, because he existed already before him, etc., but we do not find that he recognizes him now as the son of Mary and Joseph, as one who has proceeded out of Nazareth, as one who is called Jesus. It was entirely immaterial whether he knew this of Christ, or not, provided only he did not recognize him, until specially informed, as the Son of God. As such, was John to proclaim him to Israel ; in order to recognize him as such, he had received a special divine revelation ; but that he had not hitherto recognized him in this character, is placed beyond question by his own direct testimony, "I knew him not." Whether, however, he knew him also as the son of the carpenter Joseph, as a pure and moral man, as his cousin, is, as far as this expression is concerned, not at all determined. Those persons in Galilee who despised Christ, because they knew his family, because they had seen him in his childhood, because they knew that he was the son of unlearned people, did they know Christ? Yes, they were acquainted with his outward appearance, but himself, his true being, they did not know. We ourselves frequently make a similar distinction, when we are asked whether we are acquainted with a man or not, by answering, "Yes, superficially, or in a general way, but not specially": and, in such a case, we would, under certain circumstances, hesitate not to reply, "I know him not"; for we feel conscious that we do not really know a man at all, until we have become acquainted with his proper character. Here, in the case of Christ, must all the external and incidental relations which he bore have retreated into the back-ground when brought into contact with the one truth of his existence, that he was the Son of God, that he was the Messiah; and, therefore, might John have said of him, "I knew him not," with entire correctness, so long as this, the true purpose of Christ's being, was kept concealed from his knowledge.

If, therefore, we are obliged to infer from Matt. 3 : 14, that John had occasionally seen his cousin at an earlier period, and had known him as a man of moral and pure habits, we are, on the other hand, compelled to conclude from Jno. 1 : 31 and 33, that he had no correct idea at all of his dignity and his high destination, and knew not that Jesus was the one whose forerunner he had been called to become.—There is, it must be confessed, a difficulty in the way, which appears to militate against this view; it is, however, by no means unremovable. It seems hard to reconcile with this supposition the probable fact that John's mother communicated to him, at perhaps a very early period, the note-worthy promises which were connected with the birth of his cousin Jesus, and which stood in so close a connection with the divine announcement respecting his own birth ; from which representations he must have been accustomed, from the time they were made to him, to look upon Jesus as the distinguished personage whom he was to precede. Respecting the probability of such a communication, however, we must remember that, at least in the early years of the two children, nothing could be said to them regarding these promises, because they could not possibly have comprehended their import ; because, too, the parents must have feared that a divine prophecy whose meaning was only partially understood by themselves, might give to the minds of their children a totally false impression, and must, therefore, have rather awaited their appropriate development, looking for the exact time when they might venture with safety to communicate to the children the promise which had been made respecting their future connection and the nature of their employment. We must, in particular, recollect that those wonderful events which were connected with the birth of the children, were not made a subject of boasting and vaunting conversation by the mothers, and that they did not communicate them freely to other people ; on the contrary, as we so often read, "Mary kept all these things, and pondered them in her heart," and therefore we have every reason to conclude that they concealed and kept quietly in their minds the rich treasure of the heavenly promises, in patient expectation of the time when they should prove to be true and be fulfilled before their eyes. They could not, therefore, have thought of making their children acquainted with these promises before the proper time for imparting the information had arrived. When the time of the first public appearance of the two young men, now grown to manhood, was near at hand, then perhaps this communication became necessary, and even then much depended upon other relations, to us unknown, which might have happened at the time to be existing; and, besides, who is able to affirm that at this period the parents of John had not long been dead, so that he could have learned from them nothing of the promises respecting Jesus; and in such an event, is it not probable, since he withdrew himself so early into solitude and separation from other men, that Mary had found no opportunity of informing him of the facts which related to his connection with his cousin?

Various explanations of this declaration of the Baptist, "I knew him not," have been offered by interpreters of the New Testament; no one of which, however, is free from objections, while some are evidently inadmissible. That above given is, all sides of the question considered, the least objectionable; but it must be borne in mind, that in solving this difficulty, as also many others in the New Testament, the chief obstruction lies in the fact that complete historical accounts of many events and incidents alluded to in the Scriptures, have not been given us, but only scanty and not unfrequently disjointed fragments which it is often no easy task to bring into harmony with each other.—One class of interpreters adopting the most patent meaning of ᾔδειν *(I knew)*, contend that John asserts here that he knew not the *person* of Christ. This view is advocated by Dr. J. R. Beard in *Kitto's Cyclop. of Bib. Literature.** But, if John did not know the person of Jesus when he presented

* N. Y. edit. vol. 2. p. 129. Art. *John the Baptist.*

himself for baptism, how was he made conscious of his superiority to himself? To this Dr. B. replies: "The relation in which John and Jesus stood to each other must have been well known to both. When, therefore, Jesus came to John, he would naturally declare himself to be the intended Messiah. Such a declaration,—thus pointing out the person,—would, of course, conciliate belief in John's mind, and might naturally prompt the self-abasing language which he employs when requested by Jesus to give him baptism." This reply is altogether unsatisfactory; for a.) it is highly improbable that John and Jesus should have known the relation in which they stood to each other without having been already personally acquainted; and b.) there is not the slightest hint in the narrative of Matthew (3: 13, 14.), that Jesus declared himself to be the expected Messiah; on the contrary, its whole tenor gives us to understand that a personal acquaintance between the two already existed. Thus much at least must be admitted, or every attempt to solve the difficulty will be unsuccessful.

Taking a ground quite the opposite of that just considered, all the modern commentators of any eminence assume the fact as unquestionable, that John and Jesus were personally acquainted previous to the baptism of the latter; and some of them even contend that John was also previously cognizant of the Messianic dignity of Jesus. These differ not a little among themselves in the explanations of the sense in which the phrase in question (*οὐκ ᾔδειν αὐτόν*) is here employed by the Baptist. That of Neander (*Leben Jesu*, 4 te Auf. S. 107.) seems the most objectionable of all. He says: "The Baptist intends to assert by these words, in the most impressive manner possible, in consequence of the object he then had in view, that his confident conviction respecting Jesus as the Messiah and the Son of God, is not of human but of divine origin. Though he had already anticipated from what he had heard reported respecting the birth of Jesus, that he was the Messiah, the divine testimony which he had now received in his own person regarding Jesus was far more important in his eyes than all which he had previously heard of him from other sources, and, in comparison with that which he now beheld in the divine light, all that he knew at an earlier period respecting Jesus appeared to him as only ignorance." But the Baptist was too straightforward a man to make such nice distinctions ; and, if we are allowed to solve every difficulty in the New Testament interpretation by such an elastic process as this, there will be no end to the spiritualizing of Scripture, whenever its plain import is at variance with the pre-conceived ideas or the objective feelings of the interpreter.

The explanation given by Tholuck* is nearly as unsatisfactory, and finds just as little support in the narrative : "Most commentators remark here that John was indeed personally acquainted with Jesus, but that he did not know him to be the Messiah. But from Matt. iii. the latter supposition seems to be incorrect. It is better, therefore, to assume with Beza, Lampe and others, that when the decisive moment of baptism approached, the Baptist was filled with an [in substance correct]† apprehension of his character, which by the appearance of the dove became a settled conviction."—This explanation, however, comes into direct conflict with John's assertion that he did not know Jesus previous to his baptism ; for, how could

* Commentary on John, Eng. transl. by Kaufman, N. York, 2d edit. p. 86.

† There is something faulty here in the rendering of the German : we have

he say so, if he entertained a proper idea of his character, even though his conviction might have needed confirmation?

In some respects akin to this solution of the difficulty, but not carried by any means so far, and therefore much preferable, is the explanation given by Leopold *(Joh. d. T. p.* 121–123.*)* : "By the words 'I knew him not,' the Baptist did not mean to say that he had known nothing at all of Jesus until he presented himself for baptism, for we find sufficient records to prove that John had, previously to that time, made his personal acquaintance; but the expression *οὐκ ᾔδειν αὐτόν* is to be taken *in a higher sense.* The conversation of John and Jesus (Matt. 3 : 13–15.), on the application of the latter for baptism, proves a previous acquaintance of the two. Whence otherwise the brevity of the conference? Whence the hesitation of the Baptist to baptize Jesus? The former shows an acquaintance in general; the latter, a knowledge of the Messianic dignity of the Saviour. . . . . According to the Gospel of John the expression is to be taken thus: the Baptist does not mean to declare that he was unacquainted with Jesus; but intends to say that he, although initiated into the plan of the Messiah, had not hitherto recognized him *in his full greatness*, and did not, until God honored him with the disclosure."—This explanation, like that of Tholuck, infringes upon the meaning of *ᾔδειν*; and is, in fact, a mere evasion of the difficulty.

No solution of this apparent contradiction between the evangelists John and Matthew, can be satisfactory which does not proceed from the premises admitted even by the ra-

endeavored to give by the words supplied in brackets what we suppose is the idea meant to be conveyed by Tholuck; but we may be wrong, having no German copy by us for reference.

tionalizing Winer,* "that οὐκ ᾔδειν αὐτόν, Joh. 1 : 31., refers, as the whole connection, especially v. 33., teaches, to the Messianic dignity of Jesus" ; and which is not, therefore, based upon the concession that John knew not Jesus to be the Messiah until he obtained that knowledge by a divine revelation, given by the descent of the Holy Spirit in a symbol, after Jesus had received baptism at his hands.—The fact that John refuses to baptize him at first, presents no real difficulty ; for we are by no means obliged to conclude that he did so because he was conscious of Jesus' Messiahship, since, as has been mentioned above,—a view in which critics of such different characteristics as De Wette, Olshausen, and Bloomfield coincide,—John no doubt hesitated to administer the rite to him because he was aware of Christ's superior wisdom and sanctity.

Adopting this explanation of the expression "I knew him not," we have only to solve the difficulty which has been already touched upon, viz., how, considering the relation in which the mother of John and Jesus stood to each other, it could happen that the Baptist should know the person of Jesus and yet be ignorant that he was the promised Messiah. Winer considers this difficulty inexplicable ; and it must be admitted that, on account of the want of positive historical information upon this point, no explanation can be made which shall be indisputably correct, and be beyond cavil or objection. The solution above given bears at least the air of plausibility, but is not, as none can be, wholly satisfactory. It is not necessary, however, nor are we bound, to show the entire harmony of the two facts ; it is enough to have shown, as has been done, that they are not irreconcilable.

* Biblisches Realwörterbuch, 3 te Auf., erst. Band, S. 586. Anm. 6.

The English theologians, generally, adopt the view advocated by Beard ; and contend that John knew not the *person* of Jesus until he appeared to receive the Messianic baptism. Such is the opinion expressed by Horne in his "Considerations" (§ 6.), and by Taylor, in his "Life of Christ" (§ 9. 1.); the latter of whom says : "The Baptist had never seen his face. But immediately the Holy Ghost inspired S. John with a discerning and knowing spirit ; and, at his first arrival, he knew him and did him worship." Huxtable, in his "Ministry of S. John the Baptist" (p. 59.), though admitting the possibility of a previous acquaintance between the Forerunner and his divine kinsman, inclines to the same belief. He regards the fact of their being related favorable to "the supposition of some degree of personal acquaintance"; but thinks that the distance lying between their respective abodes, and, particularly, the language of Luke in 1 : 80., render "the supposition improbable."

It is possible, indeed that John may not have been personally acquainted with Jesus ; but the narrative of Matthew (3 : 14.) seems clearly to imply a previous acquaintance; and the manner and connection in which the Baptist says "I knew him not" (Jno. 1 : 31.), show that he means, "I knew him not as he 'that baptizeth in the Holy Spirit,' as 'the Son of God,' the promised Messiah."

We may, therefore, with great propriety, conclude, after this review of all the facts of the case, that John became acquainted in his early years with his cousin Jesus, that he was also aware of his great moral purity ; nay, we may even suppose that there arose within him at times an anticipation of his high destination ; but, notwithstanding he knew him not, not until the Spirit of God had revealed that he was the Messiah, the Son of God.

CHAPTER III.

DEVELOPMENT OF JOHN, AND PREPARATION FOR HIS PUBLIC MINISTRY.

As the sacred history in general represents to us only simple matter-of-fact, only the great and note-worthy appearances in the epochs of the theocratic reign, and exhibits these in their brief and simple outline, and, refraining from all further reflections upon the way in which and the reason for which these events occurred, affords us only now and then, by slight intimations, a glance into the secret workings of the divine Spirit in individuals and among the entire nation; so do we find, in the history of John, respecting the formation and development of his character until the time of his public appearance, only a few slight hints given in the evangelical narrative, which suffice, indeed, to throw light upon his ministry at a later period, but entirely cut off all speculation upon every over-curious question respecting details and unimportant circumstances. We must, therefore, content ourselves, not with attempting inquisitively to discover, by all kinds of conjectures and strange subtilties, what the divine wisdom has intentionally veiled from our eyes, but only with endeavoring to construct, out of the general hints given us respecting him, the formative process by which the character of this notable personage was produced.

Of the manner in which his domestic education was conducted, we may obtain the most correct knowledge by proceeding from the fact that he was descended from a priestly race, and of pious parents who were in possession of precious promises regarding their son; and that he was destined by the angel, even before his birth, for a Nazarite (Luke 1 : 15.). Since his father was not sufficiently rich, in all probability, to employ private instructors for his son, as was the custom at this time in Palestine, and was too far removed from Jerusalem to give his son an opportunity of receiving instruction in the public schools and from the discourses of those in that city learned in the law, he must himself have taught John in the chief subjects of instruction, and, above all, in the law, which formed at that time the principal element in a liberal education. Zacharias was a priest, and as such must have been well acquainted with the Old Testament; he was a pious man, and therefore must he gladly have occupied himself with the study of holy writ. From him, therefore, could his son have obtained an accurate and true, though, as might be expected from the stand-point of his instructor, a limited insight into the contents and character of the Old Testament; and by him might he have been inspired with a worthy zeal and predilection for this kind of study. His mother, too, was a pious and god-fearing woman; and since the first and deepest religious impressions are commonly made by the mother upon children, we may justly conclude that John was early imbued by his intercourse with his mother with the deepest reverence for God, confidence in him, and obedience to his commands. To this must be added the fact that he was a Nazarite, dedicated to God from his childhood: he must, therefore, have early accustomed himself to regard God as the one to whom alone he belonged, as him to whom he was to devote the labors of his whole life.*

* A Nazarite (*Heb.* נזיר, from the verb נזר *to separate one's-self*) was one who was consecrated, either by himself or by another, in some peculiar manner

The numerous prayers and devotional exercises which were imposed upon him by his vow must have brought him into a more and more intimate union with him whom he recognized more and more, as he studied the sacred records, in his power and holiness as well as in his mercy and truth. The deprivation of so many of the enjoyments of life, which was necessary to the fulfillment of his vow, must have served him as a protection against the numerous enticing and seductive allurements by which the season of youth is usually beset; must have withdrawn him more and more from the attractions of the outward world; and must, especially under the careful training of pious parents, have awakened in him, at an early period, that moral seriousness which afterwards formed the distinguishing characteristic of his entire life. Since, furthermore, his parents longed earnestly for the coming of the new Messianic reign, and since this expectation was particularly confirmed by the occurrences which took place in connection with the birth of their son and by those which happened in the house of their kinswoman Mary; since, finally, they knew that their son was called to act an important part in the great epoch then approaching, they must surely have taken upon themselves at an early period to call the attention of the

to the service and worship of Jehovah. The Nazarite might be either a male or a female. An instance of the latter was the mother of Samson; examples of the former were Samson himself and Samuel, which two Old Testament worthies were, like the Baptist, Nazarites from their birth. The law of the Nazarite is given in full in Num. 6: 1–21. He was, in particular, to abstain from wine, strong drinks, and from all that was made from the vine, even vinegar, and was to have his hair unshorn. When the vow of the Nazarite had been performed, the hair was shaved off and made a burnt offering to Jehovah. A similar custom was known among several nations of antiquity, and is practised among the Persians of the present day.

youthful John in particular to those prophecies of the Old Testament which relate to the Messiah, and to the signs of the times which indicated his speedy advent ; and they must have directed his thoughts and mind to the promise of a forerunner of the Saviour,—a promise fraught with deep import for him,—to which the angel had previously referred his father Zacharias (Luke 1 : 16, 17.).

In this manner John grew up to manhood, ever more withdrawing himself from all in the external world which was unpleasant to his feelings and opposed to his leading a life dedicated to God ; constantly forming for himself a strong and impressive character by the perusal of the sacred writings and by meditation on the divine promises ; developing himself independently from an early period, and impressed, no doubt, with an anticipation which gradually formed itself within his soul, that he was destined by God to uplift anew the prophetic and punitive voice after the manner of the ancient prophets.—That, however, which must specially have roused the young man and have created in him, along with the most violent indignation, a desire also to change the course of things and direct them to a better end, was, without doubt, the moral corruption which, as he perceived, had spread among all classes of the people ; the increase of all kinds of crime ; the profanation of what he deemed most holy ; and the hypocrisy and forgetfulness of God which were manifested by the leaders and most celebrated men of the nation. All this he looked upon in the light, perhaps, of the distinguished counterpart afforded by the spotless purity of his cousin,—a purity which he had as yet by no means recognized in its full perfection, which he had not himself reached, but to which he was earnestly striving to attain. In a mind swayed by such powerful feelings as was his, a daily experience of the demoralization of his people, added, probably, to the indignation which burned within him, as it did in all the noble hearts of that time, in view of their disgraceful slavery,—which, perhaps, he was wont from an early period to regard as the punishment of their sins,—and united with a deep and lively knowledge of the Old Testament Scriptures, with the endeavor to perform the divine commands in their widest extent, and with the firm expectation that a new era of the theocracy was about to be ushered in,—might, it is easy to perceive, have readily produced the resolution to withdraw himself wholly from the world and retire into solitude, there to live entirely for his God and to wait for the better time which was approaching.—Whether other external circumstances besides these, as, for instance, the death of his parents, by which he was altogether freed from family bonds and thrown back, as it were, wholly upon himself, contributed in leading him to adopt this resolution, we cannot determine, on account of the want of all indications of the fact, yet it seems to us not at all improbable.

To a man like John, who must in his youth have become accustomed to so many deprivations, it could not have been difficult to forego altogether everything which an effeminating luxury deems essential to existence, and to support in the simplest and poorest manner, the life which he purposed to devote for the future entirely to God, and to pass it in the consideration of divine things, with the view, it may be, of preparing himself for a future public appearance as a preacher among the people. In the mild latitude of Palestine, it was not so difficult, amid the richness and luxuriance of its vegetation, for him to dwell secluded from all men in solitary regions ; and we are not obliged to conclude that John sought out expressly the places which were the most unfruitful and the most valueless. It is indeed related of him that he had been in the wilderness ; but we are not to consider this a desert, like the sand-wastes of Africa, but rather steppes such as were made use of freely and with profit by nomads for pasturing their cattle, as we find that Joseph's brethren tended their herds in the wilderness (Gen. 37 : 22.),—lonely and uninhabited places, uncultivated and pathless, but affording readily a frugal subsistence to the children of nature. In Matt. 3 : 1, John's place of residence is called more definitely " the wilderness of Judea ;" and it was, therefore, the region lying to the west of the Dead Sea, which, on account of its wildness and solitude, was best adapted to the necessities of John.

Here he lived probably in caves, using for his sustenance what nature afforded,—according to Matt. 3 : 4, and Mark 1 : 6., locusts and wild honey. Among the immense swarms of locusts which had before this been a frequent plague of Palestine, we find many kinds which were esteemed edible, if they were not considered dainties, for their flesh when roasted tastes very much like that of boiled crabs, and which must have constituted an article of food for the poorer classes, especially, on account of its cheapness. Locusts were allowed to be eaten by the law of Moses (Lev. 11 : 22.). In the eastern countries besides Palestine several species of the locust were used as food. Diodorus Siculus mentions a people of Æthiopia who were so fond of them that they were called *acridophagi*, *locust-eaters* (24, 3.). Even the Greeks are spoken of by Aristophanes as using them for an article of diet (*Achar.* 1116, 1117.). They are eaten at the present time by the Arabians and Africans ; and even form an extensive article of commerce (Sparman, *Voyage* vol. 1. p. 367. ff.). They are boiled, and afterward eaten with butter ; or they are roasted and eaten with salt ; and they are even ground to flour and made into bread (Niebuhr, Arabien, S. 171.). Such locusts as these it was which afforded his daily sustenance.

So also honey was among the Jews a favorite means of sustenance, as one can perceive at once by the manner in which the promised land of Canaan is mentioned, "the land which flows with milk and honey." They had, however, not only the honey of bees, but also the honey of grapes (thickened must), and the honey of trees (the thick glutinous mass which is formed upon the leaves of certain trees.). By the wild honey here mentioned we must understand either the kind last described, or that prepared by wild bees. Several modern critics (as Kuinoel, Fritzsche, Meyer,) are of opinion that by the "wild honey" (μέλι ἄγριον) here mentioned is meant a honey-like substance which is found upon the leaves of certain trees in the East. Sometimes this substance exudes from the plants of its own accord ; sometimes it flows forth through a puncture made by an insect called the *coccus manniparous* (*manna-producing coccus*) ; and sometimes it is a deposit made by certain insects which live upon the trees.* It is better, however, to suppose that the honey of wild bees is here referred to ; for wild honey is even now, according to Schulz (Leitung v. 133.), found abundantly in the wilderness of Judea, where it is deposited by the bees in the clefts of

* Honey of this kind is found in abundance in California. It collects in the month of July on the upper surface of the leaves of willow trees and of the white oak ; from which it is gathered by the Indians in considerable quantities. A saccharine substance exudes also from a species of pine which grows upon the Sierra Nevada ; which, like the honey, or manna, found on the willows and white-oaks, has an exceedingly pleasant flavor (*San Joaquin Journal*, 1851.)

rocks and in hollow trees. That such "wild honey" as this is what is here mentioned, Winer, (*Realwört.* Art. *Honig*) and De Wette (Com. zu. Matt. 3 : 4.) are of opinion, in which they agree with Robinson (*N. T. Lex.* Art. *Ἄγριος*), who says : "Maundrell saw many bees on the flowers between Jericho and the Dead Sea (p. 115.) ; and Forskal notes that he often saw honey flowing in the woods of Arabia, Descr. Animal. p. xxiii." Josephus describes the region of Jericho as *productive of honey* (*μελιττοτρόφος*, Bell. Jud. 4. 8. 3.). *Tree-honey*, on the other hand, was never common in Judea, least of all in that region bordering on the Dead Sea.

These were simple means of subsistence, it is true ; but they were abundantly sufficient to prolong life, and more than this John did not desire.—Alike poor was his raiment, which is described to us as a garment of camel's hair and a leathern girdle. From the hair shed by camels in the spring, cloths and garments of the coarsest kind were prepared, which only the poorest and the lowest class of people wore ; but they were strong and lasting, perfectly answering the objects of raiment.—Some understand by "raiment of camel's hair" the camel's skin with the hair on, and suppose John to have worn such a garment as the ancient prophets wore sheep-skins and goat-skins (Heb. 11 : 37.) ; but a camel's skin garment would have been too heavy to carry conveniently, and so to understand the expression violates the natural meaning of the Greek (*ἔνδυμα ἀπὸ τριχῶν καμήλου*). As the leathern girdle which the Baptist wore was in imitation of that of the prophet Elijah (2 Kings 1 : 8.), so it is probable was his garment of camel's hair copied after that worn by the same Old Testament prophet ; for we may with propriety suppose that the expression "hairy man" (Heb. אִישׁ שֵׂעָר) applied to Elijah in 2

Kings 1 : 8., refers to the kind of garment with which he was clothed (See Thenius, *Bücher d. Könige S.*262.).—The second chief article of the Baptist's attire was a leathern thong by which his garment of camel's hair was fastened; and this formed a striking contrast with the girdles of the rich which were for the most part set with precious stones.

Thus is John represented to us at his first public appearance; and thus, without doubt, have we to conceive him during his previous residence in the wilderness, a complete picture of the austere prophets of more ancient times, as one of whom he must have regarded himself, namely, as the successor of Elias; and representing symbolically in his outward life and residence the spiritual wilderness in which he was to labor and the repentance which he was to require.

That it was not an altogether unheard-of and unusual thing to withdraw in this way from all human society into lonely and distant places, we ascertain among other ways from the description which Josephus, a Jewish historical writer, who lived nearly at the same time with John, gives of his own life; for, after he had thoroughly examined and tried all the three sects of the Jewish people, he also made the attempt to discover how the instruction of a rigorous ascetic, whom he calls Banus, would suit him. He thus describes him: "I was informed that a person named Banus lived in the wilderness, who used no other clothing than what grew upon trees, and had no other food but that which was produced spontaneously, and bathed himself often in cold water, by night and by day, for the sake of purification." (*Life*, 2.). In this case, then, we have a still stronger instance of asceticism and of the renunciation of all human fellowship; for the raiment of Banus was not prepared, as was John's, artificially by the hands of men; and, therefore, we can, at least, regard the Baptist as not the only Jew in whom such an idea of anchoretism unfolded itself, and as not the most rigorous in carrying it out into practice.

But, in what way was John employed during his stay in the wilderness? He was engaged, no doubt, in perfecting his character, in mortifying his fleshly appetites, in the suppression of sinful desires, and in the study of the Word of God. If, in general, the spending of life in solitude is not the surest means of overpowering sinful inclination, and of extinguishing sin, yet, in the case of John, one is authorized to conclude, from the serious earnestness which he exhibited in his whole life, and with which, therefore, he must have proceeded to the work of attaining moral perfection, that the seductive power of all sensual enticements was lost upon him on account of his living in a manner and in a place far removed from their influence; and that, in like manner, the habit of practising a morality, confessedly only Jewish, but such as was prescribed by the law, removed far from him the temptation to many sins of practice and of thought. It is just as certain, however, that he could never have attained in this way to perfect sinlessness; but, as he himself confessed in his address to Christ, "I have need to be baptized of thee," he must have remained still sinful in the inmost recesses of his heart. For this reason could he always be to the corrupt people an example and a model of moral purity, as far as such could be obtained by conformity to the Jewish law; whilst he, likewise, in accordance with the divine plan, afforded, on the other hand, a standing proof how impossible it is, without the new spirit which is conferred by Christ upon believers, to attain to a perfect change of heart. In this struggle of his after perfection, his constant employment with the Word of God must manifestly have been a great assistance:

for, in general, he who has God ever before his eyes and is always directing his senses and ideas towards him, is led away into sin with much more difficulty than the man who is engaged in the ordinary avocations of life. The chief object of this employment, perhaps, in his case, was one which was in harmony with the impressions which he had received in youth and other external motives which constantly worked upon him,—the examination of the divine promises respecting the sending of the Messiah. The truth and certainty of this mission must have been speedily confirmed in his mind, and, in like manner, a conviction of the probability, nay, necessity that the new reign should shortly commence.—At this point, however, it is proper to inquire, *what were his views of the nature of this kingdom?*

Judging by expressions uttered by him at a later period, we are forced to conclude that John, during his residence in the wilderness, had by no means raised himself completely above the more approved Messianic expectations of his people, as they had probably been impressed upon him, in his childhood, by his parents; and, therefore, that he had not, as indeed Christ alone had, a clear conception of the fact that the new kingdom was to be one wholly spiritual, destitute of all earthly power and glory. Before the true explanation of the obscure and apparently contradictory passages of the Old Testament, respecting the Messiah had been given, it was utterly impossible for a Jew to reject altogether what, especially in that time of oppression, he esteemed of most value in the Scriptures,—those announcements which represent the Christ as a king raised high above all earthly dominions and a prince arrayed in all the splendor and all the brilliancy of worldly magnificence. Neither could he bring himself to refer the representations of external dominion given in the prophecies to the inward spiritual dominion of the prince of life ; nor distinguish between the first and the second coming of the Lord, since, in the prophecies they are treated not distinctly but as a whole. We must, therefore, necessarily attribute to John also an expectation which shall correspond with these Jewish conceptions.

This expectation of the Baptist's, it must be granted, was of a higher grade than ordinary ; being such as was entertained by the noblest and most religious portion of the people, and was wholly free from the more crude, sensual and selfish views held by the Jewish nation at large. John saw distinctly that a moral change in the people must precede and become the foundation of the new kingdom ; that the happiness which it was to confer was to pertain only to the pious and repentant ; that, therefore, the haughty and the hypocritical who boasted that they, as the genuine descendants of Abraham, would be the possessors of the kingdom, would not only be excluded therefrom, but would be visited with punishment and be utterly destroyed ; and that, in general, the power of entering into the new kingdom would belong by no means to the children of Abraham exclusively, but, though that kingdom had been promised to the Jews and founded for them in particular, would appertain also to all those among the heathen who should be converted and should repent of their sins. In these respects, then, we find his Messianic expectations purer and more consonant with the truth than those usually entertained. He had recognized the true foundation of the new kingdom ; and, consequently, he must, at least, have had a presentiment of its spirituality, though it is likely that here likewise the earthly conceptions which he had imbibed from the opinions prevalent in his time and from the Messianic promises in Scripture, intermingled with and clouded his more correct intuitions.

But, we have to inquire here, whether with these conceptions of a Messiah who should possess external power and glory he could not have united an expectation that some sort of suffering must be endured by the Christ in order to secure his people's salvation.

It is scarcely possible that John, during his zealous researches into the sacred writings, could have entirely overlooked the Old Testament prophecies of a suffering Messiah ; for they are as clear and as evident as those which relate to a Messiah of royal power. The idea of David, moreover, who is expressly represented in the Old Testament as the type of Christ, must often have hovered around his soul ; and this monarch was compelled to suffer much and things hard to be borne, before he attained to the complete power and glory which were his rightful possession. Since, then, the Baptist had a lively perception of the fact that a moral change of the people was requisite, that God, who had been grievously offended, was to be reconciled once for all with the people by the expected Messiah, that this Messiah is distinctly announced in the Old Testament as the suffering servant of God ; the expectation might very readily have been created in his mind, that the appearance of the Messiah would, indeed, be accompanied externally with earthly splendor, as would become a king, and with the public declaration that he was the promised king of kings, who would collect all the pious around his person, lead them to God, and found with them a royal and happy kingdom ; but that they who possessed worldly power would fall upon, persecute and afflict him, just as it had happened unto king David, and that God would permit this suffering of his ambassador in behalf of his new people and kingdom, and would esteem it an expiation of the suffering which the people themselves deserved to receive ; and, finally, that he would allow him, when tried and approved by the fire of affliction, to proceed forward in his invincible power and majesty, as lord and king, unto whom all kingdoms are subject, and with whom all the pious and all that fear God are to rule in unbroken felicity. That such ideas as these could easily have been formed in the mind of John from his assiduous study of the Holy Scriptures, no one will deny ; for, that the theocratic king must endure suffering and persecution was a notion by no means foreign to the thoughts of the more spiritually informed class of the people, is proved by the words of Simeon to Mary (Luke 2 : 34, 35.) : "Behold, this child is set for the fall and rising again of many in Israel ; and for a sign *which shall be spoken against* ;—yea, a sword shall pierce through thy own soul also, etc." ; in which words the expectation of a bitter suffering on the part of her son is pre-supposed, so great that the sorrow which it is to produce in Mary should pierce her soul like a sword.

Nay, we may proceed a step further. Since John examined into the Psalms and prophecies of the Old Testament with all the zeal and the earnestness which were at his command, and with prayer and supplication to God for enlightenment,—which no doubt God did not refuse to bestow,—we may well expect that a light had already broken upon him revealing the divine nature of the expected Messiah. As Christ himself proved his divinity from the Scriptures, John might also have discovered it in the holy writings ; he might have had a presentiment, if he was not clearly convinced, that he who was to appear in human form as the king and saviour of the world, must be, if not equal to, at least in the highest degree like, God, a being elevated far above all mankind ; nay, he might, perchance, in accordance with the distinction,—very current at that time,—which the Jews made between God revealed and God concealed, and in accordance with the idea of personality which was in that age attributed, in some degree, to the Revelation of God, the Word of God, have anticipated that this Word of God, the everlasting, was that which, appearing now as a man among men, was to found a new regal kingdom ; or he might have conceived of him as the angel of the covenant, as he is specially called in Malachi (3 : 1.), to which prophet John so often refers in his teaching and discourses,—and this seems to be indicated as the truth by the appellation ὁ ἐρχόμενος (*he that cometh*), so often bestowed by John upon Christ, which appears to have been suggested by the representations of Malachi.

All this might John have believed without changing or retracting in any degree his ideas of an earthly and external kingdom, or his conceptions regarding the sufferings of the Messiah. This, therefore, is clearly perceptible, that John stood upon a very high step of knowledge, standing probably as high (as will appear more evident when we come hereafter to consider his public ministry) as one versed only in the Old Testament and without a divine revelation could stand,—the highest among all his contemporaries, since he was to exhibit the Old Testament in its utmost perfection before it was superseded forever. But he was far from having that which Christ himself first introduced,—the conception of a pure, moral, spiritual world-dominion, enclosed by no external boundaries, in which he who is king and lord in the right of his Father, is also the brother of all those who believe in him, and works in all by the agency of his Holy Spirit. This kingdom could no man have conceived of until it had been presented to him as an existing reality; and on this account can the least in this heavenly dominion be called greater than John, who, however, was declared by Christ himself to be the greatest among all who were without that kingdom.

There is no necessity for supposing that John received, while in the wilderness, special divine revelations regarding the character of the Messiah and the duties of the office which he himself, as forerunner, was to discharge; for, as we have seen, all the knowledge which he exhibited upon these points during his ministry was such as he might have acquired from a study of the Old Testament prophecies, and such as, in point of fact, others of the Jewish nation had in many respects attained.—Neither are we required to believe, on the other hand, that his views were not self-evolved, but received from his associations with others of the Jewish people. In accordance with this supposition, a number of biblical writers have maintained that John received his distinctive and peculiar ideas from the sect of the Essenes, who resided, as he did, in the region known as "the wilderness of Judea" (Pliny, *H. N.* 5. 17.). But, aside from the fact that we find no hint of this in the New Testament, it is clear from the representations which Josephus and Philo give of this Jewish sect, that neither the Baptist's manner of life nor his doctrine had anything in common with their peculiarities. As far as he agreed with them, he agreed also with others among the Jewish nation; and in not a few important particulars he differed from them altogether; which would not have been the case, had he received among them his mental and moral development.

So prepared on every hand for the great work which he proposed to perform,—namely, to lead the people by his preaching and his admonitions to repentance,—John at length made his appearance, not, however, by any means of his own arbitrary choice and in his own power, but specially called to his ministry by the Lord himself (Luke 3 : 2.). The words which he uses in John 1 : 33., "he that sent me to baptize, etc.," cannot, it is admitted, prove of themselves that a special revelation had been communicated to him, summoning him to his labors,—for the announcement of the token by which he might recognize the Messiah, which confessedly presupposes a particular revelation, may first have been made to him during his public ministry,—since his internal assurance that he was in this way to fulfill the will of God, might very well have been considered by him a divine call (just as we find in the case of Elijah no special summons from God, who, however, always spoke and acted in the name of the Lord and in the assurance of his divine coöperation) ; but we read in Luke 3 : 2. that he actually received a positive call from heaven ; and we have, therefore, no ground to doubt the truth of a fact which we find to have been of so frequent occurrence in earlier times in the case of the prophets. As we merely read of them, "the word of the Lord came to me," or "upon me," and are not informed whether it came in a vision, or while its recipient was in an ecstasy, or through the agency of an angel, or in what other way, so we cannot determine in what manner John received his summons from on high.

The time of the appearance of the Baptist, therefore, was not decided upon by himself ; but was determined by the Lord. The call which he received resembled that given to the prophets of the Old Testament. The word of the Lord came unto him, urging him to a certain course ; but the impulse of the Spirit then given was, as in the case of the Old Testament prophets, only transitory, and not abiding as it is under the New Testament dispensation : it was rather sudden and momentary ; not calm and continually active, as it is under the economy of grace.—This "word of the Lord", however, has a two-fold character : it is either a discourse of God's addressed to the people as though personally present, which the prophets receive at some moment of special inspiration and announce to the people, or a single positive command from God to do this or that. Of this latter kind are we to suppose the "word of the Lord" to John to have been.—He was, therefore, a real prophet, and as such was led and enlightened in an especial manner by the Spirit of the Lord, and made, perhaps, the recipient, at times, of particular revelations (as we may infer from the passage above cited from John) ; but he was not "*the* prophet" ; for he denied, as we have seen, that he was such when the messengers of the Sanhedrim questioned him on the point (Jno. 1 : 21.),—not the particular Messianic prophet promised by Moses, whom the confused and indistinct conceptions of the people were accustomed to distinguish from their Messianic king.

PART THIRD.

MINISTRY OF JOHN BEFORE THE PUBLIC APPEARANCE OF CHRIST.

CHAPTER I.

John's Preaching of Repentance.

Prepared by God, by whose voice he was at length summoned forth, in quiet solitude for his prophetic calling, endowed with power to perform the duty intrusted to him, and enlightened as far as was necessary to the discharge of the duties of his office, John made his appearance in the neighborhood of the Jordan, where contiguity to large towns and commercial roads would afford him access to great multitudes of people, where his preaching might be farthest extended in influence, and the reputation of his labors be the most noised abroad. According to Matthew, his residence was, ordinarily, that portion of the region round about Jordan which bordered upon the Dead Sea, and from which a steppe stretched away into the land of Judea ; whence it is called by that evangelist, " the wilderness of Judea."

The " wilderness of Judea" in which the Baptist resided "till the day of his showing unto Israel" (Luke 1 : 80.), was strictly speaking a district in the eastern side of the territory of Judah, bordering on the Dead Sea (Josh. 15 : 61., Judges 1 : 16.), and containing the city of Engedi and others. It is described as extending, in length, from the right bank of the

Kidron, about twelve miles above Jerusalem, to the south-western end of the Dead Sea; and, in width, from the same sea westwardly to the mountains of Judah. This region is comparatively barren, abounding in rocks which are clothed with little vegetation but are full of grotto-like caves; and containing few houses and sparsely inhabited, though well adapted to pasturage.—Here it was that John first made his public appearance; but his ministry was not long restricted to this particular theatre. He made his way northwardly until he came into the vicinity of the Jordan, where his opportunities for meeting with hearers were most numerous; and here he prosecuted during his brief career the labors which had been imposed upon him by Jehovah.

The scene of the Baptist's ministry may be readily determined by a comparison of the New Testament passages which bear upon the point (Matt. 3 : 1., Mark 1 : 4., Luke 3 : 3., and Jno. 1 : 28., 3 : 23., 10 : 40.). Two of the three evangelists first named, Matthew and Mark, speak in general terms, including under the term "wilderness" the sterile valley of the Jordan; the other, Luke, distinctly points out the neighborhood into which, on leaving the wilderness proper, the Baptist proceeded with the view of remaining permanently and prosecuting the duties of his office; "he came into all the country about the Jordan."—A comparison of the passages above noted as found in the evangelist John, will confirm this statement of Luke's, and show that the scene of the Baptist's labors was the valley of the Jordan, between the Dead Sea and the sea of Gennesareth (Galilee); now on the east bank of that river, now on the west bank, but most frequently, it would seem, on the eastern side.

Thus much in general can be satisfactorily proved from the

New Testament record ; but with regard to certain particular points, it is not so easy to come to a satisfactory conclusion. The first of the passages cited from John (1 : 28.) represents him as baptizing "in Bethabara beyond the Jordan." It is clear enough here that the east side of the river is referred to, as is put beyond a doubt by the expression "*beyond* the Jordan" (πέραν τοῦ Ἰορδάνου), which can have no other meaning (cp. Matt. 4 : 14, and Jno. 10 : 40.) ; but it is not yet ascertained with certainty what was the precise situation of the town here mentioned. Wherever situated, the name of Bethabara is not that by which it is known in the New Testament ; for the reading of the received text is derived from a conjecture of Origen's ; instead of which almost all the best MSS. have *Bethany* (Βηθανίᾳ), and this is given by all the editors from Wetstein to Tischendorf. Now this Bethany could not have been the town of that name which was distant about two miles from Jerusalem (Matt. 21 : 17., Jno. 11 : 18.) : it must, therefore, have been another place of the same name, situated on the eastern bank of the Jordan. In Origen's time no such a village as Bethany was found here ; but a town called Bethabara was then pointed out as the place where John had baptized ; hence his reason for changing the MS. reading of the passage in the evangelist. This tradition, however, may have been false. If true, it would follow either that the town in question had two names, one in one period and another at another, or that the original Bethany having been destroyed, Bethabara had been built on the same location. The related meanings of the two words, Bethany, *place of a ship*, and Bethabara, *place of a ford* or *crossing*, are favorable to either view. The precise situation of this village, which is perhaps the Bethbarah of

Judges 7 : 24., is not given by Origen : we learn from him only what we already knew from the New Testament record, that it was located somewhere on the eastern shore of the Jordan.

The next and last time that the place of John's labors is mentioned in the New Testament, we find him engaged in baptizing "in Ænon, near to Salim, because there was much water there" (Jno. 3 : 23.). The connection shows that the Baptist was now on the west side of the Jordan. If we receive the testimony of Jerome and Eusebius as trustworthy, Salim (then called Salumias), and consequently Ænon (Hebrew, *Eynon,* from *'Ayin,* i. e. *fountains),* was situated eight miles south of Scythopolis *(Bethshan,* 1 Sam. 31 : 10.). The latter place lay about two miles west of the Jordan, and eighteen from the southern end of the sea of Galilee. Ænon, therefore, it would seem, was situated very near, if not directly upon, the western bank of the Jordan, in Judea, it is most probable, close to the borders of Samaria. It was in the river Jordan that John, as was his custom, was now performing the rite of baptism, "because," as Olshausen says, "the water there, being deep, afforded conveniences for immersion," and not, as some suppose, in a fountain or stream pertaining particularly to the town of Ænon.—Here, at Ænon, the Baptist prosecuted his ministry for a time ; but soon after, crossing over into Perea, he was seized by Herod, and cast into prison. That side of the Jordan, therefore, on which he had commenced administering his baptism (Jno. 10 : 40.), was the one on which his labors at length came to a close.

Mark says nothing respecting the time at which John made his public appearance : Matthew connects his narrative of the Baptist with what he says respecting the birth of Christ with the insignificant words, "in those days" : Luke alone fixes it by a precise chronological statement. The latter evangelist dates his appearance "in the fifteenth year of Tiberius" (3 : 1.), who, it is known, succeeded to the administration of the Roman empire in the year 767 of the city Rome (19th of August) and 14 of the Christian era : it was, therefore, in the year 29 after Christ, at which time Jesus, if he was really born in the year 4 A.C., must have been 33 years old, and John six months older. It may indeed be that the number of the years of Tiberius' reign is here reckoned from the time he was made co-regent with Augustus ; and, in such event, this occurrence must have taken place from two to four years earlier. There is, however, no decisive ground for this supposition ; for it is not at all probable that the reign of Tiberius is dated by Luke farther back than the death of Augustus, who illuminated everything in such a degree by the splendor of his name, that Tiberius would scarcely have been thought-worthy of being reckoned the ruler of the empire so long as he was still alive.—Pontius Pilate governed, at this time, as procurator, the land of Judea ; for, after the banishment of Archelaus, the son of Herod the Great (Matt. 2 : 22.), his possessions, Judea, Samaria and Idumea, were ruled over by Roman procurators (from 6 A.D.) of whom the fifth was Pontius Pilate. Since this governor, on going to Rome, to plead to an accusation before the emperor, in the tenth year of his office, found Tiberius dead on his arrival at that city (789 A.U.C. and 37 A.D.), he must have been in power about two years at the period when John commenced his public preaching. If, therefore, we suppose Luke to reckon the beginning of Tiberius' administration from his co-regency with Augustus, it would scarcely give time for Pilate to have obtained his government.

The second son of Herod the Great, Herod Antipas, had obtained Galilee and Perea after his father's death; and over these he now ruled under the title of tetrarch; while the youngest son, Philip, possessed Gaulonitis, Batanea, Iturea, and Trachonitis. The Lysanias of Abilene mentioned in the same connection, appears not to have belonged to the family of Herod; at least, he could not have been his son, and still less that Lysanias of Abilene who was the son of Ptolemy, for that person had died thirty years before this period. He is here mentioned by Luke among the rulers, because Abilene had at an earlier period belonged to the kingdom of Herod; and it is his object to enumerate the rulers then presiding over each portion of that kingdom.

After speaking of the secular rulers who then presided over the land of Judea, Luke makes mention of those to whom was assigned its spiritual government; for this was important to the course of his history. It is well known that, according to the Jewish law, there could only be one high priest at a time; but we have two here mentioned. From the fact that Annas is mentioned first, and still more clearly from the representation in Acts 4: 6., it is evident that Luke considered him the actual high priest; yet he was not altogether certain as to the manner in which he should represent the relation which existed between this Annas and Caïaphas. The state of the case was this:—Annas had been deposed from his office some years previously by the Roman proconsul Quirinus: since, however, this removal was altogether contrary to the law, according to which the dignity of the high-priesthood was to belong, during his entire life-time, to him to whom it had once descended, it could not be easily decided whether Annas was still to be regarded as high priest, or not. After several other high priests had each for a short time occupied the station, Caïaphas, the son-in-law of Annas, had been appointed to the office about the year 26 A.D.; the elevation of whom to that dignity had only served to confirm the influence of Annas and to increase the respect paid him by the nation, though his son-in-law properly possessed the office, and was in fact the real high priest.

This was the time, then, in which, as Luke narrates, John was summoned from his retirement by the Lord, and began to preach publicly "the baptism of repentance for the forgiveness of sins"; that is, he invited the people to receive baptism, in order to show thereby their repentance, and that they might be able to hope for the forgiveness of their sins. In the next section we shall examine with somewhat of minuteness into the meaning of this expression, when we come to a more particular consideration of the baptism of John; while we shall confine ourself here to the special examination, by way of preliminary, of that one of the two separate and yet intimately connected offices of his ministry which constituted the preparation for the other, viz. the repentance which he required as an indispensable pre-requisite to his baptism.

The subject-matter of the preaching of John is given in Matt. 3: 2., in words consonant with the accounts of Mark and Luke: "*Repent*, for the kingdom of heaven is at hand." By repentance (Greek, μετάνοια, literally, *a change of mind*, or *purpose)*, he evidently meant to imply not merely sorrow and contrition for sins which were past, but also an earnest effort on the part of the repentant to free himself from sin, to obtain another disposition, and to act in accordance with the will of God. The repentance, therefore, which he required, included the effort to acquire a pure heart and a God-fearing disposition, which should evince itself outwardly in good works; and in the attempt to atone for former guilt of conduct by a present contrary practice of virtue.

It is agreed by all lexicographers of eminence that the word "*repent*" (μετανοεῖτε), as used by the Baptist as well as by Christ and the Apostles, means much more than it does in ordinary English usage. Indeed, *repent* can hardly be called a correct rendering of the original; for this idea is expressed in the New Testament by the verb μεταμέλεσθαι *(metamelesthai)*. Meyer in his Commentary (on Matt. 3: 2.) has the following on the word: "*metanoeite,* signifies *the change of the moral disposition* which was required in order to obtain a share in the Messianic kingdom." De Wette defines still more closely: "*sententiam mutate* (change your minds), *resipiscite* (return to your senses), *bessert euch (reform)*, a technical expression and ruling idea of Christianity, deeper and more comprehensive than the Hebrew *nicham,* (for which the Septuagint has *metanoein)* and *shubh* (which is equivalent to *metanoein* in *Aquinas* ed. quint.), and also more comprehensive than the *metanoein* of the Apocrypha (Wisdom 5: 3., Sirach 17: 24.); connecting with the idea of a new life." An examination of all the passages in the New Testament in which this word and its cognate *metanoia* (translated in the received version by *repentance)* occur, will show that the verb ought to be rendered in almost every case by *reform,* and the noun by *reformation;* for such is most clearly the sense in which the terms are employed by the inspired authors of the New Testament.*

* A very interesting and fundamental discussion of the meaning of these Greek terms and the proper mode of rendering them, will be found among the Preliminary Dissertations which Dr. Geo. Campbell (of Scotland) has published in the first volume of his judicious work on the Four Gospels (Dissert. No. VI.)

That John really comprehended all that is described above under his idea of repentance, is made particularly clear by the maxims of conduct which he inculcated upon the several classes of people who came to him, and inquired in what manner they should manifest their repentance (Luke 3 : 11–14.). He had just previously informed them that they should bring forth fruit meet for repentance, that is, that they should exhibit by their mode of life the fruit of their repentance; and they now ask of him, what they must do to meet the conditions of this requirement. John might now have insisted directly upon the necessity of a new disposition; but the principle of love had not yet appeared in the flesh as the model and representative of all races, and the people were yet too much taken up with the merely external to receive any great amount of enlightenment from such a description of the new state of mind which was implied in repentance. For minds such as theirs, which, as is evinced even by their question, could comprehend nothing beyond the outward and what occurred before their eyes, the outward had to be brought prominently forward; not because the essence of holiness and righteousness consisted therein, but because it was only by these single cases, as by examples, that it could be shown to them in what manner they were on all occasions to conduct themselves, in order that, by means of the outward expression of the disposition which they wished to obtain, that is, by their actions, they might gradually come to a knowledge of the disposition itself, and, forming themselves inwardly from without, finally make it their own. We perceive, therefore, that John adopted that same wise proceeding, the only one in fact which was adapted to the stand-point of the people,—which Christ put into operation in his sermon on the mount, when he exhibited to men an example of a perfect pious action as a mirror, in order that they might by looking in it perceive the contrast made by their own conduct, and that, in the effort to conform to this model instituted by him, they might appropriate to themselves also the disposition from which those good works flow.

As Christ did there, so did John here exhibit in the most natural manner unto each individual among his hearers the precise contrast to the vice which he most frequently practised and which was most deeply rooted in his affections.—Thus, he impressed it as a duty upon the people at large, the most of whom were either Pharisees or Sadducees, whose selfishness exhibited itself most prominently in covetousness and want of benevolence (for they only gave the alms prescribed by the law), that they should continually communicate to the necessitous a portion of their possessions and property, if they were not compelled to use it for the supply of their own necessities. To the tax-gatherers (i. e. publicans) who were continually guilty of committing the greatest injustice and extortion, he assigned it as their duty, that they should take no more from the people than was right and appointed by law. He commanded the Roman soldiers, on the other hand, who allowed themselves to be guilty of every kind of oppression and annoyance towards a subjugated people, to do violence to no man and to oppress none, to be satisfied with their pay and not to be covetous of more. Thus John understood how to adapt to the stand-point of every one, in a manner intelligible to each, that great and simple command, "thou shalt love thy neighbor as thyself;" and, if each one had only struggled with serious earnestness against his cherished sin, he would without doubt have attained to the right disposition ; and this would, in every case, have produced in each an apprehension of the right and the true.

John, however, not only required the nation in general to repent, or, as we have seen that he implied under the idea of repentance, to produce the righteous fruits which belong to its exercise, but he also assigned, as the true inducement to its fulfillment, the reason why it was so particularly necessary to repent ; "for," said he, "*the kingdom of heaven is at hand.*"

The appellation "kingdom of heaven" (ἡ βασιλεία τῶν οὐρανῶν) is found only in Matthew, though we read in 2 Tim. 4 : 18, "the heavenly kingdom," a wording entirely correspondent in sense, though not in form. Elsewhere in the New Testament, and also in Matthew, the same idea is given by other equivalent expressions, "kingdom of God" (Mark 1 : 14., and elsewhere), "kingdom of Christ" (Matt. 13 : 41., 20 : 21., Rev. 1 : 9.), "kingdom of Christ and God" (Eph. 5 : 5.), and "kingdom of David" (Mark 11 : 10.). The idea conveyed by these different forms of expression is one and the same, *the divine spiritual kingdom, the reign of the Messiah.*—The conception of "the kingdom of heaven" is based upon the Old Testament Messianic prophecies ; though the Hebrew appellation (*malkuth hassamayim*) does not occur in the Hebrew of the Old Testament, but is found only in Jewish writings of a later period (first in the Targum on Mich. 4 : 7.), in which it usually means, however, not the Messianic kingdom, but rather the Jewish theocracy. In these Old Testament prophecies* the reign of the Messiah is described as a golden age in which the authority of Jehovah would universally be acknowledged,

* Such prophecies are in particular, Dan. 2 : 44., 7 : 14, 27., 9 : 25. ; to which may be added Ps. 2, and 110. ; Is. 2 : 1–4. (coll. Mich. 4 : 1.), 11 : 1. ; Jer. 23 : 5., 31 : 31., 32 : 37., 33 : 14. ; Ezek. 34 : 23., 37 : 24.

the Jewish theocracy be established in unexampled splendor and purity, and peace and happiness prevail throughout the world. The Jews in general interpreted these prophecies too literally, assigning them a meaning almost wholly temporal. They expected a Messiah who would appear in the clouds of heaven, and, descending to earth, would free their nation from bondage, restore their ancient worship, establish a temporal dominion, and, subduing all others, rule over them in happiness and glory forever. In this expectation they greatly erred, as those who listened to the Baptist's teaching soon discovered.

What then did John understand by the phrase "the kingdom of heaven"? A heavenly kingdom had already been founded by means of the old covenant made with the patriarchs of the Jewish people, which had subsequently been renewed, confirmed and more firmly grounded upon the basis of the Old Testament with the people in the time of Moses ; in which kingdom God ruled unlimited, as the absolute sovereign of the Israelitish nation, by means of his organs and representatives. But this divine kingdom was, and from its nature could only be, imperfect. The laws of God were frequently broken through the hard-heartedness and worldly inclination of the people ; those who should have been his organs, were but too often only the instruments of sin ; disturbances and revolts of the whole nation from their heavenly king but too frequently occurred ; and if this defection did not display itself outwardly and universally, it was exhibited so much the more by individuals among the nation, and showed itself in thoughts and actions which were enlisted in the service of sin rather than in that of the divine sovereign. The kingdom of God, therefore, had never appeared in its full perfection ; and the observant must soon have become conscious of the difference between what it actually was and what it should have been. A new epoch, accordingly, had to be introduced by a new act of the divine power, such an epoch as had been long since announced in the promises of the Old Testament, and had been earnestly looked for by all believers; in which a separation was to be made in the multitude who now boasted themselves in their appellation of "people of God," and only the true servants of God were to be chosen as the citizens of the kingdom, while the rest were to be rejected; when God should, by means of an instrument truly correspondent to its vocation, rule over this new kingdom, which, on its part, should never more be subjected to change and degeneracy by sin working from within, or from enemies attacking from without; in a word, when all the precious promises respecting a happy, untroubled life and uninterrupted enjoyment, should be fulfilled in the utmost measure, so that, for the members of this kingdom, heaven should in truth have descended to earth.

Since John and a few of his contemporaries,—each of whom, however, hoped for the satisfaction of his own individual, and often not very pure, wishes, from the entrance of this heavenly kingdom,—recognized the fact that this celestial reign was to be one thoroughly spiritual; so did he, still further, recognize the additional fact, that entrance into it would be allowed only to those who turned in repentance unto God; and therefore he proposed repentance as the chief and fundamental condition of participation in its enjoyments.—Just as clearly did he perceive that unrepentant and obdurate sinners would become obnoxious to divine punishment on the coming of this new kingdom (although, as we further see, he conceived of this punishment, in a manner not accordant with the truth, as connected externally with the appearance of the Messiah ; compare, on the other hand, the words of Christ, Jno. 3 : 13—19.) ; and, in order to exhibit this more intelligibly to the people, he makes use of the two similes, or comparisons, which we have recorded in Matt. 3 : 10, and 12, and in Luke 3 : 9, and 17. He likens the people to trees, which, by the nature of their fruit, it being either good or bad, enable us to tell whether they are also inwardly pure and healthy, or not, and says : "The trees which bring forth unsound fruit, —therefore the men whose actions evince the impurity of their minds,—shall be destroyed and burnt ; and, in truth, the axe now lieth at their root, therefore their judgment is near at hand, and in a short time they shall receive their punishment."*—The second representation (3: 17.) is that of a farmer, who throws up against the wind, with his winnowing-shovel, the corn which has been threshed upon the threshing-floor, in the open air, and thereby causes the chaff to be carried away by the wind, and the pure heavy corn to fall to the ground ; who then collects together the pure corn and brings it into his granary, but burns the chaff. So also will Christ do : he will make a separation between the true wheat, the valuable and useful corn, the children of God, and the chaff, the valueless sons of the world and of vanity. The true wheat will he collect into barns, therefore will claim it as his property and under his protection ; but he will burn the chaff with unquenchable fire, which is meant, perhaps, to express the large

* The present tense as here occurring, "*is* hewn down" (ἐκκόπτεται) is used as in Matt. 26 : 2. to denote what *will immediately and certainly happen*, and not, as might be supposed and as some think, to mark *what is accustomed to happen*. The "*therefore*" (οὖν) is conclusive against the latter supposition.

amount of the matter collected and the long duration of the punishment, as well as the complete destruction of sinners.—The "*floor*" here spoken of is what is technically called a *threshing-floor*, (ἅλωνα), a circular space in the open air, the ground of which has been leveled and beaten hard. On this the grain was deposited, and, in the time of our Saviour, threshed either by the hoofs of oxen or by machines drawn by oxen. Here, it is most probable, the term *threshing-floor* is used briefly to denote the grain that lay upon it, as in Ruth 3 : 2., Job 39 : 12. So it is almost universally taken by commentators; and with this sense the meaning of the verb διακαθαριεῖ *(will thoroughly cleanse)* best harmonizes. Thus conceived the term figuratively designates either men in general (De Wette), or the *Jewish people* in particular (Baumgarten-Crusius), as the objects of purification: Meyer, however, taking the word in its strict application, interprets it of *the place of judgment.*—After being threshed the grain was thrown up against the wind with a *winnowing-shovel* (πτύον, Heb. *mizreh,* Is. 30 : 24., Jer. 15 : 7.), not "*fan*" as we read in the received translation, in order to separate the chaff from the wheat.—The "*chaff*" (ἄχυρον, Heb. *mots*) here mentioned, is not merely such in its narrow sense, but includes also the broken straw, or stubble, which was left after the operation of winnowing had been completed. This in Palestine was used for fuel.*

From these expressions of John, it seems clear that he conceived of the judgment as something external, which was to make its appearance on the coming of the Messiah; that he, therefore, thought that the Messiah himself was to come as

* See on these points Robinson, *Bib. Researches*, vol. ii. pp. 277. 371., Jahn, *Bib. Archæology*, Eng. transl. §§ 63–65.

the judge (cp. on the other hand, Jno. 3 : 17.) ; and, since he could not do this without considering the founder of the new kingdom not merely a spiritual but also an earthly, worldly, lord and ruler, he was accustomed to picture to himself the new kingdom as also worldly and earthly, though resting upon a truly spiritual foundation. We find, accordingly, that that which we established as true, in the preceding section, respecting the character of his Messianic expectations, is, in this representation, completely confirmed. This error, as we have already mentioned, proceeded probably from the fact that he was not able to distinguish between the first and second coming of Christ ; and that, in consequence, what is to happen only on the future advent of Christ, he conceived of as immediately connected with his first advent in his state of humiliation.

Neander, in his Life of Jesus,* developes in his usual felicitous manner the conception which the Baptist entertained respecting the calling and work of the Messiah and the nature of his kingdom : "He contradicts the notion, so prevalent among the Jews, that all the descendants of Abraham who outwardly observed the religion of their fathers would be taken into the Messiah's kingdom, while his heavy judgments would fall upon the pagans alone. On the contrary, he maintains the necessity, for *all* who would enter that kingdom, of a moral new birth, which he sets forth to them by the spirit-baptism ; and proclaims, as a necessary preparation for this new birth, a consciousness of sin and longing to be free from it ; all which is implied in the word *metanoia* (reformation,), when stated as the necessary condition of obtaining the promised baptism of the Spirit. He expects this kingdom to be *visible ;* but yet conceives it as purely spiritual, as a community filled and inspired

* *Leben Jesu* (Life of Jesus), Amer. transl. '48. § 40. p. 54.

by the Spirit of God, and existing in communion of the divine life, with the Messiah as its visible King; so that, what had not been the case before, the *idea* of the theocracy and its manifestation should precisely correspond to each other. He has already a presentiment that the willing among the pagans will be incorporated into the kingdom in place of the unworthy Jews who shall be excluded. The appearance of the Messiah will cause a sifting of the theocratic people. This pre-supposes that he will not overturn all enemies and set up his kingdom at once by the miraculous power of God, but will manifest himself in such a form that those whose hearts are prepared for his coming will recognize him as the Messiah, while those of ungodly minds will deny and oppose him. On the one hand, a community of the righteous will gather around him of their own accord; and, on the other, the enmity of the corrupt multitude will be called forth and organized. The Messiah must do battle with the universal corruption; and, after the strife has separated the wicked members of the theocratic nation from the good, will come forth victorious, and glorify the purified people of God under his own reign."*

* The precise meaning of the phrase "kingdom of heaven" and its equivalents, according to New Testament usage, cannot well be given in the form of a definition. Robinson (New Testament Lexicon, on the word *βασιλεία*) gives an explanation of its sense which is quite correct: "Referring to the Old Testament idea, we may therefore regard *the kingdom of heaven* in the New Testament as denoting in its Christian sense, *the Christian Dispensation*, comprising those who receive Jesus as the Messiah, and who, united by his Spirit under him as their head, rejoice in the truth and live a holy life in love and in communion with him. This spiritual kingdom has both an internal and an external form. As internal, it already exists and rules in the hearts of all Christians, and is therefore present. As external, it is either embodied in the visible church of Christ on earth, and in so far is present and progressive; or it is to be perfected in the coming of the Messiah to judgment and his subsequent

Josephus in his notice of the Baptist and his ministry makes no express mention of his announcement respecting the Messiah. His words are : "For Herod slew him [John], who was a good man, and who directed the Jews to practise virtue and to exercise righteousness towards each other and piety towards God, and in this way to submit themselves to baptism ; for thus, said he, baptism will prove acceptable unto him, provided that they received it not for the purpose of obtaining forgiveness of some sins, but for the purification of the body, since the soul had previously been thoroughly cleansed by righteousness."* It is not impossible, notwithstanding his silence, that Josephus was acquainted with the Messianic element in the ministry of the Baptist ; if so, he made no allusion to it for fear he should give offence to the Romans by speaking of a king who was, according to the testimony of John and that of his fellow-prophets, to subdue the world to himself and rule over it in triumph forever. But it is more than likely that the historian did not really comprehend the true object of John's mission ; and that, therefore, his historic representation

spiritual reign in bliss and glory, in which view it is future. But these different aspects are not always distinguished ; the expression often embracing both the internal and the external sense, and referring both to its commencement in this world and its completion in the world to come." A very able critical investigation of the meaning of this phrase is to be found in Tholuck's *Bergpredigt Christi*, on Matt. 5 : 3. p. 70–88. edit. of 1833. This edition of the Commentary has been translated into English, and published in Clark's Foreign Theol. Library.

* Antiquities, 18. 5. 2 : *τοὺς Ἰουδαίους κελεύοντα ἀρετὴν ἐπασκοῦντας καὶ τῇ πρὸς ἀλλήλους δικαιοσύνῃ καὶ πρὸς τὸν θεὸν εὐσεβείᾳ χρωμένους βαπτισμῷ συνιέναι οὕτω γὰρ καὶ τὴν βάπτισιν ἀποδεκτὴν αὐτῷ φανεῖσθαι, μὴ ἐπί τινων ἁμαρτάδων παραιτήσει χρωμένων, ἀλλ' ἐφ' ἁγνείᾳ τοῦ σώματος, ἅτε δὴ καὶ τῆς ψυχῆς δικαιοσύνῃ προεκκεκαθαρμένης.*—Whiston's rendering is wrong.

is based upon a mere scientific and not a religious insight into the character of the Baptist. Add to this the well-understood fact that Josephus adapts himself in his writings to the habits of thought and style of composition prevalent among the Greeks, and we have a reason which sufficiently accounts for the circumstance that in his representation of John, we do not find depicted the living peculiarities of that prophet, but only the general and most easily apprehended features of his character and ministry. "He saw in John," says Neander (Life of Jesus, § 33.), "only a man of moral ardor, who taught the truth to the Jews, rebuked their corruptions, and offered them, instead of their lustrations and outward righteousness, a symbol of inward spiritual purification in his water-baptism. With such a narrow view as this we could neither understand John's use of baptism, nor explain his public labors among such a people as the Jews. It is but a beggarly abstraction from the living individual elements which the gospel accounts afford."

In the expectation of the near approach of the judgment John addressed the multitude which had resorted to him, the most of whom consisted, according to Matt. 3 : 7., of Pharisees and Sadducees, and who, therefore, had, doubtless, come to the pious man in an unholy and unrepentant frame of mind, and threatened them with punishment: "Offspring of vipers, brood of serpents, children of the devil from whom the first sin proceeded,* who hath taught you to flee from the coming judgment?"; that is, who hath persuaded you, you so holy and pure a people in your own estimation, to flee from the approaching wrath of God, and that you should come to

* "*Generation of vipers*" (*γεννήματα ἐχιδνῶν*, *offspring, progeny of vipers*), hardly means as Von Rohden here and Olshausen think, *children of the devil*, but rather *crafty and malicious men* (cp. Ps. 58 : 5., Is. 14: 29., 59: 5.).

baptism in order to evince your repentant disposition?—He hints to them here with strong and bitter irony the real intention which they had in professing repentance and consequently in submitting to baptism; for they, as we shall see hereafter, were for the most part by no means of a repentant mind (cp. Luke 7: 30.), and John penetrated at once their real design in presenting themselves to him for baptism. Since they were in his presence, however, the Baptist treats them as persons who had come to him in all sincerity, and proceeds with holy seriousness: "If you would really flee from the judgment, act as a sincere change of disposition requires, and suffer not yourselves to be led away by the thought, we have Abraham for our father, and are therefore freed from all liability to punishment, and are of right citizens of the new kingdom." This was a customary boast of the Jews, the bulwark behind which they always intrenched themselves, that, in consequence of their bodily descent from Abraham, God must of necessity be gracious unto them, and bestow upon them in preference to all, if not on them alone, all the blessings which they, in their earthly misconceptions of the prophetic promises, expected from the appearance of the Messianic kingdom. The falseness of this idea, however, was evident to those who entertained the true view of the moral nature of this kingdom and of the repentance which formed its ground-work. Such a more correct insight into its real nature not only John possessed, but, as we have seen in a former section, many others, as Simeon, among the nobler-minded and more advanced of his people. "This descent," says John, "is of no advantage; it is and can be, at most, only fleshly, and, unaccompanied by a right disposition, has no worth: God could make these stones which lie around, children of Abraham as truly as you are, viz., in respect to real character, not as to physical creation: his power is unlimited; he is not bound to adhere to the fleshly descendants of Abraham, but, if you are not worthy, he is at liberty to choose from among other people the heirs of the promises made to Abraham. A total change of disposition can alone make you partakers once more of the lost heritage, and protect you from the anger of God; and indeed it is high time to make this change, for the judgment is already at your doors."

Such is the course of thought in this speech of John's, which we find in nearly the same words in Matt. 3: 7–10, and Luke 3: 7–9. The apparent discrepancies which exist here between the narratives of Matthew and Luke are easily harmonized. Luke represents the address of John as directed to the people at large, the multitude (ὄχλοις) that came out to hear his preaching; and it is entirely appropriate as so addressed, for the majority of them, being Pharisees, rejected the counsel of the Baptist, as we learn from Luke 7: 30. (coll. Matt. 21: 32., and 11: 16.). This evangelist, however, evidently speaks generally, not intending to denote the particular classes to whom John's discourse was specially addressed, just as we would say, in popular language (and such is the language of the Scriptures), "he denounced *the assembly*," when in fact we mean, and are understood as meaning, that he denounced only a particular class of persons present in the assembly. Matthew speaks more definitely, representing the discourse as addressed in particular to the Pharisees and Sadducees; and such, no doubt, was the fact. Both accounts, therefore, are correct; but Luke's is the more general—Matthew's the more specific.—Yet are we not to conclude from these representations that no Pharisees or Sadducees believed in and were baptized by John.* Only a few of the latter sect, we may infer from the nature of their religious views, could have been attracted by his doctrine ; but the opinions and feelings of the Pharisees, especially of the more honest and religious among them, were more in unison with those of the Baptist ; and from among these not a few, we may judge from the tenor of the evangelical narratives, particularly that of Mark (1 : 5., where, however, "*all,*" πᾶσα and πάντες, is not to be taken strictly, but, as elsewhere in the New Testament, Matt. 10 : 22., Acts 22 : 15., as a kind of popular hyperbole, the use of which figure is not infrequent in the New Testament and is not liable to lead to misconception), were led to profess repentance and to receive baptism at the hands of the forerunner. Whether the majority even of these, however, continued faithful to their vows, is another question, and one that does not affect the point under consideration. The probability is, they did not (cp. Jno. 5 : 35.) ; for then, as now, many that ran well at first speedily wearied in the race, and retired as soon as the immediate cause of excitement had ceased to operate.

From this discourse of John's we may form a pretty clear idea of the manner and scope of his preaching. Upright, repentant hearts he attempted to lead upward to a more perfect purity, and to a struggling with their cherished sins, by pointing them to the near approach of the heavenly kingdom, the citizens of which all pious souls were destined to be. The obdurate, on the other hand, and the haughty he sought to crush with

* On the character and opinions of the three different sects into which Judaism was divided in the time of Christ (*Pharisees, Sadducees,* and *Essenes*), see any one of the common Bible Dictionaries. Kitto's *Cyclop. of Bib. Literature* gives full and reliable information respecting each under the appropriate headings.

the whole power of his pious earnestness, to represent them in their nakedness and sinfulness, to terrify them with the threatening of that fearful punishment by which they were shortly to be overtaken, to remove from beneath them the props of their confidence, which were founded on human wisdom, and so, perhaps, by the might of his word to subdue sinners that were not yet totally hardened and callous, and bring them with anxious sorrow to repentance.

The preaching of the Baptist was an exhortation to repentance and a holy life. To each class of persons he assigned its appropriate duties,—to be performed as evidence of the reality of their repentance, and to be practised as a means of bringing them to perfection in holiness and virtue. The Pharisees, and those of a like spirit, he sharply reproved for their hypocrisy and impiety; these sins being more reprehensible in them, because "contrary to their rule, their profession, and institution." Others he guided gently into the straight ways of the Lord; leading them by mild persuasion along the most direct and shortest road into the heavenly kingdom.—By means of such preaching, he "disposed the spirits of men for the entertaining the Messiah and the homilies of the gospel."*

* A very complete and valuable Treatise on these and other points relating to the Life and Ministry of John, is contained in the "Allegemeine Encyklopädie" of Ersch and Gruber, section second, vol. xxii. (edited by A. G. Hoffman), p. 94–120. The Article was written by Wilibald Grimm. Though able and learned, it is neological in its tone; but it is by no means of the Strauss and Baur stamp. The Author characterizes Von Rohden's Treatise, disparagingly, as "streng supranaturalistisch," "strongly supranaturalistic," that is, the opposite of rationalistic or neological. This will be considered a recommendation among those who hold, as we do in America, to the divine inspiration of the Scriptures.

CHAPTER II.

John's Baptism.

John was not content with mere preaching, which might so readily be dissipated without leaving a sufficiently deep impression upon the memory and hearts of the multitude; but he sought, in addition, to work upon the moral feelings by means of an external moral action which could not so easily fail of producing a deep and lasting impression upon the minds of those who flocked to hear him preach of the heavenly kingdom.—In modern times the question has been very much discussed, whether John in making use of his baptismal rite had before his eyes, as an example, a custom already commonly practised among the Jews, namely, the baptism of proselytes from heathenism to Judaism; or whether this last-mentioned rite was introduced at a later period, and perhaps in imitation of the baptism administered by John. Since we find on this point no positive and definite historic testimony in antiquity, the question cannot, perhaps, be brought to a final and complete settlement that shall be universally satisfactory; but the preponderance of arguments upon the point goes to prove, that, though there were lustrations and ceremonial purifications in common use among the Jews altogether similar to baptism, yet there was not, before the time of John, any proper baptism.

There were various symbolical washings and lustrations practised by the Jews, some in accordance with the requirements of the Mosaic law (Lev. 16 : 4., 24, 26, 28., Exod. 19 : 10., Num

19 : 7, and elsewhere), others of their own free will, without any special directions from the Lord (Judith 12 : 7., Josephus, *De Bell. Jud.* 2. 8. 7. coll. *Antiq.* 18. 1. 5.). Such lustrations were prevalent not only among the Jews, but in the East generally ; and seem to have originated from a common religious conviction among men that they need purification before they can become acceptable to God. Of the Levitical washings enjoined upon and practised by the Hebrews, none seem to have been performed by immersion ; and all of them were ceremonies which denoted merely a purification from defilement, not one of them being a rite of initiation into the Jewish religion or into any society formed for religious purposes within the pale of the theocracy. How much soever these symbolical Levitical purifications may in their general idea have resembled the baptismal rite administered by John, they differ so entirely from it in several fundamental particulars that one can not fail to perceive that the historical connection of the two is far too slight to warrant the supposition that the one sprung from and was the complement of the other. The washings enjoined by the Law had for their object purification from ceremonial defilement ; but the baptism of John did not : the one rite was performed by the candidates themselves upon their own persons ; the other was administered to its recipient by the Baptist himself, or by one of his disciples properly authorized : the former was repeated upon every occasion of renewed defilement ; the latter was performed upon the candidate only once for all. The two ceremonies, therefore, were essentially different in their nature and object ; and, it is not unlikely, also in their outward form.*

* Such is the opinion of Stuart, *Bibl. Repository*, vol. 3. p. 341. ; of Ebrard, *Kritik d. evangel. Geschichte*, S. 284. ; and of others.

The supposition that the rite administered by John was copied or at least derived from Jewish proselyte baptism, is equally untenable. This view, though held at one time by writers of eminence, as Selden (*Jus. Nat.* 2. 2.), Lightfoot (*Hor. Heb.* p. 220.), Kuinoel, Bengel (who wrote an elaborate treatise in support of his opinion) and others, is given up at the present day by every biblical critic of eminence. According to the opinion generally received, Jewish proselyte baptism did not originate before the time of the destruction of Jerusalem (70 A. D.) ; and this view is based upon the apparently decisive circumstance that we find no mention made of such a rite either in the Old Testament, the Apocrypha, the New Testament, Philo Judæus, Josephus, in any of the ancient Christian writers, or in any of the earlier Jewish Targumists. The first testimony in its favor is found in the Babylonian *Gemara*, or Commentary of the Talmud (*Jebamoth*, 46. 2.), which Gemara was composed during the 5th century of our era (from 427 to 500 A. D.), where the rite in question is represented as existing in the 1st century after Christ ; but, it is well known, the traditions of the Gemara are not reliable, and cannot be received as valid historic testimony. Even admitting the tradition to be true, however, it does not carry the practice of proselyte baptism far enough back to make it the prototype of the rite administered by John ; and did it even do this, nothing would be easier than to show that, though the external form (i. e. immersion) of the two ceremonies was precisely the same, the object and recipients of the former were totally different from the object and recipients of the latter. In any view of the case, therefore, John's baptism cannot be correctly said to have sprung from proselyte baptism ; though, on the supposition that the latter existed and was practised at the time of

John—(an hypothesis which, as we have seen, is destitute of historic testimony), it must be admitted that the form of the one might readily have suggested the form of the other.*

But, after all, we need not resort to conjecture to discover the origin of John's baptism. It was, like that afterwards instituted by Christ, the special appointment of heaven. So it is represented in Jno. 1 : 33., Luke 3 : 2, 3., 7 : 30., and especially in Matt. 21 : 24–27. ; and the Jewish people regarded its origin as divine (v. 26.). Immersion in water, external purification as a symbol of internal, lay so near, and must have been so universally intelligible, that there is, in truth, no necessity, even had John received no special instructions on the point, for seeking out a particular model according to which John conformed in instituting his baptism. It must have been his object, rather, to present something new and extraordinary to the people ; since, partly, his appearance and the object of his mission were something beyond the ordinary, and, partly, because the people might, in this way, be so much the more easily aroused to attention, and be induced to seek an acquaintance with this unheard-of appearance and action of the Baptist's. Now, had proselyte baptism been customary at this time, it would have given offence and been a cause of vexation to many, that they who ought to be treated as Jews and not as heathen, should be placed in the same situation as the heathen, and should have to submit to the same rite as

* The most masterly treatise yet written on the subject of Proselyte Baptism is that of Schneckenburger, *Über d. Alter d. jüd. Proselytentaufe*, Berlin, 1828. This critic, in common with De Wette (*Archäologie* §. 246.), Meyer (*Commentary*, on Matt. 3 : 5.), Winer (*Bib. Realwörterbuch*, Art. Proselyten), Stuart (*Bib. Rep.*, as cited), and others of the best commentators, assigns to proselyte baptism an origin posterior to that of Christianity.

they would if they had just been converted from heathenism. The question put by the Pharisees, Why baptizest thou then? (Jno. 1 : 25.) appears, moreover, to indicate that such a custom was by no means generally known, performed by many and upon many; but that the people expected such innovations only from a man specially called and authorized by God, who should receive from God full power to found a new community, or at least to introduce a new epoch in the theocracy (cp. Is. 44 : 3., Ezek. 36 : 25., Zech. 13 : 1.); and that they were resolved not to endure any such new rites established by a man who had received no call to perform them, and who could, or would, in no way justify his claim as a divine ambassador.

It was by no means the intention of John to found a new community by his baptism; and it could just as little have been his purpose to indicate that the rite was indispensably necessary to obtaining a part in the new Messianic kingdom; for he said expressly that God could raise up from the very stones children unto Abraham, and therefore that no external advantage would afford a claim to the expected salvation. But, what object he had in view by his baptism, what signification he assigned to it, he himself explains when he calls it a "*baptism of repentance* (reformation) *for the forgiveness of sins*" (Mark 1 : 4., Luke 3 : 3.). By "baptism of reformation" is meant a baptism *which has reference to reformation*, which enjoins reformation (change of mind and of aims in life) as a duty upon its recipient. The object of the baptism, *the end to be attained*, is the forgiveness of sins; and this is conditional upon a true reformation of character in him to whom the rite is administered.

Repentance was, as we have seen, a necessary condition with

John for entrance into the kingdom of God. In order to make the reality of this repentance, that is, of the renunciation of sins of every kind, visible, and at the same time to give it a seal, those who actually vowed repentance and gave external proof of their change of mind by a confession of their sins (Mark 1 : 5.) and an assurance of their penitence, he immersed, or inundated with water, probably with his own hands,—for he remained continually in the region of the Jordan,—causing them, since they had washed themselves free from outward filth and defilement, to intimate by the action that they had also cleansed themselves from all inward impurity, and had come to the resolution to lead henceforth, at least so far as lay in their power, a life unspotted and free from every remnant of sin.

The candidates who presented themselves to him for baptism, had to make *a confession of their sins* as a pre-requisite to its reception (Matt. 3 : 6., Mark 1 : 5.). This confession was an indispensable condition for those who had no consciousness of their sinfulness could not, of course, be expected to begin a reformation in their life and conduct ; and without this promised reformation the rite could not be administered, nor could forgiveness of sins be obtained. The confession required was to be honest, full, and heartfelt ; for all this is implied in the participle *exomologoumenoi* (*ἐξομολογούμενοι, confessing out and out*, i. e. *fully*, *heartily confessing*, cp. Acts 19 : 18., Jas. 5 : 16.) ; a complete acknowledgment by the candidate of the necessity on his part of repentance and reformation. The confession may have been summary, respecting the feeling of sin in general ; or it may have been specific, respecting particular acts of transgression. It is probable that it was sometimes the former, and sometimes the latter; according as in individual cases it seemed best to the Baptist.

The river in which John performed his baptisms, is the most celebrated in Palestine. Many interesting associations cluster around its name. It is called in Hebrew *Yarden* (from *yaradh, to flow down*); and in Greek *Iordanes* ('Ιορδάνης). The present Arabic designation *esh-Sherî'ah* signifies *the watering-place.* The remotest perennial source of the river is a large fountain near Hâsbeiya in the valley west of Mt. Hermon, in about 33° 25′ of north latitude; but it is usually described (Josephus, *Antiq.* 15. 10. 3., *Bell. Jud.* 1. 21. 3.) as originating in two larger fountains near Bânias (the ancient Paneas or Cæsarea-Philippi), in about latitude 33° 16′, at the south-eastern base of Mt. Hermon. After flowing some ten miles the river enters lake Hûleh, the ancient Merom (Josh. 11: 5, 7.), the southern end of which sheet of water is distant some twelve miles from Bânias. Emerging thence, the stream flows rapidly through a narrow rocky ravine, about eight miles, to the lake of Tiberias, or sea of Galilee, into which it empties its waters. This lake is about twelve miles long and five or six broad. The Jordan issues at length from its southern end, and after flowing through a valley called after its name (in Arabic, *el-Ghôr, the valley*), empties finally into the Dead Sea, in lat. 31° 46′. The distance between lake Tiberias and the Dead Sea is a little over 56 geographical miles; but, on account of its many windings, the length of the channel of the river between the two points is estimated at more than 150 miles. Its breadth here is usually from 80 to 100 feet; its depth generally varies from three to six feet, but in many places it is considerably greater.

The valley of the Jordan, lying between the two bodies of water last mentioned, is in general five or six miles wide; and it is bordered on all sides by mountains. "Through this broad plain," says Robinson (*N. T. Lexicon*, Art. Ἰορδάνης), "the Jordan flows in a still deeper valley; which is usually from 80 to 100 rods wide, and from 40 to 60 feet lower than the rest of the Ghôr. In many places there is yet another slight descent from this lower valley to the actual banks of the stream, by a strip of alluvial or marshy ground covered with canes or other vegetation. The course of the river is skirted by a narrow border of trees and bushes on each side; never extending beyond the outer banks of the lower valley; and sometimes confined to the marshy tracts. The river rarely, if ever, overflows its banks beyond the border of vegetation; and in no possible case do its inundations rise beyond the lower valley. The general surface of the Ghôr, above this lower valley, is therefore a desert; except where watered by the many fountains which burst forth at the foot of the mountains on each side. These occasion in many parts luxuriant vegetation and fertility; as for instance around Jericho." * Such was the scene of the baptisms administered by John.

This baptismal ceremony of the forerunner's was so simple, so consonant with the character of the Jewish people, who were accustomed to represent purification from internal pollution by an external washing, and so appropriate, that it must have explained itself on the moment to all, and recommended

* See Robinson, *Bibl. Res.* vol. 2, p. 257., vol. 3., pp. 307, 347., and in the *Bib. Sacra*, 1848, pp. 397, 764. See also a well-written, popular article on the River Jordan, illustrated with a number of neat engravings, and contributed by Jacob Abbott to Harper's New Monthly Magazine for Sept. 1852

itself with success to every one who had a mind prepared or willing to comprehend its meaning.—But, what are we to understand by the expression, "*for the forgiveness of sins*"? Did John mean that he had power to grant complete forgiveness of sins by means of this external ceremony? This cannot be; he could not have presumed to look into the hearts of men and read therein how far their repentance was actually sincere; he could not have esteemed this outward action so effectual in its operation that the divine forgiveness of sins was attendant upon it with no further condition. He who esteemed Jesus, when he came to him, so much purer than himself, who declared that he needed to receive baptism at his hands, must have been but too fully conscious of the fact, that, even in connection with the best intention and with the firmest determination to root out and destroy sin, perfect purity of heart cannot be attained; he must have known well that the repentance which he required was by no means accompanied by a forgiveness of sins; for how else could he have wished to submit himself anew to the baptism of repentance? It must have been clear to him, a prophet enlightened by God, one who had searched diligently in the Scriptures, that forgiveness of sin could be expected only from the Messiah; that he alone would deliver his adherents from the yoke of guilt and iniquity, as he would also from external oppression and servitude; and if, therefore, he called his baptism of repentance a baptism for the remission of sins, he can mean by this only something like the following:—by repentance we can alone obtain a portion in the kingdom of God, in which we receive forgiveness of sins; the seal of repentance, however, is baptism; whoever, therefore, has made known and confirmed his repentance by this external action, he has a claim to the forgiveness of sins which is imparted in the kingdom of God He promised this forgiveness, therefore, only to those who came to baptism with a true and upright conviction of what they were doing, and who in the subsequent period of their lives remained continually faithful to the vow which they had made in the act of baptism; and to these he only *promised* forgiveness; he did not impart it himself, for he knew that he himself needed the same.

John's baptism possessed rather a negative and conditional character, whereas the Messianic baptism of the Holy Spirit positively imparted a new life—a distinction arising from the necessary relation of the law to the gospel, and one recognized by the forerunner himself when he declared that he baptized in water unto repentance, but that his successor should baptize in the Holy Spirit (Matt. 3 : 11., Luke 3 : 16., Jno. 1 : 33.). The rite administered by the Baptist insured forgiveness of sins indeed to every candidate who truly reformed; but this forgiveness was to be bestowed at a time yet future, viz., when Christ should have appeared; whereas the baptism of the Holy Spirit renewed the soul at once, cleansing it from sin, and imparting to it the divine life. The rite administered by John, therefore, was only a baptism of water "*unto* repentance", not, like Christ's baptism, *a regeneration* of water *and of the Spirit* (Jno. 3 : 5.). It had not the character of an immediate, but merely of a preparatory consecration for entrance into the Messianic kingdom (Jno. 1 : 31.). For this reason, on those of the early Christians who had received only the baptism of John, knowing nothing of that of the Spirit, when re-baptized, was conferred the true Christian ordinance, according to apostolic example (Acts 19: 1–7.),* in order that they

* This subject will be more fully discussed when we come to consider the re-

might be prepared to receive the baptism of the Holy Spirit.

As, then, John's entire ministry was particularly directed to exciting a spiritual revolution among the people, and to preparing a way for the Lord by arousing their minds from the intoxication of sin, so he sought, by means of the rite of baptism, to confirm this sudden change, and, through the agency of this external act, to produce an impression the more deep and the more ineffaceable. But his baptism served at the same time to quiet and tranquilize such hearts as were really sorrowful and repentant, such as had been aroused to the consciousness of their sins and also to a consciousness of the fearful punishment to which they were exposed ; in so far as they received in baptism the consolatory assurance that the coming Redeemer would accept them as his own and forgive them their iniquities. He who wished to obtain this comforting assurance by the pledge of baptism, hastened without delay to John ; he, however, who already had this hope firmly grounded in his soul, and was convinced that deliverance would come to him without his having received baptism, felt and really had no pressing necessity for submitting to the ordinance. And those who were actually baptized formed thereupon no new community, adopted no new mode of worshipping God, and differed in no respect from their contemporaries, only as regarded their upright and sincere repentance, their moral conduct in life, and the joyful expectation of a speedy appearance of the Lord, who would deliver them corporeally and spiritually ; and even in these respects, they did not differ from all their people, as has been already

lation which existed between John's baptism, that of Christ's disciples, and the Christian rite.—See Part IV., Chapter 4.

remarked, for they differed not from those who, without having obtained baptism, stood upon a level even with them in piety and in a hopeful waiting for the advent of the Messiah.

Since John sought at no time to found a new community by his baptism, since he shows by the expression recorded in Matt. 3 : 9, and Luke 3 : 8., that he by no means unconditionally limited reception into the kingdom of God to the descendants of Abraham, it is not surprising that, according to Luke 3 : 12, and 14., he appears not to have excluded from this ordinance even the heathen (for it is probable that the publicans and the soldiers were for the most part heathen Romans) who came to receive the rite. We are authorized to conclude, however, that these people bore some special relation to the Jews as regarded their views of religion; they were, it is likely, proselytes of the gate, who entertained a belief in the one true God and had undertaken to observe the laws of the decalogue, but not the whole ceremonial service and each single religious observance practised by the Jews; for had they not been such, they would hardly have come to John; and John would scarcely have ventured to baptize persons who were altogether heathens, for such would not, and could not, have known anything respecting the Messiah. Proselytes of this kind, with this knowledge and enlightenment, stood no farther from the kingdom of God than the children of Abraham; and, therefore, could he, without hesitation, administer to them, after they had uttered the vow of repentance, the baptismal rite, and point them to the coming Redeemer.

Jewish *proselytes* (Heb. *gerim;* Greek, *proselutoi*, προσήλυτοι, 1 Chron. 22 : 2., Matt. 23 : 15., Acts 2 : 10.) were of two kinds; *proselytes of the gate*, and *proselytes of righteousness.*

The former class, to which belonged such as here spoken of, consisted of converts from heathenism who had renounced idolatry and worshipped the true God. They bound themselves to the observance of the seven so-called Noachic precepts, viz., against idolatry, profanity, incest, murder, dishonesty, eating blood or things strangled, and allowing a murderer to live. Josephus (*Ant.* 14. 17. 2.) calls such proselytes, οἱ σεβόμενοι (sc. τὸν θεόν); and so they are denominated in Acts 13: 50., 16: 14., 17: 4. 17., 18: 7. (cp. 13: 43.). The Jews consider Naaman, the Syrian, a proselyte of this character (2 Kings 5: 17.). Whether Cornelius, the centurion, who is spoken of (Acts 10: 2.) as "one that feared God" (φοβούμενος τὸν θεόν), was also such, is contested.—Proselytes of righteousness were converts from heathenism who conformed to all the precepts of the Mosaic law, and became Israelites in every respect, birth excepted. The rites by which they were admitted into the Jewish community, were, originally, *circumcision* (Exod. 12: 48.) and *a free-will offering* (the latter only in the case of women): to these rites *baptism* was subsequently added, administered to females as well as males.

That John, when administering his baptism of repentance, referred always expressly to the Messiah, whose appearance was at hand, and made the forgiveness of sins dependent upon him, is proved to our entire satisfaction by the words of Paul in Acts 19: 4.: "John verily baptized with the baptism of repentance, saying unto the people, that they should believe on him which should come after him, that is, [Paul himself adds by way of explanation] on Christ Jesus." The reference to him that was to come after, is here (especially in the Greek text) placed in such close connection with the act of baptism itself, that we are compelled to believe, either that John made use of a baptismal formula, as, "I baptize thee in the name of him that is to come," or, at least, that he inculcated upon every candidate the truth that his baptism only served as a preparation for a higher baptism; that the one was only the external seal of fitness to receive the application of that other which alone brings with it the actual forgiveness of sins.

John himself gives utterance to this truth in Matt. 3 : 11., Mark 1 : 7. 8. and Luke 3 : 16., where he calls his own only a water baptism unto repentance, but that of his great successor a baptism in the Holy Spirit and in fire ; where, there is no doubt, he means to say, that, in comparison with that higher baptism, the rite which he administered is only an external baptism, an outward symbol of internal purity and of an ever-continued feeling of repentance ; and for this reason, therefore, does he call it a baptism *unto* repentance, because repentance is not to be completed all at once ; but, since sinfulness and the pollution of sin are never entirely removed, so also must repentance be of perpetual continuance ; and as, therefore, his baptism was, on the one hand, a seal of repentance already completed, so was it, on the other, an incitement to repentance ever renewed and ever continued. The baptism of the Messiah, on the contrary, would, as he clearly recognized, not only represent externally this purity, this renunciation of evil, but would itself endue with a new principle of life, with the divine Spirit, which is now the principle of life in us, and, as fire consumes the dross of metal, destroy in us all the dross of our disposition and the sinfulness that adheres to our nature. That John saw with entire correctness in this respect, and had a highly enlightened idea of the ministry of his successor as regards this impartation of a new element of life, we are especially justified in concluding from the fact that Christ applies these words of the Baptist to himself (Acts 1 : 5.), and that Peter refers to and repeats the same (Acts 11 : 16.).

The question now arises, whether John thought, in using these words, of the external rite of Christian baptism ; or only denominated the communication from Christ of a new divine element of life, baptism, by way of a figure. It is rendered very probable by many reasons that the people expected a water baptism from the Messiah (compare, especially, Luke 3 : 15., the supposition of the people that John was the Messiah, which seems, according to the answer of the forerunner, to have been based upon his administering baptism ; and, also, the question of the Sanhedrim, Jno. 1 : 25., as to his authority to baptize, if he were not the Messiah) ; and this expectation was founded upon the great ceremony of purification performed on Mt. Sinai (Exod. 19 : 10. 14.), typically conceived, and upon such expressions in the prophets as Ezek. 36 : 25., 37 : 23., Zech. 13 : 1., etc. It is quite possible that John took advantage of this expectation, applying it to himself, in order that he, as the forerunner and preparer of the way of the Lord, might himself introduce this baptism ; by which means this rite of purification would be performed, not by Christ himself, but, as would be more in accordance with his high dignity, by his servants ; from which, however, it must not be inferred that the ceremony was an arbitrary human institution, introduced by John, for it was, in fact, as we have seen, commanded by God himself (Jno. 1 : 33.). But, that John expected that the Messiah would administer a water baptism with his own hands, does not appear to be justified by the expression under consideration. He would not, it is quite certain, have instituted a comparison between his own water baptism and the spirit baptism of Christ, if he had conceived of this latter as itself outwardly symbolized, as it is in fact by a water baptism ; he would not have contrasted the form of his rite with the operation, or effects, of the rite to be administered as Christian baptism ; but, noting the similarity of the form of the two, he would have exhibited, by way of contrast, so much the more pointedly the difference between their inward operation upon the heart. This, rather, was the idea entertained and expressed by John, that, as he immersed men in water, in order to represent thereby their repentance, so the Messiah would immerse them in the Holy Spirit, and therefore fill them wholly with the divine Spirit, since this alone, moving and working in man, can induce him to act as becomes a citizen of the new celestial kingdom.

It is evident that the Baptist does not speak here of the Holy Spirit which is imparted to believing Christians ; for John knew nothing of this Spirit ; just as his disciples also, even after his death, knew naught of such an existence (Acts 19 : 1. ss.). This Spirit had not yet appeared (Jno. 7 : 39.), the Spirit of the Father reconciled to us through the Son ; the Spirit of the Mediator himself which dwells in us continually, speaks in our behalf to the Father (Rom. 8 : 26.) and brings us into continual communication with God ; the Spirit which is diffused through the whole church, lives and works in it, and makes us even here participators in eternal happiness ; the Holy Spirit which only a Christian can know, who has felt and experienced its presence within his soul. John and all the pious men who lived before and in his age knew the Holy Spirit only as a vital energy imparted by God, which excited the natural capacities, and in a certain degree enlightened them, and urged them on to repentance and improvement. In their view the Holy Spirit was always only a power coming from God, which is imparted unto men, for the most part merely for the moment ; not God himself remaining and dwelling in us ; only an effluence of the general divine existence, which is far elevated above men, not the Spirit of the Father reconciled to us by the death of his Son. We perceive, therefore, that high as John's expectations regarding the kingdom of the Messiah reached,—inasmuch as he supposed that participation in its enjoyments would be accompanied by the impartation and complete and full possession of that divine vital energy,—he yet was far removed, in this expectation, from the true conception of what Christianity actually afforded to its recipients ; for, to the idea of the continued indwelling within us of the Holy Spirit, understood and believed in the Christian sense, he could never, independently of Christianity, have possibly attained.

There is some doubt as to what John meant by the word "*fire,*" which is added in Matt. 3 : 11, and in Luke 3 : 16, to the representation : "he shall baptize you in the Holy Ghost and *in fire.*" The most natural and first-suggested explanation seems to be, that fire baptism is here contrasted with water baptism ; it would seem as though nothing further is added to the idea than what is already contained in the notion of a spirit baptism, the Spirit being merely compared to a fire which purifies and enkindles a new life, in order to bring more prominently into view the contrast between the baptism of the Spirit and that of John. But if this were the sense of the passage, we might naturally expect that John would have expressly presented this opposition by the arrangement of his words ; he would, therefore, have mentioned the baptism of fire first, and then have subjoined, by way of explanation, the baptism of the Spirit. The altogether contrary arrangement which here presents itself, entirely excludes this mode of explaining the expression ; unless, indeed, it afterwards occurred to the mind of the forerunner to denominate the spirit baptism of Christ a baptism of fire, in order to describe more perfectly and to express more pointedly the contrast between it and the water baptism which he administered. But this explanation is directly opposed by the fact, that, both in the preceding and in the following verses of the narrative in Matthew and Luke, we find the word "fire" used in a totally different sense, it being always mentioned as a fire that shall consume and destroy the unbelieving, and not as a purifying and cleansing element. It appears that this signification must be firmly retained in the present passage also ; and we must suppose, accordingly, that John announced a two-fold baptism of Christ ; the one, a baptism of the Holy Spirit, only for his disciples and companions in the heavenly kingdom ; the other, a baptism of destructive and consuming fire (naturally, a picturesque or figurative expression), for the enemies and hardened sinners whom he will exterminate and destroy. That this is here the true meaning, we perceive from the explanation which he immediately assigns, and which we have already considered in the previous section ; where he goes on to describe the separation of the bad from the good, as it was to take place on the coming of Christ, and where also he represents the Messiah as utterly exterminating the unworthy portion of the people, just as Malachi announces the angel of the covenant as making his appearance with consuming fire.

It is contended, after Chrysostom, by most of the Catholic and by some respectable Protestant commentators (as Beza, Calvin: and, in more modern times, Stolz, Eichhorn, Olshausen, etc.) that, since *fire* is used in other places of the Scriptures to denote divine influences, the *baptism in fire* here spoken of refers to the transfiguring and purifying power of the Holy Spirit. But this explanation, as well as that which interprets the phrase of the *tongues of fire* spoken of in Acts 2 : 3., is, on critical grounds, quite inadmissible ; and is rejected, after Origen and Basil, almost unanimously by the critics of the present century (as Kuinoel, Alford, Neander, Meyer, De Wette, etc.). Neander gives a fair idea of the meaning of the passage in which the expression occurs (Life of Jesus, § 39) : "He [the Messiah] it was that should *baptize them with the Holy Spirit and with fire;* that is to say, that as his (John's) followers were entirely immersed in the water, so the Messiah would immerse the souls of believers in the Holy Spirit, imparted by himself; so that it should thoroughly penetrate their being, and form within them a new principle of life. But this spirit baptism was to be accompanied by *a baptism of fire.* Those who refused to be penetrated by the Spirit of the divine life, should be destroyed by the fire of the divine judgments. The 'sifting' by fire ever goes along with the advance of the Spirit, and consumes all who will not appropriate the latter."

That this is the correct and indeed only tenable explanation which can be given to the expression, will be shown by an examination of the passage as it occurs in the evangelists. In Mark and John (1 : 33.) the words *and with fire* are wholly wanting ; and so also is the explanatory representation which immediately follows in Matthew and Luke (cp. Acts 1 : 5.).

Here we have the key which unlocks the difficulty. The representation in question is the simile or comparison explained in the previous section. We perceive in this that a discrimination is to be made between the substances lying on the "threshing floor", after the operations of threshing and winnowing have been completed: the *wheat* is to be stored away in a granary; but the *chaff* is to be consumed. Now, by universal interpretation, the storing away of the wheat corresponds to the *baptism in the Holy Spirit:* the burning of the chaff, therefore, must, according to a just criticism, correspond to the *baptism in fire.*

The *baptism in fire*, then, refers to the destruction of those who, under the Messianic government, should refuse to receive the baptism of the Holy Spirit, those who should oppose themselves to the reign of the Messiah. The "unquenchable fire" spoken of, may indeed, as Meyer thinks, be meant to represent the fire of eternal punishment in Gehenna; but neither the meaning of the expression nor the tenor of the passage demands such a reference. On the contrary, the simile would rather indicate an extermination of the unbelieving and opposing from the earthly kingdom of the expected Messiah. Such is the view of Neander, De Wette, Baumgarten-Crusius, etc.

We come, therefore, here also, to the same results respecting the Messianic expectations which we have already obtained in the historical representation of the formation of his character: that, namely, with the highest and most spiritual ideas of the kingdom of God,—his conception of the baptism of the Holy Spirit being one of them,—he united yet other earthly and material notions respecting a worldly and external dominion of the Messiah, as he does here respecting the destruction of sinners; and we perceive here also, that he was by no means in a condition,—as at that time, indeed, he could not possibly have been,—to separate and distinguish from each other the first and the second appearance of the Lord.

NOTE.—John's baptism is briefly but justly described by Taylor, (*L. C.* § 9. 1.) as "a ceremonious consignation of the doctrine of repentance, which was one great part of the covenant evangelical, and was a divine institution. The susception of it was in order to the 'fulfilling all righteousness': it was a sign of humility: the persons baptized confessed their sins: it was a sacramental disposing to the baptism and faith of Christ."—The Forerunner preached "a baptism of repentance for the forgiveness of sins"; and every true penitent whom he baptized received, no doubt, the pardon of his iniquity. The right to grant "remission of sins" is, indeed, the prerogative of the Messiah, and their forgiveness is the distinguishing characteristic of the Messianic times; yet was sin also pardoned under the O. T. dispensation, on the manifestation of repentance. Repentance and faith in God were made the only conditions of forgiveness. This "remission of sins,"—which, however, was not visibly secured until the atonement was actually made and fully completed; and, hence, was, even when John began to baptize, to be outwardly and visibly "bestowed at a time yet future," (v. p. 126),—is the distinguishing doctrine of the Christian religion, as revealed in the Old as well as the New Testament. In the former, it is announced rather in "types and shadows"; in the latter, it is openly and plainly proclaimed and exhibited in the atoning sufferings of the Messiah; for, as Horne well remarks in his "Considerations" (§ 2.), "the doctrine of salvation 'by the remission of sins,' through faith in a Redeemer, was, from the beginning, the sum and substance of true religion, which subsisted in promise, prophecy, and figure, till John preached their accomplishment in the person of Jesus."

Huxtable opposes the view that the phrase "for the remission of sins," as applied to John's baptism, refers to a forgiveness "afterwards to be received from the Christ"; and thinks that the results of the repentance required by him, "are most naturally conceived as immediate rather than prospective." "The Jews were as yet dealt with," says he (*Ministry*, p. 22.), "according to the principles of the O. T. revelation; and according to these, forgiveness had ever been promised upon the simple condition of repentance."

CHAPTER III.

Effects of the Ministry of John among the People.

An appearance so new and striking as that of John, could not long have remained unobserved by the people ; the multitude had always exhibited special honor for the prophets, whose whole exterior air and conduct, their rigid abstinence, their wretched raiment and rugged mode of life, their bold language, regardless of consequences, and the pointedness of their addresses, could not have failed to make a deep impression upon the minds of the nation at large. In a time so stirring as that in which John commenced his ministry, when the expectation of a new and significant æra of the theocracy was so general and so deeply rooted, when, on this very account, every circumstance of an unusual nature must have produced great excitement, it was entirely consonant with the order of things that even the first appearance of the Baptist should produce an immense concourse of the people. His advent was truly national ; the remembrance of the old time when the prophets lived and acted, was awakened ; a desire for something else, for something better, was prevalent among the greater part of the people, and, therefore, they were eager to visit and examine into whatever promised to contribute to the introduction of a better and happier epoch.

John entered upon the prosecution of his labors in the populous and much-visited region of the Jordan, near the Dead Sea, preaching at first, it is probable, only to individuals and to families, whom he met there ; but the report of him must have soon spread farther into the circumjacent cities, and have brought to him the inquisitive of every class. His preaching and his new ceremony of baptism drew others to him from a distance more removed ; and so we read, in the beginning of the history, in Matt. 3 : 5, and Mark 1 : 5., that all the citizens of Jerusalem, all Judea, and all the inhabitants of the region round about the Jordan, came flocking to him from their respective abodes. Though we are, as is natural, not to understand this according to the strict letter, as representing that no individual was left behind, the expression yet indicates clearly that the great mass of the people and by far the greater part of the inhabitants of the country round about Jordan came to him ; and we may well conceive that, when the new appearance was made generally known among the people, and had obtained considerable renown, but few, if any, would have remained content without beholding the forerunner. All must have visited the wonderful man and observed his conduct for themselves, were it only in order to become able to converse about him, to conform to the prevailing fashion ; each, in order that he might not be the only one who knew nothing from personal knowledge of that which was throwing the whole surrounding country into excitement. That, therefore, the multitude which flocked to see John was quite as great as it is represented, is altogether credible and easily explained. But, the question is, *in what state of mind did the most of these people come unto John, and what impression did they carry away on their departure?*

That many, very many, if not driven to him by the necessity of their hearts, yet overcome by his preaching, actually exercised repentance, and applied themselves diligently to producing a change in their disposition, is rendered certain by the question which, according to Luke 3 : 10. ff., so many people of different classes put to the Baptist, "What shall we do then ?" From this it appears evident that they really intended to perform the injunctions of John ; and therefore they asked his counsel as to the manner in which they could best exhibit their repentant frame of mind. What he required of them was not, as we have elsewhere seen, difficult of performance, no rigorous abstemiousness, no painful ascetic practice,—and in this we must, as has been previously remarked, wonder so much the more at his wisdom, because one must naturally have expected from him, the stern ascetic, that he would require all to adopt a similar mode of life,—but the renunciation of such sins as were most cordially cherished by each class of the inquirers ; and this, if they were truly serious in their repentance, they could easily perform. We may, therefore, take it for granted that many, and especially those who found themselves sunk deepest in the mire and pollution of sin, wrought upon by his solemn preaching of repentance and alarmed by the threat of approaching judgment, busied themselves seriously with the work of conversion and reformation.

Many others, on the contrary, who perhaps had only come to him from curiosity and in company with the multitude, and who, moreover, overcome for the moment by his preaching, had actually vowed repentance and suffered themselves to receive in baptism the seal of their earnest striving after repentance and moral improvement, might, perhaps, have preserved within them, at the beginning, the impression of this occurrence and their good resolutions ; but the natural inclinations and desires of their hearts were not so entirely repressed as to allow us to conclude that the remembrance of what they had experienced had a lasting influence upon their minds and conduct. The great mass of the people who came to him very soon forgot in their practice his teachings and his threats, though they did not cease on that account to honor him as a prophet sent from God; for we perceive from Matt. 14. 5. (cp. Matt. 21 : 26., Mark 11 : 32.) that John was regarded in this light by the people at large, in which passage the Pharisees are represented as fearing to say anything against the Baptist, because the people in general looked upon him as a prophet, and, therefore, also, as we learn from the context of the same passage, considered his baptism a divine institution. All this, however, could not prevent his ministry from being productive, in most instances; of no abiding conversion. Were not this the case; had, on the contrary, this entire multitude which is represented as having hastened with eagerness to his presence, believed in his words, and conducted themselves in accordance with his commands, how could it have been possible that Christ should not have been joyfully hailed from all sides as the Messiah and as the deliverer from sin, and that all should not have turned to him in the exercise of their repentant feelings; and how could it have been necessary for the Messiah himself in the very beginning of his ministry to preach so constantly the strictest repentance and to rebuke and threaten with punishment the sins which were then prevalent among the nation? From the treatment which Christ met with at the hands of the people, who, on one day, cried "Hosanna!" before him, strewed palm-branches in his way and spread their garments beneath his feet, and yet, on the next, cried with united voice, "crucify him, crucify him!" we may ascertain with sufficient clearness in what estimation we ought to hold their enthusiasm for John; and how in his case their fickleness must have manifested itself in their speedy forgetfulness of their vows, as it did in the case of Jesus by their rapid transition from the warmest zeal in his behalf to the most destructive hate.

The people, moreover, were inclined to consider the Baptist himself the Messiah (Luke 3 : 15.). As the expectation of his coming was very generally spread among the nation, the over-excitable and credulous part of the people would be inclined to find him in every thing strange which met their sight; and as John appeared in the guise of the old prophets, while the Messiah was also frequently represented as a prophet and teacher of the people in the ancient prophecies, especially in the prophecy of Moses; and since, moreover, a ceremony of purification was also probably expected to be performed by the Messiah, they could scarcely help concluding that in John they had found the promised Christ. Because he separated himself outwardly from all other men, and because he rebuked with a severity regardless of consequences the faults of the people, even of the most distinguished, it was looked upon as an indication amounting to proof, that he would also oppose himself to their external rulers and oppressors and nowhere suffer injustice or tyranny; and this thought must naturally have greatly encouraged the earthly hopes of the people. John, however, gave them that noble answer which has already been considered in another connection; he baptized only in water, but he who was to come after him, the latchet of whose shoes he was not worthy to loose, for whom he was not worthy to perform the most menial offices, he was to baptize in the Spirit and in fire. He points here most distinctly to one infinitely higher than himself, whom they should expect, one who would bring unto them altogether different blessings and appear among them with an altogether different power from that which he possessed; and who, as John further shows in the parable of the farmer with his winnowing-shovel, would make a distinct separation between the good and the bad, the just and the unjust, conferring upon the former eternal life, but inflicting upon the latter destruction as the punishment of their sins.

To represent himself as the Messiah to the people, who were ready to receive him as such,—a course which vanity might have prompted him to follow,—was a part which the Baptist disdained to act, preferring to yield implicit obedience to the divine call, which had conferred upon him the office of a forerunner and nothing more, and, in his modesty, announcing himself as the most menial servant of him whom God had appointed his successor. "The great, the god-like feature of his character," says Neander (Life of Jesus, § 38), "was his thorough understanding of himself and his calling. Filled as he was with enthusiasm, he yet felt that he was but the humble instrument of the divine Spirit, called, not to *found* the new creation, but to *proclaim* it; nor did the thronging of eager thousands to hang upon his lips, nor the enthusiastic love of his own immediate followers, ever ready to glorify their master, in the least degree blind his perceptions of duty, or raise him above his calling. Convinced that he was inspired of God to prepare, and not to create, he never pretended to work miracles (Jno. 10 : 41.), nor did his disciples, strongly as he impressed them, ever attribute miraculous powers to him."

John appears to have made frequent use of the expression "*whose shoe-latchet I am unworthy to unloose*," and to have given it as a constant reply to all those who wished to assign to him a higher office than that which he was called to undertake. At least, we find precisely the same expression in his answer to the question put to him by the Sanhedrim (Jno. 1 : 26.), and which was urged by that body after Jesus had been baptized, though he had not as yet entered upon his public ministry.—The relation which these leading men in the state bore to the Baptist, it will be well to examine here with some attention. Since John commenced his labors altogether in the manner of the ancient prophetism, practising a rigidly ascetic life and presenting an unusual and striking appearance, and since he announced the near approach of the Messiah, whose kingdom he, with all his enlightenment, both conceived to himself and proclaimed to the people as earthly as well as spiritual in its nature, the Pharisees and their associates supposed that they had found in him the man whom they needed, who would enter into their ambitious plans and make common cause with them, in order to make sure forthwith of the expected Messiah, and, by his means, to attain that respect, power and authority which formed in them the main object of their efforts and their existence. That they must renounce their sins in order to attain this end, did not occur to them ; or rather they had succeeded in persuading themselves that they were without sin ; and therefore they entertained not a doubt but that they, as descendants of Abraham, would have in their own right an inheritance in the Messianic kingdom. Their only care now was to make sure that they should be invested with the highest honors in this kingdom. At first, they allowed John to follow his own course without bringing him to account for his ministry ; nay, they even went so far as to go out to him in person (Matt. 3 : 7.), Pharisees as well as Sadducees, in order to bring him into friendly connection with themselves. The Sadducees, although they ridiculed what they deemed the superstition of the people, and through their love of worldly pleasure had become dead as to all that was heavenly, yet sought to promote their own advantage by means of a man so influential as was the Baptist, and therefore endeavored to secure his friendship.

But, what answer did John give to both parties? Did he fall in with their ambitious plans? By no means; but, on the contrary, he holds up their sins before their eyes, reproves them in the presence of all the people, threatens them with exclusion from the Messianic kingdom, in case they were not converted and turned not to repentance (Matt. 3: 7–10.), in words of the severest and most positive character, and utterly casts to the ground all their hopes of making him an instrument for accomplishing their purposes. Perhaps they came to him frequently, and sought to bind him to their interest with all their arts of cunning; but every time with the same result. Yet they did not dare to call him to account, because the respect which the people had for him forbade such a procedure; and in this way John was enabled to continue laboring for some time among the nation without any hindrance being offered on their part. But at last he became too dangerous, his influence among the people increased more and more every day and threw that of others into the shade; nay, he even took advantage of the hold which he had on the feelings of the nation and made use of it to degrade the Pharisees and their friends in their estimation, and to expose their falsehood and hypocrisy. Voices were heard among the nation speaking of him as the Messiah; and, although John distinctly disclaimed all right to this high dignity, yet must the members of the Sanhedrim, judging him from their knowledge of their own hearts, have feared that the Baptist would not long resist this enticement; and from such a Messiah, they well knew, they had every thing to fear. Threatened, therefore, in their very existence, they resolved to venture their last move, to bring him to account for his conduct, and, if he could not prove that he was acting under divine authority, to prevent him from proceeding in his ministerial labors, and to make him as much as possible an object of suspicion among the people.

Accordingly we read in Jno. 1 : 19. that the Jews, that is, the representatives of the Jewish people, the members of the Sanhedrim,* sent to him priests and Levites, therefore a deputation of the whole clergy of the State, to Bethany (Bethabara, in the ordinary text) on the farther side of the Jordan, where John was then exercising his ministry. This deputation belonged, as we are informed expressly (v. 24.), to the sect of the Pharisees, and therefore to those who were most strongly interested in establishing an influence among the people, and in reducing, in every possible manner, the authority of the Baptist. Christ himself refers at a subsequent period to this embassy to John (Jno. 5 : 33.). The Sanhedrim, beyond a doubt, had the right to bring John to such an examination ; for it was the office of that body to be on the watch and prevent any false prophet from deceiving the people ; and therefore every prophet had to prove to them, either by a miracle or by some special evidence of a divine call, that he had a right to perform his ministry ; and if he could not produce such proof, he was forbidden to prosecute further the labors of his office (cp. Matt. 21 : 23.).

* Throughout John's Gospel, the expression "the Jews" (*οἱ Ἰουδαῖοι*) is used to designate the party which made opposition to the Son of God. The appellation usually means, as here, the *Sanhedrim*, or representatives of the people, an assembly of seventy-two persons, composed of *chief priests*, *elders*, and *scribes* or *Pharisees*, which had the superintendence in matters of religion and law in Jerusalem.

To the question, *who he is*, John answers freely and candidly that he is not the Messiah (v. 20.) ; and so too he refuses the other titles of honor which the deputation would have conferred upon him, as not of right belonging to him (vs. 21, 22.), and gives them finally, when they insist upon a positive explanation, no other answer than what had already long since been said by the prophet Isaiah (40 : 3.) : he is "the voice of one crying in the wilderness, Prepare ye the way of the Lord, make straight in the desert a highway for our God" (v. 23.). Such an appeal to this passage was new to them ; in all their study of the Scriptures they had certainly never learned to interpret the expression in such a manner, and to find in it an announcement of a forerunner of the Messiah. At any rate, they seem to have been unable to urge against it any serious objection ; yet they were not willing to let John escape so easily. They asked him, therefore, *what right he had to baptize* (v. 25.) ; for, even admitting that he was the forerunner of the Messiah, he had not, they thought, acquired on that account the right to introduce a new ceremony. A baptism administered by the Messiah himself they would, perhaps, have allowed to pass unquestioned ; nay, they even expected, it is probable, that baptism would be performed in his name, not, however, by him in person, but by some prophet.

The Baptist replies briefly and laconically, but with sufficient precision, that he baptizes only in water ; as his whole ministry is preparatory, his baptism is also preparatory, as he had previously and frequently declared that it was the Messiah who was to baptize in the Holy Spirit.—And now, in order to do away once for all with further questions and inquiries respecting his ministry, he gives to them a sign by which they might shortly discover whether he had a right to exercise his office or not; for he proclaims to them with the most confident assurance, that the Messiah, his great successor, is standing even now in their midst, and therefore will speedily make himself known and will bear witness both for him and for himself. John had then already baptized Jesus; he knew that in a short time he would come forth in public as the Messiah, and he could therefore appeal with the greatest confidence to his approaching appearance (vs. 26, 27.). The Pharisees, however, had to wait for the fulfillment of his assertion; and could undertake nothing further against him, if he proved himself, by the result of his prophecy, to stand in a specially near relation to God. At a later period, when Christ had actually appeared in public, when all the people hastened to him in crowds, the Sanhedrim had to struggle against a yet more dangerous enemy, on whose destruction they had to risk their all; at this period they let John pass unattacked, and soon thereafter his career came to an end.

If now we bring together and view at once the consequences of the ministry of John, we shall find that he roused against himself the opposition of the Pharisees and of those who clung most firmly to their sins, and found a hearty reception among only a very few of them, and only among such as were Pharisees merely in name and not in conduct (Luke 7 : 29.); that, however, his reputation was spread widely and fixed firmly among the people, that all honored and commended him as a prophet, and many were led by his repeated exhortations to repentance and to a better mode of life. The great mass, it must be confessed, rested content with outwardly honoring him, and with taking the vow of repentance, without seriously and faithfully fulfilling it; but yet it was a fact of great importance and full of significance for the time, that by means of the preaching of the Baptist the expectation of a deliverer was extended more widely than it had ever been before ; and all the people entertained at least this expectation, that his kingdom would be not merely an earthly one, but in its main features spiritual, in which no one could obtain citizenship except by possessing a pious, God-fearing disposition, and by true repentance of heart ; so that Christ, when he came, had a foundation in some respects already prepared, from which he could enter upon the ministry and upon which he could build his church.*

* The impression produced by John was remarkable. The people "went out into the wilderness" in crowds ; and, professing repentance, received baptism at his hands. Not only their religious sentiments, but their more worldly passions, were aroused ; for, as Huxtable remarks (*Ministry*, p. 29.), "the prospect of the speedy appearance of the great Deliverer of their nation, kept back only by their sins, was calculated to stimulate their minds to an apparent ardour of reformation, far exceeding what would be produced by the genuine impulses of conscience and piety." The people seemed, accordingly, to have suddenly become devout.

Bishop Horne presents us with a picturesque, but rather over-wrought, description of the effects produced among the people by the preaching of the Baptist. It may be found in the fifth section of his "Considerations on the Life and Death of John the Baptist" (Am. ed. pp. 494. 495.): "Jews and Gentiles, Pharisees and Publicans, Sadducees and Soldiers, all confess their sins, and partake of the same baptism; all struck with apprehensions of some impending evil, all flying from the wrath to come ; forgetting their mutual hostilities and antipathies, and, like the creatures in the days of Noah, taking refuge together in the ark. As if the prophecy of Isaiah had now begun to receive its accomplishment, the publicans, who, before the preaching of John, were ravenous as evening 'wolves', became innocent as the 'lamb.' The soldiers, who had been formerly fierce and cruel as the 'lion', became tame and tractable as the 'ox', and submitted their necks to the yoke of the Gospel. Such of the Pharisees likewise, who, before their baptism, had been venomous as the 'asp' or 'cockatrice,' did, by the worthy receiving of this baptism, and the grace which God gave them, become mild and gentle as the 'sucking infant' or 'weaned child.'"

CHAPTER IV

The Baptism of Jesus.

John had fulfilled the first part of his vocation, the preparation of the people for the coming of the Messiah, he had invited them by his preaching to repentance and baptism, and had referred them to a Redeemer who was soon to appear. He was, however, charged with another commission, one which did not indeed supplant and utterly exclude the other, but which from this time onward became especially prominent; *he was to bear witness of the Messiah when he should appear* (Jno. 1: 31.). With the evangelist John this seems to have been the most important office of the Baptist; for in the very beginning of the introduction to his Gospel (v. 7.), where the characteristics of the great and universal Light of the world are exhibited to view, he makes express mention also of the forerunner of this Light in the following words: "The same came for a witness, to bear witness of the Light, that all men through him might believe"; and, after adducing the proofs that Christ and none other is the Light, already made manifest, and the Word come in the flesh, he mentions again in v. 15., as at the commencement, the testimony borne by the Baptist, who had been expressly called by God to bear witness to the Messiah.

In order that John might be prepared to announce with unshaken confidence and firmness that Jesus was the Messiah, it was necessary that he should receive assurance by means of a special sign from heaven, which should also leave behind it a deep moral impression, that Jesus and no other than he was the person whom he expected. On this account, the divine indication that was given to him was to the effect that that person would be the Messiah upon whom he should see the Spirit descending and resting (Jno. 1 : 33.) ; and this information was imparted unto him by a divine revelation, perhaps in a dream or by a vision. It was natural that this particular sign should be chosen, because it most precisely expressed that which it was intended to prove. It was meant to intimate that he who should receive it was endued to the utmost with the Holy Spirit, and, since the Spirit appeared abiding on him, that he would partake without interruption of this divine Spirit ; and,—what would be to John either new information or a confirmation of his previous expectations,—that the Messiah would be no ordinary man, distinguished perhaps, as some others had been, by remarkable spiritual gifts, but that the Holy Spirit would actually dwell in him, and that therefore he must be as much God as man. The sign itself was given to him at the baptism of Jesus. It could not well have been given on any other occasion ; for, since he was constantly engaged in preaching to the people who came to him, and in baptizing them, since he did not go in person to this one or to that one, seeking out individuals, but all came to him, Jesus must also have come to him in person, and in such a manner that the attention of the Baptist should be specially and wholly directed to him, and that he should be particularly engaged with him when the sign should be exhibited.

The baptismal scene is represented with most details by Matthew (3 : 13–17.) ; Luke mentions nothing respecting the baptism itself, but merely speaks of the sign which was given after the ceremony had been performed: "Now, when all the people were baptized, it came to pass, that Jesus also being baptized, and praying,"—which was a very natural and probably a universal custom among those who had just received the rite,—"the heaven was opened, etc." (3: 21, 22.) Mark, on the other hand, gives an account, it is true, of the baptism (1: 9–11.), but without mentioning the conversation which had previously taken place between John and Jesus, which we find recorded only in Matthew. He merely relates the bare fact, making, however, the account of Matthew somewhat more complete by changing the altogether indefinite "then" of that evangelist (v. 13.) into the confessedly not much more definite expression, "in those days" (v. 9.), and by subjoining the observation that Jesus had come out of Nazareth. The Son of God appears, therefore, to have passed his whole time up to this period in that city, in all stillness and quietness, forming his character from within; distinguished in particular, however, for nothing else save his righteous behavior and the spirituality which, without a question, was exhibited even at that day in all the conduct of his life. Since now he had been assured by the voice of God, that the time at length had come when he should appear openly as the Saviour of the world; and since, perhaps, he also knew, in consequence of his perfect knowledge of all that had reference to the completion of his calling, that it was John who, taught respecting him and his divine dignity by a sign from heaven, should bear witness for him in the presence of the people, he left his retirement and repaired to the Baptist at the Jordan, not only in order to occasion the sending of this sign, but also,—and this was the second great signification of the baptism of Jesus,—in order to receive, by means of the rite, a consecration to his cailing, and to distinguish, through this ceremonial act, the beginning of his public ministry.

Naturally, the baptism administered by John could not have had for Jesus the same signification which it had for the others who received it ; for he was already pure, and needed to take no vow of repentance, nor to have conferred upon him any seal of that repentance, nor any assurance that his sins were forgiven. It was nevertheless entirely accordant with his humiliation that he, having taken upon himself the form of sinful flesh, should accomplish in his own person all that it was incumbent on sinful man to perform. For this reason was he circumcised ; and for this reason did he frequent the festivals and conform to the Jewish temple worship ; but confessedly without bending himself to a slavish adherence to every single precept, as for example, he showed most clearly in the expression "the Son of Man is lord also of the Sabbath !" All this was intended only for sinful men ; but the Lord, who through his eternal love to man entered into the entire community of sinful men, took upon himself the whole yoke of the law, became in this respect altogether like any other man, and fulfilled, yet without sin, all the precepts which had been given for transgressors. He himself said as much to John, when the latter would have restrained him from receiving baptism at his hands ; "for thus it becometh us to fulfill all righteousness," that is, in consequence of my present condition. He does not deny, therefore, that baptism administered to him by John, a man who morally was inferior to himself, could not be performed on him in the same sense as it was upon others ; but it was for another reason, because it was consistent with his present circumstances to fulfill in his own person all the obligations of humanity, that the

Baptist should, as Christ expressed it, "suffer it to be so now."

It is impossible that our Lord could, as Strauss thinks he did, have submitted himself to the baptism of John from a consciousness of indwelling sinfulness, for how then could he have afterwards professed himself to pardon sins; neither could he have done so from a feeling that sin slumbered within him, and might, therefore, by some means, be aroused into action (De Wette); nor, finally, could he have sought the reception of the rite from a conviction of the necessity of purification from internal defilement of any kind whatever. That there resided in Jesus, on account of his finite nature and his human organism, an abstract possibility of sinning, can not be denied; for this possibility is inseparable from humanity, and this is so far just the state in which our first parents were before their fall: but such a possibility was in the case of Christ always and of necessity restrained from passing into action by the inflexible firmness of his immutable will; and, on this account, it cannot be true, and indeed it is quite inconceivable, that he should have experienced any consciousness of the need of internal purification.

Various opinions are entertained as to the object which Jesus had in mind when he submitted himself to this baptismal ceremony; in other words, what, when viewed with respect to him, is its intended signification.—It cannot have been received, as Paulus thinks, *as a testimony to his Messianic dignity;* nor, *for the purpose of grounding the faith of others on him, because baptism is a symbol of the regeneration of its recipients* (Ammon, *Leben Jesu*, I., S. 268.); nor, *to indicate that he was subject to death* (Ebrard); nor, *to honor by his example the baptism of John* (Kuinoel, Kern); nor, *to bind himself to an observance of the Jewish law* (Hoffmann, Krabbe, Osiander); nor, because he had not represented himself as the Messiah previously to the descent of the Spirit, but merely *as an Israelite who conformed to the divine ordinances* (Hess, Kuhn, and in part Neander); but, as the expression in Matt. 3 : 15., "for *thus* it becometh *us*, [viz., you by baptizing me, and I by receiving the rite at your hands] to fulfill all righteousness," would seem to indicate, *because he knew that his baptism by John was willed by God, in order to inaugurate him formally and solemnly as the Messiah* (Neander, Jacobi, Baumgarten-Crusius, Meyer), and because "it became him, being in the likeness of sinful flesh, to go through those appointed rites and purifications which belonged to that flesh" (Alford). This action of Christ must unquestionably be ranked among those properly pertaining to his Messianic calling; and the Baptist expressly testifies to that effect, when he says: "that he should be made manifest to Israel, *therefore* am I come baptizing in water" (Jno. 1 : 31.). "It was," as Lücke has well remarked, in explanation of this passage, "only by entering into that community which was to be introductory to the Messianic, by attaching himself to the Baptist like any other man, that it became possible for Christ to reveal himself to the Baptist, and through him to others."

The baptism which John performed upon Jesus, had however, as we concluded *a priori* from his sinless nature, an altogether different signification from that which the same act possessed when administered to its other recipients. For all other candidates this immersion, whether received before or after that of Christ, constituted a preparatory consecration to and preparation for the kingdom of the Messiah; for Jesus, on the other hand, it was "a direct and immediate consecration, by means of which he manifested the commencement of his career as the founder of the new theocracy, which began at the very moment of his baptism, the initiatory character of which constituted its general principle and tendency."* Yet, whether administered to others or to Christ, this baptism had the same substantial element; for it marked in each the beginning of a new course of life; but, in the former case, "this new life was to be received from without through communications from on high; while in Christ it was to consist of a gradual unfolding from within; in the former, it was to be receptive—in the latter, productive. In a word, the baptism of the members prepared them to *receive* pardon and salvation; that of Christ was his consecration to the work of *bestowing* those precious gifts."†

While in this occurrence we wonder at the friendliness and condescension of the Word which was manifest in the flesh, who became, in a yet higher sense, all things, like Paul, to all men, we cannot fail to observe anew the upright conscientiousness of the Baptist, who expresses himself in the words, "I have need to be baptized of thee, and comest thou to me?" What inferences may be drawn from this expression respecting the acquaintance of John with Jesus, and what relation the words bear to the testimony given by the Baptist, "I knew him not," we have already seen in another place. Here we have only to remark for the second time that they form incontrovertible proof that such an acquaintance existed between the two, that John had become convinced of the fact of the

* See Jacobi, in *Kitto's Cyclop. of Bib. Literature*, Art. Baptism, in which the subject of Christ's baptism and that of baptism in general is discussed with marked ability.

† Neander, *Life of Jesus*, § 42 (5).

high moral purity of Jesus, and had attained to a consciousness how far he stood below him in this respect; and that, moreover, he speaks out freely and openly his conviction, confessing before the whole world, that he, the rigid ascetic who preached repentance to all the people, is himself a sinner, needs himself a baptism of purification; and this confession must place him, if not in the estimation of men, yet in the eyes of God, high above all the arrogant leaders of the people, who had nothing more important to engage their attention than to boast of their righteousness before the people and before the Messiah.

What, however, so conceived, is an expression of the purest humility, would evidently be merely an example of the lowest hypocrisy, if we take the position, as some do, that this whole meeting took place in accordance with a plan previously concerted. It may be said that it was not the intention of Christ to deceive the people by such an exhibition, but only to have himself accredited by John as the Messiah; yet even in this case the question,—which John put in a tone of surprise,—if he knew beforehand that Christ was coming to him and for what purpose, was calculated shamefully to deceive the people, who must have been induced by the mode of the occurrence to believe that it had all been brought about by the direct agency of God; and John could not have justified his conduct in representing that the pure and the just had come to him, the sinner, for baptism. The explanation above alluded to, therefore, we must pointedly contradict and oppose; for nothing in the narrative authorizes us in casting such spots upon a character so noble and so distinguished as that of John; and, as we have elsewhere seen, we need no further explanation than that which has been given, in order to understand in their whole significance these simple and natural words of the Baptist, and to find them altogether appropriate in the connection in which they stand.*

Obedient to the will of Jesus, John hereupon admitted him to baptism. A longer hesitation would have been unbecoming, and would not have partaken of the appearance of humility. The rite was performed, without doubt, altogether in the customary form. We have no reason to suppose that Jesus was not baptized with reference to the coming of the Messiah (εἰς τὸν ἐρχόμενον); only, the confession of sin which usually preceded the rite, must of course have been omitted.

When Jesus had ascended from the water and had prayed, John beheld, as he himself informs us (Jno. 1 : 32.), the Spirit descending from heaven, like a dove, and resting upon him whom he had baptized; he received, therefore, at this moment, the sign which had been promised to him, so that he recognized Jesus as the Messiah, and was prepared to bear witness of him as he had been divinely appointed to do.

It becomes a question whether we have to think here of a real dove flying down from heaven;—for, that the "*like* a dove" cannot refer, as some suppose, to the *mode* of descent, that is, that the Spirit flew down as a dove flies, is disproved by the addition made to the account by Luke, "the Holy Ghost descended *in a bodily shape* like a dove" (3 : 22.), and

* "Quite erroneous," says Olshausen (on Matt. 3: 13. Note), "is the notion which assumes that Jesus made his appearance in public according to a plan which had been minutely calculated and carefully pre-concerted. His internal life only obeyed the will of his heavenly Father; whatever he inspired him to do was immediately done by the son. The clearest knowledge of what he did was, it is true, connected with it; but every calculation, or speculation, and human plan-making, must here be considered as excluded, inasmuch as all this makes an inroad on the immediate unity of life in Christ and God."

by the fact, moreover, that the Spirit must have made himself outwardly visible in some form or other, if John was to discover that he had actually descended from heaven. The most important difficulty in the passage is the fact that John should have recognized, without some additional circumstance, the Spirit in the dove ; especially since we find on no occasion before this, the dove spoken of as the symbol of the Spirit. There can be no question that the recognition will seem quite natural, if we take into account the voice which, according to Matt. 3 : 17., proceeded from heaven, saying, "This is my beloved Son, in whom I am well pleased."

But, there still remains to be solved the difficulty that John, according to his own account, saw not a real dove, but only the Spirit *like* a dove ; so that what he saw had indeed the closest resemblance to a dove, but yet must have been to the view something different from a dove, which latter would not have remained sufficiently long upon Jesus ; whereas it was to be for John one of the principal evidences of the Messiah that the Spirit should descend and *abide* upon him whom God would recognize.—There is, moreover, yet another difficulty, which it is important to explain : John relates (Jno. 1 : 32.) this occurrence to his disciples as something altogether new and unknown to them ; whereas we might pre-suppose that these disciples,—of whom we shall have to speak more in detail hereafter,—as they were generally present when he baptized, were present also on this occasion, and that therefore they must themselves have beheld the whole miracle. It would, consequently, be remarkable, in case all the people round about had witnessed the entire occurrence and had heard the voice, that we have no account of their surprise and excitement on the occasion ; since, in that event, the eyes and thoughts of all must have been directed towards him of whom so many and so great things had been predicted.

When urging this and the other difficulties which have been mentioned, objectors forget that they are all founded on an uncertain basis; namely, upon the pre-supposition that the disciples as well as a multitude of people were present when the baptism of Jesus and the divine acknowledgment of his Messiahship took place. Is this supposition, however, necessary? How can it be proved to be true? John must by this time have been prosecuting his labors for six months; the first feeling of curiosity on the part of the people must have become measurably stilled, and even though large crowds yet resorted to him, we need not suppose that the press of the multitude was wholly uninterrupted. Jesus was no doubt able, since he knew that John would receive at his baptism the proof of his Messiahship from his Father, to have chosen for the reception of the rite a time when he was certain to meet the Baptist alone and unattended by his disciples. To assert that John's disciples were constantly with him is to assume not only without proof, but also contrary to positive evidence. We read in Jno. 1 : 35. : "the next day John stood, and two of his disciples." Here we find that only two of his followers were with him, and the rest absent: as the others could remain away from him for some time, so also could these: they went away with Jesus, and then, at least, was John alone. Why could not this have frequently happened on previous occasions?

There is, therefore, a good reason to be assigned in explanation of the fact that John, some time after the miracle had occurred, related it to his disciples as something unknown to them and to the people; and as to that which appears to some to form an objection to the precise correctness of the narrative, that, namely, according to his own account, he saw not a *real dove*, but the spirit *like a dove*, and that, as Luke adds, *in a bodily form*, it is readily and satisfactorily replied, that he might just as well have seen this supernatural appearance which he could compare to nothing else so aptly as to a dove, with open bodily eyes as to have been made acquainted, —as it is often contended he was,—with the truth which it was necessary he should know, by means of the same apparition exhibited in a vision. Now, no one will assert that when John saw the apparition with his corporeal eyes he beheld nothing else than an ordinary dove ; and there is no good reason for supposing that he could have been made better acquainted in a vision with the spiritual element which had appeared to him in a corporeal form, than he could have been in his customary bodily condition. We are not justified, even where we read in the Old Testament so frequently of theophanies, or appearances of God, made unto mortals, in concluding that those to whom the theophanies were made invariably fell into a trance and saw in a vision ; for when this was actually the case, it is expressly mentioned, as for example in Gen. 15 : 1. : much less are we justified in drawing such a conclusion here, in the New Testament, where we have not the slightest indication that John, after he had baptized Christ, was thrown into a state of ecstasy, and while in this condition beheld the apparition. Just the same is the case with regard to the voice from heaven, which, it will be remembered, was heard again at the transfiguration of Christ (Matt. 17 : 5.) and during the last conversation which he held with the people (Jno. 12 : 28.) ; on which occasions the disciples who heard and understood the voice had not fallen into an ecstasy. And, finally, how inappropriate and unsatisfactory to himself would it have been, if John should have received while in a morbid condition that sign which was to prepare and induce him to be a witness, firm, immovable, and consolatory to all the world, that Jesus is the Messiah : how easily, at a later period, might the doubt have arisen within him, whether after all that which he had observed was not the mere play of his heated imagination which saw just what it wished to see. It was necessary that he should see and hear all while in a sound and conscious state of mind, in a mode of view at once clear and natural, and in a manner that could not be mistaken, in order that he might remain firm and unhesitating in his evidence.

If we take this view of the occurrence and hold, as is most natural, that the whole apparition was externally perceived, we do not involve ourselves in the difficulties to which, on any other supposition, the different accounts of the evangelists appear to lead. According to the narrative of Luke it was John who saw the Spirit descending upon Jesus ; according to Mark, on the other hand, it was Jesus himself ; and Matthew leaves it doubtful which of the two, or whether both, beheld the apparition. If, therefore, we do not take the ground that the evangelists contradict each other, we must admit that both observed the appearance. Are we, in consequence, to suppose that both had one and the same vision? Such is the position which they must take who, while admitting the correctness of all the accounts, contend that the whole occurrence took place in a vision. But, not reckoning the improbability that the two should have beheld in their trance one and the same thing,—since a vision, of whatever nature it may be, is grounded always upon the subjective character of the individual, and accordingly must, in this instance as in others, have appeared differently to the two persons,—it is altogether impossible to suppose that visions were used as a means of communicating knowledge to Jesus, without wholly denying that he possessed perfect and constant information in virtue of his divinity.

If this view should fail to give satisfaction, it is quite allowable to offer another explanation ; for we may hold that an external apparition took place indeed, and that in the presence of the people, but that it was intelligible only to these two divinely-enlightened men ; it was indeed a dove externally which appeared, in which, however, they alone recognized the Holy Spirit ; it was in truth a clap of thunder which was heard, but they alone understood the voice. If we have recourse to this view, because not able to free ourselves from the supposition that John's disciples and the people in general were present on the occasion, it must nevertheless appear surprising, nay, altogether inexplicable, that with regard to these extraordinary apparitions, which must have produced not a little noise and sensation,—for it is by no means a usual occurrence for a dove to come flying to a man and to settle upon his head ; nor is it more usual for a thunder-clap to be heard from a serene sky,—that we are nowhere informed what effect they had upon the people, what they thought of Jesus, etc. ; and it is equally surprising that John does not, in his subsequent narration of the occurrence to his disciples, refer to what they themselves had observed at the time, and explain to them what signification it had with respect to him that was initiated.—If we suppose, on the other hand, what is on many accounts most probable, that the people and the disciples were not present, there is no reason to be assigned why one thing outwardly and another inwardly should be exhibited to John and Jesus, externally a dove but internally the Spirit like a dove, externally the noise of thunder but internally distinct words from God ; why, in fact, that which it was necessary for them to see, could not have appeared to them outwardly altogether in such a way as it was necessary that they should see and hear.

Accordingly, that John could have recognized perfectly the Spirit of God in the form which externally appeared, we cannot by any possibility doubt when we take into consideration the prophecy which had been given to him for this very purpose, the otherwise singular circumstances of this event, his knowledge of Jesus' high moral purity, and above all the explanatory voice from heaven which pertained only to this occurrence.—Provided that we think of only John and Jesus as being present when this solemn act of consecration took place, we may conceive of the whole event in a manner exceedingly simple and satisfactory. The heaven appears to open (Matt. 3 : 16.) ; evidently a symbol of the communication now and forever opened between earth and heaven : the Spirit comes down ; a symbol of the divine existence now revealed in Christ (because the Spirit will be perceptible outwardly by human eyes, it takes here a definite form, just as God appears in some particular shape in the Old Testament, now as fire, now as a cloud of smoke, now in human form, etc.) : in a form which is compared to a dove, because this would be in the highest degree the representation of the soft and mild manner of the Spirit which dwelt and operated in Christ : the Spirit abides upon him ; a symbol of the constant and equable operation of the Spirit of God in Christ, not fitful and interrupted, as in the case of the prophets, but thoroughly penetrating him and exhibiting itself in all his conduct. To these we must add, to finish the picture, the clear and infallible voice from heaven, "this is my beloved Son," or, as it is most probably reported with more exactness in the narrative of Mark and Luke as being addressed personally to Christ, "thou art my beloved Son"; from which words, by relating them indirectly, the form of expression which appears in Matthew doubtless originated.

Some of the Apocryphal Gospels relate the circumstances attendant upon the baptism of Christ at greater length than they are recorded in the New Testament; adding much that is fabulous to the true accounts, but in such a way that their connection with the original and trustworthy sources is readily traceable. The Ebionitish Gospel of the Hebrews, for example, quoted by Epiphanius (30. 13.), inverts the order of the occurrences, and represents the miraculous appearances as preceding and occasioning John's conduct. According to its account, a light shines around the place, and a voice addresses itself first to Jesus and then to John, who thereupon falls at the feet of Christ. The Spirit, as here described, not only descends upon but *enters into* Jesus; expressing still more strongly than the original the permanent dwelling of the Spirit in the Messiah. The same idea is made still more prominent in the Nazarean Gospel of the Hebrews, quoted by Jerome (*Adv. Pelagium*, 3. 2.): "All the fountain of the Holy Spirit, descending and resting upon him, said, 'My son, I awaited thee in all the prophets, that thou mightest come, and that I might rest in thee. For thou art my abiding-place, thou art my first-born son, that reignest forever.'" Here indeed a fine Christian sense is given, but the historic facts are evidently distorted.

The whole apparition, it is clear, though perceptible to

Christ as well as to John, was notwithstanding given, according to its symbolic character, only to the Baptist for his gratification and instruction. It was intended to convince him that he whose coming he had anticipated, and for which he was preparing the way, had at length appeared. He was alone with Jesus ; and the latter could have needed no revelation. The apparition, therefore, was intended for the Baptist alone: others needed it not, and them it could benefit only mediately through him, and only then in case they regarded him as a prophet worthy of credence.—To Christ himself, however, there was imparted by the apparition no new element of life. For we cannot admit the supposition that Christ, either before this occurrence or after it, was either more or less God-man ; but, as from his birth onward he was the Word revealed in the flesh, so could there, at a later period, nothing be added to and nothing taken away from his divine nature.—It seems to be an inadmissible view to hold that Jesus was at first in possession of the Holy Spirit only sufficiently far to make him susceptible of preparation for his calling ; but that now he received the Spirit which was to induce him to undertake his external ministry to the world, and to lead him on to his public activity ; as though this susceptibility and this activity were divided in the Holy Spirit, and as though it were possible to think that Christ at one time possessed the Spirit only by halves.

The first three evangelists indeed would seem, by connecting the history of the baptism with that of his temptation, to insinuate that there was an immediate and direct operation of the Spirit upon Christ on the occasion of his receiving this ordinance. This, however, is by no means, a necessary inference from their representation of the event ; for the difference that exists between their narrative and that of John is mainly owing to the character of their individual conceptions respecting the Messiah. "The former rest their views of him more on the Old Testament: he is therefore with them a king and prophet acting in the name of God, by whom he is anointed with the Holy Spirit and power (Acts 10 : 38.), and becomes manifest through miracles, and is finally raised to divine majesty. Not so the more sublime conception of John in that matter: he sees in him the incarnated *Word (logos)*, the independent source of his divine manifestations, to the execution of which he wanted, it is true, such external calls as present themselves in the relations of practical life, but by no means a new communication of the Spirit."* The link which connects the two representations is that doctrine which Paul expresses when he represents Christ as "the seed of David according to the flesh" but "the Son of God with power according to the Spirit of holiness" (Rom. 1 : 3, 4.). The evangelists, then, do not at all com into contradiction. The first three declare as truly as John does, the superhuman generation of Christ; only they do not lay so much stress upon the doctrine as is done by that evangelist, nor do they seem to have comprehended so clearly, or, we should rather say, so *feelingly* as he did, the full extent of its import and significancy.

But, even admitting that the narratives of the first three evangelists do imply an immediate and direct operation of the Spirit upon Jesus, it does not at all follow, as Lücke has shown, that this fact is at variance with his superhuman generation. An examination of John's account of the testimony of the Baptist, will show now the difficulty may be solved; for it is quite allowable to infer from the words of that evangelist,

* Jacobi, *Cyc. of Bib. Lit.*, Art. on Baptism.

as Lücke does, that he "makes a decided distinction between the divine *Logos (Word)* in its existence before it was incarnated, and the Spirit. The former is a *person* of whom it may be said 'he was made flesh', but not so of the Spirit, which stands in contrast to flesh, and constitutes the principle of communication and manifestation to an already existing person. Jesus, having within himself the *Logos*, as *the divine subject*, was therefore, capable of receiving the everlasting communication of the Spirit. As man, subject to human development, he stood in need of an external excitement and animation by God, such as took place at his baptism."*

"The personal Logos," says Alford (Com. on Jno. 1 : 34.), "which σὰρξ ἐγένετο (*became flesh*) in the Lord, and which was subjected to all the laws of human development in infancy, childhood, youth,—evermore in an especial degree under the leading of the Holy Spirit by whose agency the incarnation had taken place,—was in the Lord the recipient (τὸ δεχόμενον) of this fullness of the indwelling of the Holy Ghost : and herein consisted the real depth and propriety of the sign ;—the abiding of the Spirit *without measure* (ch. 3 : 34.) on him indicated beyond doubt that he was the λόγος σὰρξ γεγονώς (*Word become flesh*),—for no mere human intelligence could be thus receptive of the Holy Spirit of God ;—*we* receive him only *as we can*, only as far as our receptivity extends,—*by measure;* but he into the very fullness and infinite capacities of his divine being."

Though we hold, however, to this opinion, as the most simple and upon the whole the most satisfactory, that nothing new, as to being and nature, was conferred upon Jesus by the

* Lücke, *Commentar über Johannes, I.*, S. 433. Lücke treats this whole subject with great ability in an Excursus of ten pages (S 433–443.).

descent of the Spirit upon him at his baptism, we are not obliged to assert, on the other hand, that the event had no signification whatever for Christ. In the whole of his subsequent life we see Jesus by no means so entirely independent of the influence of circumstances and events calculated to affect conduct and character ; we see him by no means so completely locked within himself and so little moved from his repose by external events, that he was beyond the reach of receiving various impulses from without which would be of no little moment to his self-development ; we see that he also needed strengthening in his calling, that he frequently retired into loneliness in order to pray. This notable occurrence, therefore, must have been, beyond a doubt, a not unimportant event for his personal preparation as the redeemer of humanity, by the strengthening of his conviction that he was called to that office. Hitherto he had lived in constant retirement, developing himself from within himself by means of the influences which wrought upon him richly from without and from within : unprompted he came to the assurance that he was the Saviour of men, and that he was called at this time to enter upon his public ministry. This internal assurance must, however, have attained a much firmer hold upon his conviction by means of this superadded external attestation on the part of his heavenly Father ; the development of his Messianic consciousness was brought by the same means to an end and sealed ; the symbol of the impartation of the Spirit was the sign that the divine Spirit had now developed itself in him to its utmost extent, that he possessed the fullness of the Spirit of God, the Spirit without measure (Jno. 3 : 34.) ; and, accordingly, his baptism was for him a divine confirmation that the time had now come for him to begin his duties as the Messiah, a consecration to his entrance upon this great office ; and, at the same time, a definite act by which he for the first time showed that he was something higher than that which men had hitherto regarded him, and that he himself was conscious of the fact, that, however, he would enter entirely into the weakness of the human race and take upon himself all their duties in order that he might bring them freedom and salvation. As such a person he appeared for the first time to John the Baptist, and obtained in him the first witness to his dignity, though not his first disciple, as we shall have occasion to notice hereafter.

With regard, however, to the outward significancy of the ordinance, it is quite evident, that, as a symbol of internal, spiritual or moral, purification, baptism could not, as we have seen, have been performed upon Christ ; but as a sign of outward purification, or separation from all common and secular employments, in order to engage in those which were spiritual, the rite could not have been irrelevant even when it was administered to the sinless Jesus. Viewed in relation to the work in which he was about to engage, there was connected with the ordinance a peculiar appropriateness. This view is happily carried out by Huxtable : *Ministry*, pp.52.53. "Our blessed Lord had hitherto passed his life amid secular engagements ; for from the question of the Nazarenes, recorded Mark 6 : 3., 'Is not this the carpenter ?', it is clear that he had himself carried on the business of his reputed father. He had thus, and in other ways as a fellow-inhabitant of the town, been mingled with the people of Nazareth in the various engagements of social life ; laboring, and selling and buying, and taking part in the offices and intercourse of neighborhood. In short, he had been completely assimilated to his sinful brethren (except in their sins), associated and blended with them. But now he was about to assume the divine functions of the Lord's Christ; if we may venture thus to apply the language which St. Paul has used with reference to his actual death, he was "to die unto sin that he might live unto God: (Rom. 6: 10.). It therefore seems fitting that such a transition should be accompanied by his passing through a rite which so graphically expressed purification; in which, in his instance, it was set forth that he washed himself clean of worldly associations, and came forth pure and entire as the Christ of God."—A symbol of such a purification as this the baptism of Jesus might well have been; and, no doubt, in an indirect manner and by implication, it was; but, in its main object and import, it was a rite of inauguration as the Messiah and of consecration to his theocratic reign.*

* The views of Jeremy Taylor on the significance of our Lord's Baptism, as given in his "Life of Christ" (§ 9. 1. 2.), are striking; and are worthy of quotation: "Jesus wanted not a proposition, to consign by his baptism, proportionable enough to the analogy of its institution; for as others professed their *return* towards innocence, so he avowed his *perseverance* in it: and, though he was never called in scripture a sinner, yet he was made sin for us; that is, he did undergo the shame and the punishment; and therefore it was proper enough for him to perform the sacrament of sinners. . . . . . . He was now manifest to Israel; he confirmed the baptism of John; he sanctified the water to become sacramental and ministerial in the remission of sins; he by a real event declared that to them who should rightly be baptized the kingdom of heaven should certainly be opened: he inserted himself by that ceremony into the society and participation of holy people, of which communion himself was head and prince; and he did, in a symbol, purify human nature, whose stains and guilt he has undertaken."

PART FOURTH.

JOHN AFTER THE PUBLIC APPEARANCE OF THE MESSIAH.

CHAPTER I.

JOHN'S TESTIMONY RESPECTING CHRIST.

By means of the revelation which was imparted to John on the occasion of the baptism of Christ, not only was he, as we have seen, placed in the condition, but it was made a duty incumbent on him, to bear distinct and public witness that this Jesus was the Messiah whom the people had expected, and whom he himself had constantly announced. Confessedly, however, he was not to do this in such a manner as to make it his sole business to bear testimony that Jesus was the Christ; nor was he compelled to leave his former employment, and, accompanying the Messiah every where, to give witness respecting him to all the world; nor was it even his duty to tell at once to all those who came to him from this time onward, that Jesus of Nazareth was the Messiah whom he proclaimed. He was called, on the contrary, to baptize in water, and to make ready a way for the Lord, (Jno. 1: 23, 33.), and he could not leave this employment until God himself should summon him away from it. He was commissioned to prepare the people for the coming of the Messiah, and this preparation would not have been accomplished in the case of very many of them, if he, instead of exciting within them, as heretofore in general, more correct expectations than they had previously entertained concerning the Messianic kingdom, and making their hearts susceptible for receiving it when it appeared, had pointed them immediately to a particular person as the Messiah. It was his duty, rather, to continue inciting men to repentance and announcing the near approach of the Messianic kingdom, until Christ should publicly establish his kingdom, and should declare before all the people, "I am the Messiah." Until such a time, he was to continue to baptize with the baptism of repentance, and to refer the people to him who should come after him and who stood already in their midst (Jno. 1 : 26.); and was to announce to only a few single faithful souls, when a proper opportunity presented itself, that it was this Jesus who was soon to appear openly revealed as the Messiah.

Since the Baptist adopted this procedure it could not possibly remain long concealed from the people that he considered Jesus of Nazareth the Messiah, especially since Christ himself began from this time to collect disciples, and soon obtained a considerable number of adherents. It cannot be doubted that John was from this period asked by many what he who was even then proclaiming the near appearance of the Messiah thought of him who was now supposed by others to be the Anointed ; and we cannot hesitate to think that every time he was so questioned the Baptist returned ever the same answer, that he was in truth the expected Messiah. In this way must all the people have gradually become acquainted with what John said from time to time respecting Jesus ; and that they really did so in general, we see in a manner especially clear from Jno. 10 : 41. f., where the adherents of Christ adduce the truth of the testimony of John respecting him as a prop for their belief ; and from Matt. 21 : 25. ff. (cp. Mark 11 : 30 ff. Luke 20 : 4. ff.), where it is necessarily implied in the reasoning of the Pharisees,—to the effect that if they admitted John to be a true prophet, Jesus might reply to them and ask, why then they had not believed in him,—that they were fully aware that John had announced Jesus as the Messiah. Had they only known that he had borne witness in a general way that the Messiah had come, they would have been able to respond to Christ: "he prophesied truly, but he did not say that you are the Messiah; we look, therefore, for another."

When we examine with some degree of minuteness the single expressions of John regarding Jesus, we are, in general, brought to the conclusion that he was a prophet in whom the Spirit did not operate in a quiet and uniform manner, as it did in Christ and the Apostles, but who, though in general standing higher and more enlightened than his contemporaries, experienced at times special operations of the divine Spirit within himself which were not vouchsafed to him at other periods, so that he attained in moments of prophetic inspiration to a clearness and certainty respecting the nature of the kingdom of God, which in more quiet states of his mind must have been succeeded by other moments of uncertainty and doubt. We must, however, hold fast to this, that nothing that he said even in those periods of inspiration can have been totally foreign from his character; that his mouth could have uttered nothing which was unintelligible to himself; but that all had in his mind a point of connection; that the insight which he obtained into the Messianic character was elevated and increased by the divine operation, but that no idea contradictory of his former stand-point was ever for a moment entertained or uttered by him.—We are not, perhaps, possessed of sufficient data to enable us to decide with certainty as to what and how far particular expressions of his were the utterance of thoughts which were the consequences of his education and general habits of conception, or how far they were due, on the other hand, to special momentary operations of the divine Spirit. We must remain content, therefore, with showing that every conception which the Baptist uttered respecting the kingdom of the Messiah, is consonant with that idea of his character which has already been presented.

John seems to have commenced his testimony (Jno. 1 : 19–34.) immediately after hearing the words which sounded in thunder from heaven when Jesus was baptized : "This is my beloved Son, in whom I am well pleased." Speaking of the ceremony, he says afterward, "And I saw and bare record that this is the Son of God" (Jno. 1 : 34.). Now, what did the Baptist mean by this appellation ? Did he use it only in that signification according to which kings and judges are and may rightly be called sons of God, or gods (cp. Ps. 82 : 1 6.), or did he use it in a more exalted sense ? That the former supposition is not correct, but that, on the contrary, he really saw in Christ a divine being, is evident from the expression which he had already, as we read in John, applied before this time to the Messiah and frequently repeated : "After me cometh a man which is preferred before me ; for he was before me" (1 : 30. cp. v. 15.). The intentionally ambiguous expression which John subjoined to the words "cometh a man," viz., "is preferred before me" (ἔμπροσθέν μου γέγονεν), and which may be understood just as well of precedence in order of time as of precedence in rank, is further explained and rendered definite by the addition which succeeds, "for he was before me ;" from which it follows that John, who certainly did not mean one and the same thing by the two expressions, and who would not have attempted to prove an assertion by means of a mere change of words, employed the expression here as indicative of rank, as if he had said "he is my superior", or "he is greater than I"; and he would thereby intimate distinctly by the words which follow that he regarded the Messiah as one who existed before his birth, and, therefore, as an eternal being. The words were uttered altogether in the brief and piquant manner of the prophets, who were wont to express with something of rudeness ideas which were unexpected and contrary to appearances, without subjoining a prolix explanation. According to customary relations one would expect that he who follows another has less authority than he who preceded: here, on the contrary, the successor is represented as the higher, and that for the unexpected reason that the successor had already existed previous to his predecessor. In these words, therefore, the Baptist openly gives testimony to his recognition of a pre-existence, an eternal existence, of the divine being dwelling in the Messiah; and in this way greater light is thrown upon those passages in which John places himself so far below his successor as to assert that he is not worthy to loose his shoe-latchet, or to perform for him other menial services (Matt. 3: 11., Mark 1: 7., Luke 3: 16., Jno. 1: 27.). He assigned the Messiah a rank so superior to his own because he recognized in him a divine personage.

But, how came John by this conception? He clearly could not have derived it from the words which he heard at Christ's baptism, because the appellation "Son of God" there bestowed might possibly be taken in another and a lower sense. If we do not resort to a special divine revelation, for which, however, we have no ground in this case, we must refer his knowledge to a study of the prophecies of the Old Testament, from which a man as enlightened as John could readily educe the correct idea of the godhead of the Messiah. We may make mention here of the passages which occur in Ps. 2, and Ps. 45. (which are certainly to be explained as referring to the Messiah, for they would not otherwise have been admitted into the canon of holy songs), in which the great king whose glory is there celebrated is expressly distinguished from the highest God, and yet is himself called God. Furthermore, we may refer to Ps. 110. which Christ interpreted himself, and adduces it as proof of his divinity (Matt. 22 : 44.) ; furthermore, to those predicates, in particular, which are employed in the description of the Messiah in Is. 9, and 11. and the divine attributes therein assigned ; to all those passages, moreover, in which the Messiah is spoken of as descended from the Almighty, a person closely connected with God, and in which eternal dominion and divine judgment are predicated of him ; and, finally, to Micah 5 : 2., where the pre-existence of the Messiah, his eternal existence, is expressly asserted. Could the meaning of all these prophecies have remained concealed from so diligent a searcher of the Scriptures, so enlightened a prophet, as we have found John to have been ? Must he not rather have been led by them with power to the recognition of the divine personality of the Messiah ? Though his ideas respecting the mode of this union of the divine and the human in Christ were not entirely clear, yet he was perfectly sure that the connection existed. This assurance he exhibited and expressed, as we have seen, in all the rest of his doctrine ; and for this reason we are not compelled to ascribe its rise and duration to a moment merely of high prophetic inspiration ; though it must not be forgotten that John, as a prophet, and therefore as an organ of the

Spirit of God, had, when under its influence, an intuitive perception of divine truth.

Apparently in direct contradiction to this recognition of the godhead of the Messiah, John utters another expression recorded by the evangelist: "Behold the Lamb of God, which taketh away the sin of the world" (Jno. 1 : 29.). But this contradiction is no greater than that of the prophecies of the Old Testament themselves which represent both attributes of the Messiah in close connection with each other; nor than that of the appearance of Christ itself, who actually fulfilled the two opposite and seemingly contradictory prophecies in his life and death. In Is. 53. we find the key and explanation of this expression of the Baptist's. That this passage, whether we take it typically or directly, cannot be referred to any one else than the Messiah, is now-a-days more and more acknowledged by biblical critics; and why, then, may not John also have discovered this reference in it? The subject there spoken of is a servant of God, who is punished on account of the sins of the people, and by whose expiation for sin we have peace; and contains, therefore, the idea of the Messiah atoning for iniquity. This servant is compared to a lamb which is brought to be slaughtered, on account of his mildness and gentleness, and on account of the patience with which he takes upon himself undeserved sufferings and tortures. Now, it is related to us here by the evangelist that John saw Jesus coming to him after he had baptized him and after Jesus had undergone the forty days' temptation in the wilderness. The expression of humility, mildness and gentleness which he perceived in the countenance as well as in the whole person and appearance of Christ, no doubt impressed the Baptist powerfully and called up in his memory this passage in Isaiah, which he without a question referred, though not with a full understanding of its meaning, to the Messiah, so that he could not refrain from breaking out in the words, "Behold the lamb of God (i. e. the Lamb consecrated, or dedicated, to God) which taketh away the sin of the world." This idea, that the Lamb of God, or the Messiah represented by this metaphor, should bear the sins of men, is expressed in almost the same words in Is. 53 : 11, 12. ; and, that he should bear the iniquities of another can mean, according to the original text, nothing else than that he should take upon himself the guilt of the sins of another, and therefore should suffer the punishment which this guilt induced, should make atonement for sin.

The idea that one person can make expiation for the iniquity of another, and thus free him from guilt and punishment, an idea which is not at all foreign to the Old Testament, but which lies in fact at the foundation of the whole system of sacrificial worship,—is necessarily to be pre-supposed in order to understand this expression aright ; and in this sense must the Baptist, if he gave any reflection to the point at all, have understood it and applied it to Christ. Nor could this conception have been, as some think, totally foreign from the expectations of such among the Jewish people as applied themselves diligently and earnestly to the study of the Scriptures (cp. Luke 2 : 29. ff.). They could hardly, as they did, have applied Is. 53. to the Messiah without deriving therefrom at least a notion that the theocratic king was to undergo sufferings and death. Traces of this thought are found in the early Jewish writings (cp. 2 Macc. 7 : 37, 38.) ; and "the whole history of the sacrifices and devotion of the heathen world abounds with examples of the same idea variously brought forward ; and to these the better informed among the Jews could be no strangers." Since he stood so near to the Messianic reign, his own spiritual vision penetrated yet farther than that of Isaiah : he saw that the sins, not of many, as it is expressed in that prophet, but of the whole world, were to be taken away by the Lamb of God ; just as this idea of the uncircumscribed limits of the sphere of Christ's operation is indicated in Matt. 3 : 9, and Luke 3 : 8., and was not unknown also among the more enlightened of the people, although among the latter there still lay at the base of their expectations the belief that the heathen world could and would attain to a participation in the kingdom of the Messiah only through the medium of Judaism, and only after it had received Judaism either wholly or at least partially. To this fact refer those numerous passages of the Old Testament which announce a universal turning of the heathen to the temple and worship of Jehovah.

It has been almost universally held by Christian commentators that this declaration of the Baptist's which has just been considered, refers to the atoning sufferings, and perhaps also to the death, of Christ ; this view being opposed in general only by the Socinians and by some among the Arminian school of theology. Certain recent interpreters, however, influenced chiefly by doubts as to the possibility of the Baptist's having had an insight into the doctrine of the atonement,—the distinguishing doctrine of the New Testament,—have insisted upon quite a different explanation. According to their view the words "behold the Lamb of God which taketh away the sin of the world," represent the Messiah as *taking away the sins of the world* (αἴρειν being construed as equivalent to *removere) by his teaching*. The predicate "Lamb of God," expresses, they think, the mildness and patience exhibited by the Son of God in his life and actions. So explain Kuinoel, Paulus, and others. This explanation, however, though sufficiently accordant with the meaning which *airein* (αἴρειν) sometimes bears in the New Testament and most frequently in the Septuagint, does not preserve the reference to the figure involved in the phrase "*the Lamb of God*," which evidently is based upon the representation in Is. 53 : 7., "he is brought as a lamb to the slaughter, etc.," and is clearly intended to picture Christ as undergoing sufferings like a victim which is slaughtered for the sins of others, (cp. Matt. 8 : 17., Luke 22 : 37., Acts 8 : 32., 1 Pet. 2 : 22–25., Rev. 5 : 6, 12 ; 13 : 8.). Gabler offers, in his Melet. in loc. Joh. 1 : 29., an interpretation which better suits the figure implied in "the Lamb of God," but gives a rather unnatural and forced signification to the phrase ὁ αἴρων τ. ἁμαρτ. τ. κόσμου ("that taketh away the sin of the world"). This critic renders : "he, the innocent martyr, who endureth the sinful treatment of the world" ; the *airon* (αἴρων) being interpreted after the analogy of 1 Macc. 13 : 17., where ἔχθραν αἴρειν means *to endure hatred.* It does not follow, however, that, because ἔχθ. αἴρ. signifies *to endure hatred*, αἴρειν τὴν ἁμαρτίαν means *to endure the sinful treatment*, for *sinful treatment* is not, it is sufficiently clear, a proper rendering of ἁμαρτία in this connection.

But even among those who refer this expression of the forerunner's to the atoning sufferings of Christ, there is a difference of opinion as to the proper rendering of the latter part of the declaration. Some translate, as in the received version, "who *taketh away* the sin of the world" (Robinson, in his New Testament Lexicon, Meyer, and in part Olshausen), giving *airon* the signification which it commonly bears in the Septuagint, and consequently, agreeing so far, but only so far, with the interpretation offered by Paulus and Kuinoel.—Others adopt a different signification of the verb *αἴρειν*, viz., that which it has in Gen. 45 : 23., Job 21 : 3., Lam. 3 : 28., and render the phrase, "who *beareth* the sin of the world." This idea is precisely correspondent with that expressed in Is. 53., "he shall *bear* their iniquities" (v. 12.), "he *bare* the sin of many" (v. 12.) ; and the allusion of the words of the Baptist to this passage of the Old Testament prophecies is too direct to allow of any other interpretation than that which answers exactly to the Old Testament conception. The meaning of the phrase, therefore, is, "who beareth the sin [i. e. the punishment of the sin] of the world"; and in this particular sense the evangelist John elsewhere (1 Jno. 3 : 5.) uses the similar formula *αἴρειν ἁμαρτίας*, the idea expressed by which must be the same as that which he gives in 1 Jno. 2 : 2. of the death of Christ (cp. Rev. 5 : 6. 12. ; 13 : 8. ; 1 Pet. 1 : 19.). Such is the view of Tholuck, De Wette, Bloomfield, Alford, and others ; and it is that which accords best with the manifest allusion of the passage to the sufferings of a piacular victim.—Olshausen attempts to unite the two meanings of *αἴρειν*, *to bear* and *to take away*. "The sacrificial lamb," says he, "which bears the sin, also takes it away : there is no bearing of sin without a taking of it away." In a certain sense this is true ; but it is not true because *αἴρειν* means here *to take away:* it is only true as a consequence. To unite two meanings so diverse, is illogical ; and is only an evasion of a difficulty in interpretation.

Jesus is here spoken of by the Baptist, as a lamb offered for sin. This animal, though not the usual sin-offering, is selected because it best represents the holy innocence and mild dignity of the Saviour, and because it is that which forms the chief figure in the representation of Isaiah which suggests the expression here uttered by the forerunner. Christ is depicted as a piacular victim offered for the sins of the world. "Such a victim," says Bloomfield, "was solemnly brought to the altar, and then the priest put his hands over the head; which was a *symbolical action*, signifying that the sins committed by the persons expiated were *laid upon the victim*; and, when it was slaughtered, it was then said *to bear* the sins of the expiated; by which it was denoted that the victim paid the penalty of the sins committed, was punished with death in their place, and for the purpose of freeing them from the penalty of sin. Therefore when Christ is called *the lamb bearing* the sins of the world, it is manifest that we must understand one who should take upon himself the sins of men, so as to pay the penalties of their sins, and in their stead, for the purpose of freeing them from those penalties."

That the idea of a suffering Messiah was by no means wholly foreign to the thoughts of the more pious Jews of John's time, we have already seen when noticing the prophecy of Simeon respecting Jesus (Luke 2 : 29. ff.). We must, however, admit that John did not conceive the words which he here uttered in their full and complete sense, for this could have possibly been done by man only after the fulfillment of the prediction; but that he connected the idea of a suffering which the Messiah would undergo with the conception of a divine kingdom which he was to establish, no one surely can deny. We have to fall back once more upon the fact, that, as in the Old Testament, so in the prophetic insight of the Baptist, the second and first appearances of the Lord are not kept distinct; that John must, therefore, in consequence of the ancient prophecies respecting the spiritual working of the Messiah, have thought of a terrestrial glory which, though struggling to victory at first through suffering and even through death, should at length necessarily develop and establish itself upon earth and found an earthly spiritual, perfect theocratic kingdom which should extend itself visibly and externally to all nations and have an eternal duration. If, therefore, the period of the suffering of the Redeemer kept itself for the most part in the back-ground in his mind, forgotten as it were in the presence of his more lively hopes and expectations respecting the everlasting glory which was to proceed from the divine Messiah after he had come forth victorious from suffering, the remembrance of this period was yet by no means entirely lost in him, and here, powerfully excited by a sight of the meek Redeemer, it exhibited itself with so much the more force and feeling, giving acuteness for the moment to his prophetic vision, if not unraveling the whole riddle of the future. This, then, was a prophetic intuition, bordering indeed on Christianity, but yet, perhaps commingled with wholly heterogeneous elements. We are not, consequently, compelled to resort to any artificial explanation of the words of the Baptist, nor to fall back on the supposition that he had received some special instruction from Christ himself with regard to the necessity of his future suffering. Of such instruction we find not the least mention in the sacred records; and such John could not have received without renouncing his own calling and becoming a disciple of Christ's, and this, according to the divine intention, he neither was nor could be.

If we understand aright John's conception regarding these

two periods, the one of suffering and the other of divine glory, which the Messiah was to experience, we will know at once how to estimate that other more full expression of his regarding his successor (Jno. 3 : 27–36.), and will discover that it is altogether out of the reach of cavil, and perfectly consonant with his habits of thinking. The testimony in question he gave to his own disciples, and in opposition to their views and expectations, when they complained to him that he respecting whom their master had at an earlier period borne witness,—who, therefore, as they supposed, notwithstanding the Baptist's distinct declaration to the contrary, ought, in accordance with the usual course of things, to have honored and attached himself to John as his master,—instead of joining himself as a disciple to the Baptist, was collecting a band of adherents around himself, was intrenching upon the office of John, since he had himself begun to baptize, and was attempting to overshadow him in every way.—These reproaches against Christ the Baptist repelled with the observation, that, if Jesus was collecting so great a body of disciples around him, this must be the will of God ; and that the same was true, if his own authority was decreasing ; for it stood in the power of no man to obtain in any way an important part to act in the kingdom of God, unless God himself had called him thereto and given him the capacity to perform it. He appeals then to his own earlier testimony respecting Christ, that he was only commissioned to go before him, but was not himself the Messiah ; in which it is distinctly implied that he stood far beneath the Redeemer, and could not attain to power and glory equal to his.

In order to render this relation comprehensible to them, he makes use of a figurative representation which was very current in that age, particularly among the theocratic nation, by which the Lord and God of his people is depicted as at the same time the spouse, or as the bridegroom,. of his people given to him in truth and obedience as his spouse or bride. Applying this idea to the Messiah, John represents himself as the friend of the bridegroom (Heb. *shoshbhen*) or conductor of the bride, whose especial business it is to arrange the preliminaries of the marriage,—who conducts the bride to the bridegroom, and then modestly retiring finds his reward in the joy of the bridegroom in the possession of his beloved. "This pleasure I now enjoy in full measure," said the noble, modest John, "I have conducted the people to the Messiah, and removed from the way the hindrances which prevented the union of the two ; now is my office completed, I must again retire by degrees into my former obscurity ; my authority must decrease in the same measure according to which the Messiah, the husband and lord of his church, shall increase in power and influence ; my reward consists in the consciousness of the faithful fulfillment of my duty and of the joy of the Messiah in the union which has been so happily completed."

This was sufficient to show the impropriety and groundlessness of the complaints of his disciples. In order, however, to give a still more complete explanation of his relation to the Messiah, and to exhibit still more plainly the dignity of the latter, there are added yet other remarks (vs. 31–36.) of a concise, sententious brevity ; of which, however, though the matter is probably John's, the form is rather to be attributed to the evangelist.

Reference is here made first of all to the divine nature of Christ, of which John had previously borne witness in the words which have been already examined. He that cometh from above is by that very fact elevated above all men, above all creatures : he, on the contrary, who has his origin on earth is according to his nature earthly, and belongs to that which is created ; his word, therefore, his doctrine, partakes of an earthly character, and even if it proceeds, as it does in the case of the Baptist, from divine illumination, it never attains nevertheless to perfect purity and clearness, but is troubled and obscured by the weakness and sinfulness of its earthly organ. On the contrary, only he who comes from heaven, and, as the ruler over all, is possessed of all wisdom and a divine insight into things, can teach and bear testimony to that which he in consequence of his divine nature has heard from and seen with the creator and ruler of all things. Casting a glance, half sorrowful, half reproachful, at the disciples who had taken offence at the appearance of Christ and found fault with his conduct, the Baptist adds : "But his testimony, divine though it is, has no one received (v. 32.)."

Evidently "no one" (οὐδεῖς) is not to be taken here absolutely ; for the very ground of the complaint of John's disciples and of the conversation which they held with him, was that multitudes were resorting to Christ (v. 26.) ; the remark must, therefore, have been made with reference primarily to those disciples who were then standing around and conversing with the Baptist ; but since, as we have seen, the prophetic vision of John foresaw the ignominy and persecution which Christ was destined to endure, so there is good reason to think that this expression was employed by him in view of the opposition which the testimony of the Messiah was yet to meet with from every quarter, notwithstanding that the excitable multitude now crowded around him in great numbers.—That the Baptist himself intended this expression to be understood with a limitation we perceive from the testimony which he immediately subjoins, that whoever should give ear to the teaching of Christ should experience within himself its divine truth in a manner that would be powerful and unquestionable, and would sanction and confirm as with a seal the fact that God is true and his words true (v. 33.); for Christ's words are God's words, they are not intermingled with errors and untruths, such as human teaching cannot be wholly free from; for he in whom God has so implanted his Spirit as John saw it in an image on the occasion of his baptism, is possessed of the perfect and infallible Spirit; he possesses it not partially, but has received it in an unlimited measure; and therefore all his words are wholly divine, and must convince all those who follow him of their perfect correspondence with divine truth (v. 34.). The reason why God has so highly exalted the Messiah, whom John had heard divinely announced as the Son of God and whom he himself declared to be such, and has endowed him with dominion over all things, is based in his love to his Son, unto whom as being of his being and existence of his existence he has imparted the highest power upon earth (v. 35.), so that now all who would attain to happiness must believe in him and submit themselves to him with faithful confidence; he that does not believe, who, on the contrary, opposes himself to the Messiah, has incurred the wrath of God, which so long as he does not turn in penitence unto the Son will continue to abide upon him (v. 36.).

It might now be asked, especially in view of the last observation, if the Baptist perceived so clearly that salvation could only be found in a believing resignation to the Messiah, why did he not now resign himself wholly to him, and seek from him salvation? Perhaps on no other ground than because he did not suppose that the precise time had come when the Messiah,—whom he with all his spiritual conceptions expected, as did Christ's own disciples even after his resurrection (Acts 1 : 6.), to make his appearance before the nation in earthly power and glory,—would with a loud summons collect around him all his disciples ; and because, moreover, he could not have conceived of faith in him in the sense in which it was afterwards portrayed by Paul, but meant only in this recognition of the Messiah to exhibit him as the one in whom dwelt perfection. On this point more will be said in the following chapter. Here it is only requisite to observe, that, as has been shown, there is properly found in this full testimony of John's nothing which is not consistent with the other expressions of his respecting Christ which have been previously examined, nay, nothing which is not necessarily contained in the same.

The *form* of these words, however, appears to belong more to the evangelist John than to the Baptist. If one will only compare the expressions of the evangelist in the prologue to his Gospel, which in several points, coincide almost verbally with the form of words which is adduced here as that used by the Baptist ; and if, furthermore, he will compare the verses which constitute the conclusion of Nicodemus' conversation with Jesus (3 : 16–21.), and other single expressions of Christ himself (as in Jno. 15.), he will perceive that the entire impress and coloring of the words from v. 31 to v. 36. indicate the mind of a believing Christian, rather than of a prophet who stood as yet without the pale of Christianity. They, therefore, do not think amiss (Kuinoel, Tholuck, Olshausen, Meyer, etc.), who suppose that the form of John's testimony has been to some extent obliterated from v. 31. onward, by the evangelist in giving his narrative. It must have been difficult for a disciple of the Lord who was accustomed to a mode of contemplation altogether Christian, to have preserved for us perfectly true to their form the precise conceptions of the Baptist, which bordered so very closely on what are in all respects genuine Christian thoughts ; unless, indeed, these expressions were limited to such short pithy sayings as those given in the examples which have been previously considered, or to such peculiar Old Testament images as that presented in vs. 28–30. Provided we do not, on this account, doubt that the evangelist has preserved for us in these verses the true contents of the expressions of the Baptist, if we do not suppose that he has interpolated among them foreign and false thoughts, we do not in fact nor do we appear to cast any doubts either upon the character of the evangelist or upon the historical truth of his Gospel, when we admit that the *form* of the words as they have been delivered to us, pertain to him and not to the Baptist. That, on the other hand, the evangelist does not give us his own reasoning from v. 31. onwards, is clear from the fact that he in no way lets us understand that here the remarks of the Baptist cease and his own begin, and from the further fact that he speaks throughout in the person and in accordance with the relations of the Baptist. He intends to represent to us the continuation of the testimony of John, and this he does ; only, his style and mode of narration, either consciously or unconsciously to himself, no longer retain firmly and give back in their precise original form the almost perfectly Christian expressions of the Baptist, but his own Christian consciousness gradually seizes and conducts his pen in the representation

CHAPTER II.

The Disciples of the Baptist.

We have hitherto spoken on several occasions of the disciples of John, but have delayed till now treating of them in full and regular connection. It was very natural and customary in ancient times for special adherents to collect around a distinguished man who proposed some new doctrine or introduced some particular mode of living, in order that they might learn from him, and form themselves under his conversation by friendly intercourse. As this happened among heathen nations in the case of philosophers, who always collected around them a chosen circle of scholars, so also it took place among the Jews of that age in the case of distinguished teachers of the law and in the case of ascetics, with whom many, either from inclination or impelled by some necessity, were wont to associate, as we have already had occasion to see in the example of Banus and Josephus. Just so had it been at an earlier period with the prophets, who established their prophetic schools in which they instructed their disciples,—who came to them sometimes of their own inward impulse, and sometimes were called by them,—in the things which pertained to the kingdom of God and its requirements (cp. especially the history of Elijah and Elisha). These prophetic schools "were institutions to which the children or the disciples of the prophets resorted ; and they were the most numerously attended and the most celebrated under Samuel, and subsequently under Elisha and Elijah. Their residence was in the country, where they had all things in common, and lived a life of frugality, poverty, and toil. Yet they had always sufficient leisure to devote to study and contemplation, because their desires were easily satisfied, and because, removed from frivolous pursuits, they still found time enough after their bodily labors for the loftier exercise of mind. Thither the people came to have doubts removed, and duties taught. They found in the prophets precept enforced by example,—the moral beauty of a holy life ; they found instruction for time and preparation for eternity. They were the most trustworthy and most enlightened interpreters of the law. Their whole being was radiant with radiant instruction ; their sermons, their prophecies, their denunciations, their life, their very external demeanor."*

In this same way also did there collect about John, who made his appearance after the manner of the prophets of old time and separated himself distinctly from the common people by his doctrine and his mode of life, individual adherents with dispositions like his own, who connected themselves with him in close familiarity, either urged on by a true feeling of their necessity for a deeper insight into the divine will and counsels, or for training in a rigid moral life, or else,—since among many of them more impure grounds governed their conduct,—connecting themselves with him in order to derive some personal advantage from the reputation of being the intimate associates of a master so highly distinguished. The tie which existed between these and John must not be supposed to have been of such a nature that they, chained, so to speak, continually to their master, never left him, and had estranged themselves from all their customary relations on his account. On

* Journal of Sacred Literature, vol. 3. (Jan. 1849) pp. 91, 92.

the contrary, there is no doubt that they attended to their ordinary avocations just as before, and only now and then delayed for a season longer than usual in his company. Only such youths as had to perform as yet no fixed duties of a civil and social character remained with him, perhaps, in more constant companionship, assisted him, it is not unlikely, in his baptismal employment, and were instructed by him in the exercise of rigid repentance, and especially how to exhibit such conduct as would be pleasing to God. The wealthy among his disciples took upon themselves, no doubt, the supply of the few and simple necessities of the self-denying Baptist; and, perhaps, many gifts were brought to him by the people who flocked to his ministry.

Of the training which the disciples of John received from their master we have very few indications in the Gospels. Without doubt he instructed them more fully and thoroughly than he did in his short addresses to the people regarding the expectations which he must have cherished respecting the coming Messianic reign after the training he received in the Old Testament and after the partial divine enlightenment which he had enjoyed. That many of his instructions, however,—especially those which related to his own inferiority to the Messiah, and to the ignominy and suffering which the latter would have to undergo,—were and continued to be totally foreign to the fleshly sense of his disciples, we readily discover, partly from the complaints which they made, as we saw in the previous chapter, of the arrogance on the part of Christ in collecting around him a greater number of adherents than John himself, and partly from the apparent incapacity of the disciples of Christ,—who had for the most part been at an earlier period the disciples of John,—to comprehend the repeated announcement of Jesus respecting his sufferings and death, to which they could not in any way reconcile themselves until they saw its fulfillment take place before their eyes.

Independently of this, the chief aim and end of the instruction given to his adherents by the Baptist, were, perhaps, a training in rigid practices indicative of repentance. He himself stood yet, even as they did, upon the Old Testament legal stand-point, according to which the inward repentant disposition must be rendered distinct and definite by outward action, be openly exhibited, and be thereby so much the more confirmed and established. Accordingly, he required of them in particular the practice of rigid fasting, as we read in Matt. 9 : 14., Mark 2 : 18., Luke 5 : 33. ; which is the most universally understood and wide-spread token that man, feeling sorrow for his sinfulness, would mortify the flesh by rigid restraints, in order that it may not with ever greater wantonness, with ever increasing violence, contend against the soul ; and with these fasts were connected, without doubt, special deprivations of the ordinary enjoyments and even necessities of life, as also, perhaps, washings and lustrations.

We learn, moreover, from Luke 11 : 1. that John held with his disciples special exercises in prayer, and himself taught them how they ought and for what they should pray, in order that they might obtain from God power to conduct themselves aright, a reception into the new divine kingdom, and the forgiveness of their sins.* While, therefore, with Christ, direc-

* On the margin of the Philoxenian (Syriac) Version of the New Testament we find a formula of prayer, which, it is said, of course falsely, that the Baptist and his disciples were accustomed to use in their devotions. It runs as follows:

"Father, show unto us thy glory !
"Son, grant that we may hear thy voice !
"Spirit, hallow our hearts forever : Amen."

tions respecting the form in which God ought to be worshipped were kept as far as possible in the back-ground, with John they seem, as might naturally be expected from his more external legal stand-point, to have played an important part, and to have formed one of the chief points of the training which he gave to his disciples.

The sect which the disciples of the Baptist constituted after his death, becoming separated and excluded from Judaism, was treated with ignominy by the people at large: their master John, on the contrary, was constantly, and with a unanimous and fixed decision on the part of the nation, regarded as a just man and a prophet (Matt. 21: 26., Josephus, *Antiq.* 18. 5. 2.). This recognition his followers subsequently urged to the utmost extreme, departing from the clear light of history and ascribing to him higher and more wonderful attributes than he possessed; attributing to him miraculous powers, and adding to what he taught other doctrines of a theosophic character, especially after the Gnostic systems, which had been created from the intermingling of Christianity with the dogmas of heathen philosophy, had thrown all the speculative minds of that age into confusion, and led them astray from the pure doctrine of Christ, more or less according as they possessed greater or less knowledge or had experienced in a greater or less degree the regenerating influence of the Gospel. To such persons as continued from the beginning to live and act in full or partial opposition to Christianity, this recognition furnished a welcome pretence for continually depreciating Christ according to their pleasure, and on the other hand for elevating above him men chosen from among themselves, whose character and acts were more in correspondence with their own. In this way, especially, it is probable, through the accession of heathen oriental philosophers, who found in the history of John the Baptist a useful historic foundation for their accustomed and favorite speculations, was formed the Gnostic sect of the later disciples of John, or Zabians, whose views corresponded in general with those of the other Syriac anti-Jewish Gnostic systems, retaining a peculiarity for the most part only in the deification of John.

The sect here alluded to, the so-called *Sabeans* (*βαπτισταί*, *Baptizers*, from the Hebrew *tseba'*, *to dip*, *to immerse*), or, as they are also denominated, Nazareans, Mendeans, and Disciples of John the Baptist, or Christians of St. John, has existed in the East from the earliest period of Christianity. The people themselves, as well as their holy books, which are written in Syriac, have been known to Europeans only about five hundred years. "This sect," says Neander, "evidently took its origin from those disciples of John the Baptist, who, contrary to the spirit and intention of their master, adopted, after his martyrdom, a course hostile to Christianity. We find traces of them, mixed up with fabulous matter, in the Clementines, and in the Recognitiones Clementis, perhaps also in the *ἡμερο-βαπτισταῖς* and *γαλιλαίοις* of Hegesippus. From this sprung up afterwards a sect, whose system, formed out of the elements of an older eastern theosophy, has an important connection with the history of the Gnosis."* The holy books of the Sabeans, six in number, are thoroughly penetrated with the leaven of Gnosticism. One of them, *Sidra Jahia, the Book of John*, gives the history of the Baptist whom the Sabeans claim as the founder of their sect, from his birth to his death. To John they ascribe the origin of their rites and ceremonies; and they say that they received from him all their sacred

* Church History, Prof. Torrey's transl., vol. I. p. 376, note.

books. The Sidra Jahia is, of course, quite different from the evangelical account, and is filled with legends of the most improbable character. With regard to Jesus, as well as John, whom they represent as superior to Christ, the views given in these books are altogether at variance with those of the New Testament. The difference is not so great, however, as to warrant us in doubting the historical connection between the Sabeans and Christianity.—Valuable information, but such as is not pertinent here, respecting the religious opinions of this sect, is to be found in Leopold, *Johannes der Täufer*, p. 182–195.*

* There is, as far as we know, no full account in English of the Sabeans and their religion. L. E. Burckhardt has written a work on this subject which is, on the whole, the best for general circulation; it is entitled *Les Nazoreens appelles Zabiens et Chretiens de St. Jean, Secte Gnostique*, Strasburg, 1840.

Note to the Fifth Edition.—The author of the present Treatise has prepared and published an elaborate article on the Sabeans,—their history, condition, literature, and religious rites. It will be found in *The Christian Review* for January 1855, under the title "The Nazoreans, or Mandai Jahia,—Disciples of John the Baptist."

CHAPTER III.

Reference of his Disciples to Christ.

When now Christ had actually made his appearance and was entering upon his ministry, John was sufficiently modest and self-denying to point his disciples away from himself to him who was greater, from whom they could obtain better nutriment for their hearts and spirits. It is narrated in Jno. 1 : 35. ff. that he stood with two of his disciples in the place where he was accustomed to baptize, and, seeing Jesus passing by, he called the attention of these disciples anew to his dignity, speaking of him as he had done previously when bearing witness of him in their hearing (v. 29.), "behold the Lamb of God." It is probable that he uttered these words with such a tone and gesture that the disciples understood it to be their master's will that they should make themselves acquainted with Jesus. They followed him, therefore, in order to discover his dwelling, after which they purposed to choose a fit opportunity to gain further information from his own lips respecting his views and his doctrines. Jesus anticipates their modest discretion, and, taking them at once to his house, he plants in a long interview the first seeds of the divine word in their susceptible souls ; then he dismisses them from his presence in order that they may feel this first impression working within them in its full power, and that the seed sown may shoot forth into life. One of these disciples, Andrew, is expressly named (v. 40.) ; the other was, there is little or no doubt, the apostle John. By their means Simon Peter, the brother of Andrew, who was also a disciple of John's, is made acquainted with the Lord ; and in this way there was formed from these adherents of the Baptist the first band of Christ's disciples, at first indeed having no closer connection with him than followed from their being now and then in his company, but soon bound to his person by indissoluble ties, since it was in him alone that they found the words of eternal life.

The question now demands consideration, *why John did not now refer all of his disciples to Christ, and not merely certain individuals among them.*—We must in the first place consider that John, when he called the attention of these two disciples specially to Christ by repeating the words, "behold the Lamb of God," by no means intended to say, "separate yourselves henceforth from me and become followers of Jesus" ; for it was not possible for every one to become at his own pleasure an intimate disciple of Christ, since he himself chose them and called them to that office. The Baptist meant to hint to them that they should make the acquaintance of Jesus, and keep him in their eye as the one by whom signal changes were in a short time to be produced. There is, moreover, no reason why we should not suppose that others also of John's disciples sought Jesus and heard his teachings as long as he remained in their neighborhood ; but Jesus called them not, and they on their part supposed that they must wait for a public signal from him at the time when he would actually establish his kingdom.—It is to be remarked, furthermore, that John would have referred to Jesus only the better instructed of his disciples and those who were farthest advanced in their longing for and knowledge of the kingdom of God,—only such as had a true disposition and susceptibility for the heavenly, and would with meek resignation cling to the Messiah in the period of his humility ; and this it was clearly impossible to expect from all the disciples of the Baptist. There must have been many among them who, notwithstanding all the instructions which they had received from John respecting the Messianic kingdom, had none other than altogether fleshly conceptions, and in their minds by no means associated with the external rites and ceremonies which they practised, that idea of which those rites were intended to be the outward expression. Such persons as these, since Jesus had not as yet accredited his dignity by external manifestations, John could not possibly have directed to him as the Messiah. Many of them, moreover, would have found fault with the manner of life adopted by Jesus, one altogether simple and exhibiting nothing that was particularly striking or strange ; for their master John appeared to them to be in his rigid asceticism the ideal of perfect morality. From this feeling which was ever directed to what was external, and which had no lively consciousness of the higher importance of the inward disposition, might have easily proceeded at a later period an opposition to Christ, a denial of his Messianic dignity ; and so much the more surely, if the humility which distinguished John should have been wanting in his disciples, and if they could not and would not endure that it should be said that their master was less elevated than he who had himself needed his baptism and his testimony. And history, as we have seen, actually relates to us how this opposition was carried to its extreme at a later period by the adherents of the Baptist. We have already remarked, and shall in the sequel have further occasion to notice, how enviously they expressed themselves against the great popularity of Jesus ; and this envy must, from the nature of the case, have increased more and more in those of them who came not to a knowledge of the truth ; for the more heavily misfortune pressed upon their master, the higher did the fame of Jesus rise. Surely such as these could not have been the last to hasten the execution of the sentence which deprived the Lord of life, and to persecute the followers of him they had crucified.

It is time now to examine somewhat more minutely the reasons *why John did not, after giving his public testimony to the Messianic dignity of Jesus, publicly declare himself his disciple, and attend upon his ministry.*—Perhaps one of the reasons which has been assigned already in explanation of the fact that the most of John's disciples did not come into a close connection with Christ, will also account for the Baptist's not becoming his immediate follower. Jesus, as we have seen, chose his own disciples ; and did not receive such as came to him merely from their own impulses (cp. Luke 9 : 57–62.). A man could be an adherent of Christ's and recognize him as the Messiah, without being on that account an intimate disciple and living with him in constant intercourse ; and in this sense was John an adherent, but Jesus chose him not as a disciple. But, why not ? On this account, perhaps—because he would collect around him only such susceptible hearts as, feeling within the living need of a Redeemer and filled with a desire to find him, were yet engaged in searching him out, and still had, therefore, an open ear and ready mind for the new and unexpected teachings of the Messiah ; who could yield themselves to him with undivided hearts, and devote their whole existence to the love and imitation of their great master . Such an one was not John. He had already struggled powerfully in contemplation and thought within himself, and from this inward reflection he had developed a view, not to say system, respecting the kingdom of God which, because it was the product of his own spirit, could with so much the more difficulty be discarded by him and exchanged for another. His entire being, his life and his conduct were something prepared and decided upon within himself; in him, therefore, the new claims and new doctrines of Christ could with difficulty find entrance; and in no case was he qualified to become himself a proclaimer of the gospel. Adopting this view of the matter, we are not obliged to suppose, as some have done, that Jesus at a later period gave John special instruction,—a supposition which is destitute of support from the narratives of the evangelists, and which comes into direct conflict with the doubts which John is represented as having afterwards entertained. It was not in general Jesus' manner of teaching to impart ready-fashioned ideas and scientific dogmas respecting himself and his kingdom, as must have been the case with John, whose doctrines nevertheless sound very much like those which are truly and wholly Christian. Jesus, on the contrary, inciting the mind to attention, scattered here and there a word of life into susceptible souls and waited until it had germinated, in order that he might lead each in his own individuality to a full knowledge of salvation.

John, as has been already remarked, was called by God to baptize in water, and to prepare the people for the coming of the Messiah; and as long as he could do this from his own stand-point, God left him in this position and took not the office from him. He was still to prepare the way, still to announce unto those who had as yet no knowledge of the fact, that the kingdom of the Messiah was at hand, and that they must exercise repentance in order to be received into it. He it was, according to the testimony of Christ himself (Matt.

11 : 10.), who was to arouse the people to a desire of obtaining admission into the kingdom of Christ ; and this he could do as well now as before the public appearance of Christ ; he could still by his testimony respecting Jesus accredit him as the Messiah, and point the better prepared among the people to his dignified character ; he could still elevate those who heard him to his own stand-point and impress upon them the truth that the Lord would establish not a mere earthly kingdom, but one in its outlines and essential character altogether spiritual ; and, afterwards, Jesus himself could by degrees teach those who had been previously so prepared, that he had come to found a purely spiritual kingdom, and that the earthly power which John supposed would be connected with it should be first outwardly exhibited at his second advent.—"This preparatory position of John," says Neander, *Life of Jesus*, § 41. (2.), "had to continue until the time when the entrance of Jesus as theocratic king, upon the establishment of his kingdom, gave the signal for all to range themselves under his banners. The Baptist, true to the position that had been assigned to him in the theocratic development, had to continue his labors until their termination, a termination which external circumstances were soon to bring about." A similar view on this point is entertained by Winer, (*Bib. Realwörterbuch*, Art. Joh. d. Täufer) ; and is assented to by De Wette (*Com. on Jno.* 3 : 36.).—Meanwhile, however, John's testimony, though given to the Messiah, continued to be altogether private, and was not made in the presence of the people at large. It is for this reason, perhaps, and because, moreover, the value of the testimony depended entirely upon the recognition of John's prophetic calling, that no mention is made in those public proclamations of the gospel described in Acts 10 : 37, and

13 : 25., of the Baptist's inspired testimony concerning Christ, while, on the contrary, his exhortations to repentance and his announcement of the coming Messiah are particularly spoken of as the preparation for the Messiah's public ministry.

Finally, we must, in accounting for the fact under consideration, bear in mind what has previously been noticed, that the imperfect and in some respects incorrect expectations of John respecting the founding of the kingdom of the Messiah, must have prevented him at this time from coming into closer connection with Christ. He still expected that Jesus would by some public act declare himself a king, the promised son of David, and would then summon all his disciples under his colors, in order to establish again the fallen kingdom of Israel. Then, he thought, would be the time for him to follow the call ; then indeed would he not hesitate to share with his monarch the sufferings and persecutions, which, according to his conceptions, the Messiah was to undergo ; in order finally to come forth victorious with him, and to receive a share in the glory which was then to be imparted to him by the Father and in his eternal dominion over all lands and over all spirits. Until this time should arrive, the Baptist continued performing the duties. of the office which had been assigned him ; he pointed the people to the Messiah ; he persevered in bringing them into a more and more complete state of preparation, in order that all might be ready, when the great hour should strike in which Jesus would place himself at their head, and commence the struggle with the world and the devil ; waiting for this time to come, he continued performing as before his appropriate work, preaching, baptizing, and bearing testimony to the Messiah.

CHAPTER IV.

Relation of the Baptism of John to that of the Disciples of Christ and to Christian Baptism.

We cannot close our consideration of the public ministry of John without treating somewhat more minutely of his baptism, which, as we have seen, seemed to come into conflict towards the last with the baptism administered by the disciples of Christ (cp. Jno. 3 : 22., and the supplementary correction of these words in Jno. 4 : 2., where it is said that Jesus himself did not baptize, but only his disciples.). We have seen that the baptism of John was, in its distinctive features, a summons to repentance, a seal of the resolution to exercise it and of the constant performance of this resolution with continual reference to the Messiah who was soon to come in order to confer upon all faithful hearts the forgiveness of their sins. This signification the Johannean baptism continued to retain ; for even after Christ had publicly appeared, the Messiah must still have been represented to all those who came unto John as yet to come, yet to appear in the future, especially since there was rooted in the hearts of all those that attended upon John's instructions the expectation that the Messiah would usher in, by some political act, the beginning of his grand and imposing ministry. John, therefore, continued to baptize all that promised repentance, referring, as he had done before, to him who should come after him,—just as, according to Jno. 1 : 26, 27., he speaks of Christ, who had already appeared and had been recognized by him, as one still to come, and in the same way at a later period at the sending of his disciples on a mission of inquiry to Jesus (Matt. 11 : 3.) ; at the same time, however, pointing the more susceptible among them to Jesus, as we have seen he did, and proclaiming him to be the one that was promised, and the one that should be his successor.

Those followers of John who had afterwards become the disciples of Jesus, and from their own contemplation and conviction had recognized the Saviour of the world, must have regarded the baptism of John which still referred only to him who was to come, as imperfect ; since he whom the Baptist proclaimed had actually made his appearance. When, therefore, they came, in company with Christ in his wanderings, to the river Jordan near the place at which it empties into the Dead Sea, in which region John also was then holding forth, taking advantage of this favorable opportunity for baptizing in order to carry out here and perfect the act of their former master, they baptized those who acknowledged that they recognized in Jesus the Saviour of the world, not indeed with reference to a coming, but in the name of a present Redeemer. Nothing else than this could they have had in view or attained by this baptism ; for the Holy Spirit, according to the testimony of the same evangelist who relates this occurrence, was not yet given (Jno. 7 : 39.) ; the rite, therefore, could have been nothing more than a water baptism with a requirement and promise from the candidate that he would exercise repentance, and an acknowledgment on his part that Jesus was the Christ, and the one from whom alone salvation was to be expected. In substance, consequently, this baptism of the disciples of Christ did not differ from that administered by John ; but only in this, that the latter only pointed to the Messiah from afar as one that was about to come, while the former, on the other hand, represented him as now present, and required from its recipients a confession of faith in Jesus personally as the predicted Messiah. It is evident that both such as had previously received the rite administered by John and such as now came for the first time to baptism, could become the subjects of this rite of the disciples ; for not only could those who had at an earlier period given evidence of their eager desire to receive in a manner worthy of him the coming Messiah, now confirm by their reception of baptism their belief that this Jesus was the Christ, but those who now heard for the first time of the expected advent of the Messiah, since they were able in general to attain to a belief in this announcement with little more facility than they could to a conviction of the realization of the expectation in the person of Jesus, could readily be induced to allow themselves to be enrolled by baptism among the community of believers in his divine mission and authority.

Jesus himself did not, it is clear, administer this baptism ; in such a case he would have had to baptize in his own name, and then he of whom John proclaimed that he would baptize not in water but in the Holy Spirit and in fire, would have commenced again a rite which was only preparatory to entrance into his kingdom, and not very different from that administered by John. He did not, however, prevent his disciples from baptizing ; for it must have consisted with his ideas of propriety that as many as possible should be made ready, be it by means of John or by means of his own disciples, for the coming of his reign, in order that he might find every where a better-prepared foundation for the reception of the divine word. During the time, therefore, that he himself taught near the river Jordan, his disciples baptized ; and the people, powerfully moved by the words of Christ, and discerning that the Spirit of God abode in him, submitted themselves the more zealously to this baptism, and testified in the act that they truly believed in this their divine teacher. In this way the number of those who by baptism acknowledged themselves the adherents of Jesus, kept constantly increasing, and more and more persons kept continually resorting to him instead of going as before to the Baptist ; so that the number of those who were baptized by Christ's disciples soon became greater. than those who had received the rite from John (Jno. 4 : 1.). On this account, therefore, the envy of such of John's disciples as stood as yet upon a lower and more fleshly stand-point, was powerfully excited ; and when now a contest respecting the worth and efficacy of this ceremony arose between them and a Jew (i. e. a member of the Sanhedrim and of the College of representatives of the people), and when the latter probably insisted upon ranking the baptism of the Apostles higher than that of John, they hastened in anger to their master, and complained to him of the assumption of his former scholar. We have seen how victoriously and with what humility John repelled their charges.

This baptismal ceremony of the disciples of Christ appears, moreover, to have been only temporary, and by no means to have continued during the whole life-time of Christ. We find no where else either in John or in the other evangelists the least trace of the further practice of the rite. It was not until after the resurrection that Jesus commanded his disciples to baptize ; but this is quite a different ceremony, genuine Christian baptism, of which we shall have further occasion to speak. Since this, therefore, is the only passage where this baptism is mentioned, and since even here it is spoken of rather incidentally, we are perhaps warranted in concluding that the more the disciples came to a knowledge of the character of Christ and of the divine word, the more they hesitated to make use of this external symbol; and they soon perceived, it is probable, that Jesus' teaching and miracles were a more powerful and better means of arousing and of confirming faith in him than this merely outward ceremony.

The disciples were, it is likely, incited to the performance of this rite by a feeling of opposition to the baptism of John, which they regarded as imperfect; but this opposition must speedily have ceased, for John was soon after cast into prison. They were still at this time too much involved in the circle of ideas which they had received from their former master, and too much accustomed to the manner of his ministry, not to fall into the error of laying too much stress upon mere outward water baptism; and from this feeling arose their opposition to the incomplete rite that was performed by John, and their institution of a new baptism in the name of the Messiah who had already appeared on earth. They were incited, moreover, to the performance of the ceremony not a little by their contiguity to the Jordan, the sight of which stream irresistibly impelled them to make use of its waters for baptism, which was at that time performed by a total immersion. As soon, however, as the disciples had removed from the neighborhood of the Jordan,—which they soon did, because Jesus feared that the enmity of the Pharisees would be aroused by hearing that such numbers were attending upon his ministry (Jno. 4 : 1.),—and had come into other regions where a suitable quantity of water was not so convenient of access; this physical hindrance must of itself have called their attention to the fact that the administration of baptism was by no means necessary to the advancement of the cause of Christ, but that Jesus had within himself the means of gaining admission and favor among the people. The more zealously they pressed around the person of the Redeemer and feared to lose a word from his lips, so much the less did they feel themselves called upon to prosecute this baptismal labor ; especially since Jesus himself, though he had not previously hindered them from baptizing on the ground of its impropriety, but on the contrary had considered the act as in many respects useful, did not at a subsequent period urge them to renew the performance of the ceremony.

What relation, now, did these two baptismal rites sustain to Christian baptism? That both of them were only preparatory we have already seen ; since they only pointed to the Messiah, (the one, as yet to come ; the other, as having made his appearance,) who should bring forgiveness of sins. Christian baptism, on the other hand, was the actual impartation of all that salvation which had been obtained for men by the life and death of Christ : it did not merely promise the forgiveness of sins, but included it within itself, and was a baptism in the Holy Spirit. Here also was immersion in water still a symbol of purification, but there was added to this negative another and a positive element : it was also the symbol of immersion into a new spirit of life ; or, as Paul has somewhat differently turned the figure, the immersion was a symbol that our old man is dead and buried with Christ, while the emersion is a symbol of resurrection and of acting in newness of life.—Besides operating thus objectively, the Christian rite had yet another signification : it was a sign of the reception of him that had been baptized into the Christian community. Those other two preparatory-ceremonies founded, as we have seen, no new community, for they could at most only betoken a greater or less spiritual advancement in their recipients ; but Christian baptism, on the contrary, introduced a new spiritual element into man and made him thereby an altogether new creation ; and consequently an entirely new community must have originated from these adherents and followers of Christ who differed so essentially from the rest of men.

We are impelled, therefore, to this conclusion, that the impartation of the Holy Spirit is always the chief thing in Christian baptism, that immersion in water as being an outward symbol is not wholly essential, and that just in the same proportion as the significancy of the rite as a sign of reception into the visible Christian community retreats into the background ; in that same ratio it becomes less and less a ceremony of absolute necessity.—In this way it becomes explicable to us why Christ did not himself baptize his apostles and the disciples who joined themselves to him during his earthly life, and yet why his followers after him administered the rite. They had been once for all openly acknowledged by Christ as his disciples, had actually and visibly, as was demanded in that time of the infancy of the Church for its confirmation and advancement, received the Holy Spirit, and there had been imparted to them by that Spirit all those miraculous powers and gifts which distinguished that early period in the history of the Church. Since they possessed the reality, they needed not the external symbol, whether they had received, or not, at an earlier period the baptism of John. For, whether each of them had, or had not, confirmed his earlier preparation for entrance into the kingdom of God by the baptism of

John or by that of the disciples of Christ, was of comparatively little importance ; but it did import much whether each had entered into the communion of the Spirit and of life with Christ ; and in whomsoever this was not evinced by other facts, as was the case with the apostles and the first disciples of Christ, upon such baptism had to be performed anew, but it became in such a case an altogether different ceremony, the proof of entrance internally and externally into the kingdom of God. If, therefore, those who had at a previous time received the baptism of John or that of the disciples, received also at a later period Christian baptism, we cannot with any show of reason find therein any proof of the propriety of repeating that initiatory rite ; for it was not Christian baptism which was performed a second time in such instances of repetition ; and, though the ceremony in its outward appearance was in both cases the same, the signification and essential character of the two were altogether different, and each was independent of the other. Christian baptism, it is certain, was never performed but once on any, and was never repeated.

To this view no objection that is valid can be urged from what is said in Acts 19 : 2–6. of the baptism of certain disciples of John at Ephesus. These had received the baptism of John, probably on the occasion of their travelling up to Jerusalem to attend the Passover, and had heard from him and believed the announcement that the Messiah would shortly appear and bring forgiveness of sins to all repentant hearts ; they had, moreover, beyond a doubt heard at a later period that the Messiah had actually appeared, they had, perhaps, even seen and heard him at some time during the yearly feast at Jerusalem, and believed that he was the promised Messiah (a conclusion which seems warranted by the fact that they are in v. 1. called "disciples") ; they might also have heard of his death and his resurrection, and expected it may be, that he would now, according to his declaration, soon establish his kingdom before the eyes of all men, just as Christ's own disciples inquired of him after his resurrection whether he intended then to found his kingdom (Acts 1 : 6.) ; but that this kingdom was to be for the present wholly spiritual and to be established by the working of the Holy Spirit in those that believed, they had not the least conception. On this account they answered Paul, when he asked them whether they had yet received the Holy Spirit, that they knew of no such thing as a Holy Spirit. They knew, perhaps, of a Holy Spirit of God spoken of in the Old Testament, by means of which God works upon the souls of men ; but of the Holy Spirit, which was first communicated to men through Christ's act of redemption and which brings them into immediate connection with the Redeemer and Saviour of the world, they as yet knew nothing. It was necessary, therefore, that they should be made, by means of the appropriate external rite, the true disciples of Christ. They were accordingly baptized with Christian baptism ; and they were at the same time endued, by the laying on of the hands of the Apostle, as well morally as outwardly and visibly, with those wonderful powers and gifts which were accustomed at that time to accompany the imbuing of the human soul with the Holy Ghost.

Less clear than this example is another which immediately precedes (Acts 18 : 24–28.). In this case, there came to Ephesus, during the absence of Paul, a learned and eloquent Alexandrian Jew who had likewise received the baptism of John, who was, perhaps, acquainted also with the external events of the life of Jesus, and really recognized in him the Messiah, since it was his custom to bear witness to these facts in public; but the internal character of Christ and the significance of the work of the Messiah he did not as yet understand, and he knew nothing yet of the Holy Spirit which was imparted to all believers. For this reason, Aquila and Priscilla, two true disciples of the Lord who had continued residing for some time in Corinth in friendly intercourse with Paul, took upon themselves the office of enlightening his ignorance, and of disclosing to him more carefully and accurately than had yet been done the true way of the Lord, the true signification of the appearance and ministry of the Messiah. Of nothing further than this does the narrative speak, and we are not informed whether he received Christian baptism from them or not. It would seem that, because no one of the Apostles, through the medium of whom alone the gifts of the Spirit appear to have been at that time capable of being imparted, was then present, Apollos did not at this period become a recipient of the rite; and we have no positive and direct evidence whether or not, subsequently to this, he received the ceremony and at the same time the laying on of hands from an Apostle.—It is possible that he never became a recipient of the Christian rite; for, in the condition and circumstances of the churches of that early time, such a case might have easily occurred; and believers were not at that period so much accustomed as they afterwards became, to look rather at the perfect completion of all external ceremonies than to the truthfulness and sincerity of the inward Christian life; and we have already seen that the outward sign of baptism is by no means something essential to Christianity, but that its essence always consists in the impartation of the Holy

Spirit. That Apollos was endowed with this is shown by the manner in which his ministry in Corinth is represented (Acts 18 : 27, 28.), by the manner in which Paul speaks of him, calling him "brother" (1 Cor. 16 : 12.), and by the fact that the church at Corinth earnestly desired to see him after his long-continued labors in its behalf, a part of the Corinthian Christians having even united themselves so exclusively to him that they rejected every other instructor (1 Cor. 1 : 12.). As regarded the possession of the Holy Spirit, therefore, Apollos, was in fact a Christian, whether the external ceremony of baptism was performed upon him or not, and whether he had been put into possession of the miraculous powers of the Spirit by the laying on of an Apostle's hands, or not. This one fact, however, we must have fixed in the mind, that, if he was not baptized,—and this must, from the silence of the history upon this point, always remain doubtful,—this rite was not omitted because he had previously received the baptism of John,—for whether he had done so or not was altogether indifferent to the question of the propriety of his receiving the Christian rite, as we have seen entirely to our satisfaction in our examination of the preceding example,—but it was omitted, if omitted at all, only because he showed by his life and conduct that he was endowed with the Holy Spirit, the impartation of which is not necessarily connected with the external act of baptism, and the possession of which made the superaddition of outward baptism, not indeed impracticable and impossible, but no longer necessary.

ANOTHER VIEW OF THESE RELATIONS.

What has been so far said respecting the relations existing between the baptism of John, that administered by Christ's disciples, and the Christian ordinance, is translated directly from the German of Von Rohden, without the incorporation, as in the other parts of the book, of additional matter. The view which is here given by Von Rohden, though in many respects correct, is not, we think, altogether correspondent with the Scriptural representation. It needs, therefore, some modification.

In order to estimate aright the connection which exists between these baptismal ceremonies, it is necessary that we first clearly understand what, according to New Testament authority, is the nature of Christian baptism. It may be stated in few words to be *the immersion in water of a believer in Christ, by a properly authorized administrator, in the name of the Father, Son and Holy Spirit* (Matt. 28 : 19., Mark 16 : 16.) or *in the name of Christ* (Acts 8 : 16., 19 : 5.). This and nothing else is the Christian ordinance. It *is* not, and never *was*, as Von Rohden states, "the actual impartation of all that salvation which had been obtained for men by the life and death of Christ"; nor did it, as the same writer further supposes, "include within itself the forgiveness of sins," nor was it "a baptism in the Holy Spirit." All this, however, and more, was and is *denoted by* Christian baptism; for the ceremony is *a symbol* of the regeneration of him to whom it is administered (Jno. 3 : 5, 7.); of his participation in the divine life of Christ and in the promises which are grounded upon the atonement which the Saviour has made (Gal. 3 : 27. coll. Rom. 6 : 4., Col. 2 : 12.); and of the spiritual union of its recipient with the other members of the Church of Christ (1 Cor. 12 : 13., Ephes. 4 : 5., 5 : 26., Gal. 3 : 28, and elsewhere). This is what the ordinance *denotes;* but of itself it does not, and never did *produce*, as an *opus operatum*, the effects which have been enumerated. These blessings are bestowed by the operation of the Holy Spirit upon the heart of a believer, or by what is in the New Testament denominated in a figure *the baptism of the Spirit*,—to confer which is the prerogative of Christ, and the object of his sufferings and death. Whenever the external baptism of water and the internal baptism of the Spirit unite, then and then alone we have an example of such baptismal regeneration as is spoken of in the New Testament (Titus 3 : 5.).

Since in the days of the Apostolic Church the impartation of the Spirit was usually coincident with, or rather immediately consequent upon, the reception of baptism ; and since the one implied the other, the implication being in a majority of cases really correspondent with the reality, the immersion itself, though only an outward symbol, is sometimes represented in the New Testament, by metonymy,—a natural, and, in the Scriptures especially, quite frequent figure of speech,—as the direct agent by which regeneration is produced ; though even in these cases the connection usually shows that the real efficacy of the ordinance is to be ascribed to the accompanying operation of the Holy Spirit (cp. Titus 3 : 5., "the washing of regeneration, *and renewing of the Holy Ghost*").—But, notwithstanding this, the baptism in water and the baptism in the Holy Ghost were not the same operation ; nor did the one necessarily accompany the other. The latter generally succeeded the former, and was usually bestowed by the laying on of the hands of an Apostle (Acts 8 : 18., and elsewhere).*

* The Spirit was not conferred upon Paul by the laying on of the hands of another Apostle ; but was received immediately from the Lord (Gal. 1 : 12.). How and when it was communicated we know not positively ; for we are not prevented by the representation in Acts 9 : 17., from supposing that it was

In one instance at least, however, the baptism of the Spirit preceded, and was the warrant for the bestowment of the baptism of water (Acts 10 : 47.). Sometimes the two acts were separated by a considerable interval of time as may be proved from Acts 8 : 14–17. directly, and as is implied in the question put by Paul to the disciples at Ephesus (Acts 19 : 2.). Nay, even in Apostolic times, the baptism of water was sometimes conferred without the subsequent impartation of the Spirit (Acts 8 : 13., 18–23.).

It is the *Spirit*, then, and not *baptism*, which imparts the divine life to the believer. This impartation, indeed, is *presupposed* and *symbolized* by his immersion in water ; but it is not *effected* by it. What, then, *is* the *effect* which baptism produces in and of itself? Only this : *it initiates its recipient into the visible community of Christian believers.* Baptism, therefore, as an external rite, an immersion into water in the name of Christ, is nothing more or less than a rite of initiation into the Christian Church. The *import*, the *signification*, of the ordinance is something different and of more vital interest: it is such as has been described.—Having determined the nature of the Christian rite, we are now prepared to examine the relation which it bears to that of John and to that administered by Christ's disciples.

The characteristics of the baptism of John have already been stated with sufficient distinctness. It was, as Jerome calls it, "a baptism of repentance for the remission of sins, that is, for their future remission, which was to be obtained by the sanctification of Christ," the sins being remitted in hope

imparted to him before his baptism. The account, however, seems rather to intimate that the Spirit was conferred simultaneously with the reception of that ordinance.

merely, and on condition of reformation. It was a baptism in which its recipient professed a belief in the Messiah as about to appear (εἰς τὸν ἐρχόμενον), but not in Jesus personally as that Messiah already manifest in the flesh.* It was, therefore, not the same in its most important element as the Christian ordinance; and was consequently, decided by an Apostle to be insufficient to constitute one a member of the Christian community (Acts 19 : 4, 5.). This example is decisive of the whole question; for the disciples of John here spoken of seem to have been comparatively well grounded in biblical truth, and yet, having received only the baptism of John, they were adjudged by Paul not to be in a state which was consistent with the reception on their part of the Holy Spirit.

The case of Apollos (Acts 18 : 24–28.), is in all important respects similar to that of these disciples; like them he "knew only the baptism of John"; but he appears to have been better instructed than they "in the way of the Lord". Judging from what was done in the latter case, we may infer that Apollos was baptized by Aquila, as the Ephesian disciples were by Paul; though we are not informed in so many words of the fact, being told only that the way of God was expounded unto him more perfectly (v. 26.). There was no necessity for mentioning expressly that he was baptized anew, this time in the name of the Lord Jesus; for this, of

* Matthies (*Baptismatis Expositio*, p. 86–88.), supposes that John, after his recognition of Jesus as the Messiah, baptized directly with reference to Jesus in person; but this view is contradicted by all the subsequent history of the Baptist. Had such been the fact, the dispute mentioned in Jno. 3 : 25. could never have arisen. The supposition, moreover, comes in direct conflict with what Paul says of John's baptism (Acts 19 : 4, 5.).

course, is pre-supposed. Such is the general opinion of biblical critics; but Meyer and De Wette think differently, supposing, with Von Rohden, that at this early stage in the history of the Church the ordinance may have been omitted; but such a supposition is, on many accounts, quite improbable. We are rather to rank this among numerous other cases recorded in the New Testament, where the belief of the converts to Christianity, or their addition to the Church, is alone mentioned, their baptism being taken for granted, because it was well understood by all that without the reception of that rite no one could become a member of the Christian community.—No doubt, too, Apollos received the baptism of the Holy Spirit; not, however, it is probable, by the laying on, at a subsequent period, of the hands of Paul in Corinth, as Olshausen supposes, but directly from the fountain-head, without human interposition.—We have no positive ground for concluding that his case differs in any important particular from that of the Ephesian disciples. He must, accordingly, have met with substantially the same treatment on being admitted as a true member of the Christian community.

Our view of the connection of John's baptism with the Christian rite, it will be seen, does not differ essentially from that of Von Rohden. With regard, however, to the relation which the baptism administered by Christ's disciples (Jno. 3: 22. 26., 4: 1, 2.) bears to the Christian ordinance, there is a much wider difference in our opinions.—In few words, our view is the following:—John baptized with reference to a Messiah that was yet to come. The disciples on the other hand baptized with reference to Jesus, the Messiah already come; and by this rite they initiated into the Christian community which was forming around Christ as its central-point, the Christian Church in fact, the foundation of which was laid when our Lord began to select his Apostles. This Church did not, it is true, exhibit itself as such in its full power and glory until the outpouring of the Spirit upon the day of Pentecost; but still it existed, Christ himself being witness (Matt. 18 : 17. coll. 16 : 18.), feeble indeed in its beginnings but yet containing the germ of mighty things.

This baptism was in all respects, save perhaps, its direct internal significancy, the same as that administered by the Apostles on the day of Pentecost; for both rites were based upon repentance and belief in Christ Jesus, and both initiated into the Christian Church. Those who had received it needed not to have another baptism performed upon them before they could be made partakers of the Spirit; for, as we have seen, even in the confessedly Christian rite, the baptism of the Spirit was not a necessary part of the immersion in water, but was in fact a separate and distinct operation which was in general, though not always, attendant upon the Christian ordinance. Without water baptism, it could not, except in particular cases, be conferred; and even when water baptism had preceded, it was not invariably bestowed.—Even in respect to internal significancy, however, the rite which was administered by the disciples *may* have been the same as that performed by them afterwards as Apostles; for it is not impossible, nay, it is rather probable, that it was understood by them and by those to whom they administered it as symbolizing that baptism of the Spirit which, according to John's testimony, the Messiah was to perform.*

* Matthies (*Bapt. Expos.* p. 57, Note) contends that the disciples actually baptized in the Spirit (ἐν τῷ πνεύματι); but this is impossible, even sup

The rite in question was performed indeed by Christ's disciples; but it was not without his sanction, according to the representation of John the evangelist (3 : 22.). Jesus did not baptize in person, because, perhaps, being the Lord and king of the theocracy, it would have been unbecoming his dignity to administer the rite with his own hands. Neither was it necessary that he should do so; for his disciples were fully qualified for the task.—But, how were they qualified? According to Clement of Alexandria (*Hypotyp.* lib. 5.), they were fitted for it by baptism received from Jesus himself when they were admitted to his fellowship; but, notwithstanding that the expression "though Jesus baptized not" (Jno. 4 : 2.) may be limited in its reference to this particular occasion, and does not, consequently, compel us to suppose that our Lord never administered the ordinance at any time or to any person, yet this traditional testimony of Clement's cannot well be founded on truth; for, had Jesus himself baptized, it is hard to explain how the fact could have been passed without notice by some one of the evangelists. They were qualified for the task, we should rather say, by being the chosen Apostles of Christ. They needed ever after this no water baptism; for the baptism of the Spirit which they, in common with the whole infant Church as then existing in one company in Jerusalem, received on the memorable day of Pentecost, fully supplied all their deficiencies and prepared them for the work of evangelizing the world.

It is likely, as Von Rohden thinks, that after leaving the vicinity of the Jordan the disciples ceased baptizing; not,

posing, what is not true, that the external Christian rite is itself immersion in the Spirit; for the Holy Spirit had not yet vivified the Church (Jno. 7 : 39.)

however, for want of facilities for performing the rite, but because it was not Christ's intention to have many initiated into the newly-established Church until after his death and the actual bestowment of the Spirit. He preferred preparing the way for the labors of the Apostles, laying the foundation upon which they were afterwards to raise the superstructure of the theocracy. This he could do by teaching those who resorted to him for instruction in the relations in which they already lived, and without incorporating them formally into his theocratic organization.

NOTE.—The foregoing chapter on the "Relation of the Baptism of John to Christian Baptism," as far as the bottom of p. 215, is translated, without addition, directly from Von Rohden. It was thought best, upon the whole, to make no alteration in this portion of his Treatise; although the views expressed in it,—particularly as regards the relation which the Baptism administered by Christ's disciples (Jno. 3 : 22, 26; 4: 1, 2.) bears to what is universally admitted to be Christian Baptism, and as regards the efficacy of the Christian rite, and its connection with the forgiveness of sin,—are not correspondent with the sentiments of the Translator. The doctrine of Von Rohden upon these points is distinctly dissented from by the Translator in the latter part of the chapter, under the heading "Another View of these Relations." It did not seem proper to do more than this in a book which professes to present "the *whole* of the treatise of Von Rohden."

In holding that the Baptism of John was not identical with Christian Baptism, though the same in outward form, the Translator and Von Rohden agree in sentiment. No ecclesiastical writer, from the time of the Apostles to that of the Reformation, has expressed a contrary opinion. All who have spoken on the subject, represent the two rites as different and distinct ceremonies. And no modern biblical critic of eminence thinks otherwise. The weight of evidence tending to prove a difference in the signification of the two ordinances, is too strong to be resisted. If the passage in Acts (19: 1–6.) which represents them as not identical, were wholly wanting, John's own testimony would abundantly prove their diversity, "and indeed essential diversity." Outwardly, that is, as to form, the two rites were the same; in signification they were different.

PART FIFTH.

CLOSE OF THE BAPTIST'S MINISTRY.

CHAPTER I.

JOHN'S IMPRISONMENT.

THE evangelist John, as we have seen, has alone given us information respecting that part of the Baptist's ministry which was prosecuted after the public appearance of Christ. The other evangelists appear, on the other hand, to intimate that John was imprisoned by Herod immediately after the baptism of Jesus, and that it was this very act of violence which induced the latter to make his first journey, spoken of in Jno. 1 : 44. ff., into Galilee (cp. Matt. 4 : 12., Mark 1 : 14.). In Luke (3 : 19, 20.) the imprisonment of John is evidently mentioned only by way of anticipation, because the writer wished to mention here at once and in connection all that he intended to say respecting the Baptist. That he did not intend to follow any historical order is made clear by the fact that he reverts, immediately after his observation respecting the imprisonment of the Baptist, to the baptism which he had performed on Christ, and relates nothing further regarding his subsequent fortunes and death.—With these representations, and especially with those given by Matthew and Mark, what the evangelist John relates to us in 3 : 23, 24., appears to come into direct conflict; that even after Christ had returned from his first journey into Galilee, John was still engaged in baptizing; and that Apostle even appears, by mentioning expressly that John was not yet cast into prison, to have intentionally forewarned his readers against the erroneous opinion to the contrary propagated by the other three evangelists.—What, now, have we to think of this narrative, and how must we clear away the difficulty?

The easiest and most satisfactory expedient which we can adopt, is evidently to suppose that it was not the first journey to Galilee (Jno. 1 : 44. ff.), but the second (Jno. 4 : 3.) which was prompted by the imprisonment of the Baptist; in favor of which view in particular is the fact that John himself (4 : 1.) assigns as the reason of this second journey the knowledge which Jesus had that the Pharisees had heard that he was making more disciples than the Baptist. Wherefore could this be the ground of Christ's leaving so hastily those regions, if he did not think that he had reason to suspect some act of violence from the hands of the Pharisees; and on what could this fear have been more rationally based, than on the example of bold and violent despotism which he had before his eyes in the imprisonment of the Baptist? For the first journey to Galilee (Jno. 1 : 44. ff.), on the other hand, no such motive is assigned: Jesus appears to have gone thither at that time with the intention of giving the first proof of his divine power and glory to his friends and his near acquaintances in the land of his youth, and to collect here his first disciples, at a distance from the injurious influences of the Pharisees. The narrative of John moves on in this chapter in such a manner, step by step as it were, after the fashion of a diary, that, since the imprisonment of John could not have been to him,—he having been one of his disciples,—of little importance, he must have made express mention of it, had it occurred at this time ; instead of doing so, however, he speaks out in 3 : 24. expressly against this idea, and testifies that John still baptized in the Jordan at the same time with Jesus, after the latter had returned from Galilee and after the feast of the Passover had been finished at Jerusalem (Jno. 2 : 13. ff.).

We are, therefore, obliged to suppose that the other three evangelists either knew nothing at all of the first journey into Galilee, together with the miracle that was wrought at the marriage in Cana, the return to Jerusalem to attend the Passover, and the expulsion of the sellers of merchandise from the temple and the conversation with Nicodemus which occurred in that city ; or that they were not sufficiently acquainted with these events to give a narrative of them in their Gospels ; and that, therefore, overleaping this period altogether, they began their representation of the ministry of Jesus with the second journey that he made into Galilee, which was occasioned by the imprisonment of the Baptist.

When we consider the form and nature of the Gospels,—which are not by any means constructed upon the plan of registering with the greatest precision and scientific exactness, in its proper succession and chronological order, every single occurrence in the life of the Redeemer, but are meant to represent to us in bold outlines an exciting picture of his life and acts,—this supposition is encompassed with the less difficulty ; especially since Jesus was, at this early period in his ministry, but little known, and had but few Apostles, who either were for the most part first chosen upon his second journey (cp. Matt. 4 : 18–22., Mark 1 : 16–20.), or because now for the first time his constant attendants, and since this whole first journey to Galilee and back thence to Jerusalem and to the Jordan might have been accomplished within the space of a few weeks.

The imprisonment of the Baptist is narrated only incidentally by all three of the evangelists. Luke, as we have already seen, barely mentions the fact, and with it closes his account of the ministry of John before the public appearance of Jesus. Matthew and Mark, on the other hand, introduce the occurrence in connection with the course of their narrative respecting the labors and influence of Christ, while they are mentioning (Matt. 14 : 1, 2., Mark 6 : 14–16.) the various opinions which were in circulation respecting the person of Jesus. Among these opinions one was that Jesus was John risen from the dead, which, according to Matthew and Mark, Herod, who without doubt was reproved and stung by his conscience for the murder of a man whom he acknowledged to be just, himself expressed ; but which, according to Luke, who also mentions these ideas respecting Jesus (9 : 7–9.), was held only by the people, while Herod did not express himself so pointedly and definitely, but only wished to see him who had now a greater number of the people in attendance upon him than at an earlier period John had,—in which desire it is quite likely that there was included a sort of wavering conjecture that Jesus might perhaps be the Baptist himself upraised from the dead.—On this occasion, then, when they make mention of the death of the Baptist, Matthew and Mark subjoin a supplementary notice respecting the motive of his imprisonment and execution, the latter evangelist, who appears to have had the most exact information on the subject, giving the narrative most at length. John passes over the fact in silence, because he takes it for granted as known to his readers from the accounts of the two evangelists who had written of it before his Gospel was published.

The following is given to us as the motive which prompted to his imprisonment:—Herod the Great had by Aristobulus, one of his sons, a granddaughter named Herodias whom he gave in marriage to his son, her uncle, Herod Philip, who, destined at first to be his father's successor, but afterwards disinherited by him, remained a private man, whilst the other three sons of Herod, Archelaus, Herod Antipas (the person here mentioned by the evangelists), and Philip,—whose name was the same as that of his eldest brother, but who was probably distinguished from him by some other special appellation,—divided amongst themselves, as tetrarchs, the greater part of their father's kingdom (cp. Part III., Chap. I.). The ambitious and sensual Herodias, preferring a tetrarch to a private man for her husband, persuaded her uncle, Herod Antipas, tetrarch of Galilee and Perea, to put away his lawful wife, a daughter of Aretas, the Arabian king, and to marry her, the eloping and unfaithful wife of his brother.* Such an incestuous union (cp. Levit. 18 : 16.) and, according to Luke 3 : 19., at the same time many other wicked acts of Herod, John, the public preacher of repentance, could not let pass unreproved: he who had lifted up the voice of condemnation and warning against Pharisees and against members of the Sanhedrim, could not be deterred by fear from declaring freely

* This iniquitous proceeding of Herod's produced a war between him and his father-in-law, which, however, did not break out till a year before the death of Tiberius (in the year of Rome 790, A.D. 37.). In this war Herod was totally defeated and his army cut to pieces by Aretas; a calamity which the Jews in general attributed to the vengeance of God, inflicted upon Herod on account of his treatment of the Baptist (Jos. *Ant.* 5 1–3.).

and publicly that it was not right for Herod to have his brother's wife ; and we may well suppose that he reproved this wickedness with by no means soft and honeyed words.

We are not obliged to suppose that the Baptist went with this express intention to the palace of Herod—to such a work had he not been called ; and we find no proof that it was his custom to interfere in this way with family affairs, or to seek out particular individuals for special reproof. There is no objection to our supposing, what is not so improbable, that Herod travelling on some occasion in his own land in the neighborhood of John, had gone out of his way, together with his attendant escort, in order to see this remarkable man, and that on this opportunity the Baptist had addressed to him these unwelcome words of reproof.—We are not obliged, however, to resort to either of these conjectures ; for it does not contradict our narrative, if John spoke only in a general way publicly before the people respecting this improper act of Herod's, since what he said could not easily be kept concealed from the king. The direct form of the words, "it is not lawful for thee to have thy brother's wife", does, it is true, seem to indicate that the remark was made by John in person to Herod ; but we are not compelled to press so strongly upon the expression ; for the words might have been reported to Herod by a third person in that form which they would have taken if they had been addressed to him in person.

Mark represents the matter as if Herodias had been the chief agent in producing the imprisonment of the Baptist and the cause of the hastening of his execution, while Herod himself remained rather passive in the transaction, and in the hours of his better emotions even gladly listened to the discourses of John : Matthew, on the other hand, speaks of

Herod as the prime author of his imprisonment, and as being eagerly desirous to put him to death as soon as possible thereafter. We may readily conceive how an ambitious and sensual woman like Herodias, feeling herself wounded to the quick by the monitory reproaches of John, must, in the glowing bitterness of her hate, have sworn destruction against the man, and on that account have urged on her husband by all the arts of coquetry to throw the Baptist into prison, and, after she had obtained this request, have ceased not to seek his execution. Herod, the slave of sensuality, was no doubt often tempted by her and often incited by his own wishes to remove the bold reprover out of the way, as Matthew expressly informs us (v. 5.) ; but the weak prince was constantly kept in check by the fear which he had of the people, who regarded John as a prophet, and who might have risen in insurrection at his cruel execution. Add to this, moreover, that, whenever the seductive arts of Herodias had not drawn him within the circle of their influence, and he looked at the matter more fairly and with more consideration, his own better judgment which still preserved with him something of the feeling of right and wrong, spoke out in favor of John : he recognized in him a just and holy man, and often he did not hesitate to allow him the privilege of conversation, nay, he even sometimes listened to him as a counsellor. Thus vacillating between a just regard for John and the desire to oblige the blood-thirsty will of his wife, the weak man continued for a long time undecided, until at last the seductive arts of Herodias gained the victory.

The historian Josephus, when he relates this occurrence (*Archæol,* 18. 5. 2.), assigns a different reason for the imprisonment of the Baptist ; that Herod was fearful lest John, since he had so many adherents among the people, might at length excite an insurrection, which he sought to prevent by putting him in confinement. We see at once, however, that this was only the nominal ground, the pretext which was given out in public ; for, since he was obliged to assign to the people some reason for having thrown into prison a man so beloved by them and so revered as the Baptist, and since the true reason, the just judgment and reproof by John of the incestuous marriage of the prince, could not well be declared, he was compelled to seek for some other ground, be it tenable or not, in justification of his conduct ; and fear of disturbance among the populace seemed to him the most welcome and the most likely to answer his end.

Guarding himself in this way against the anger of the people, Herod awaited a moment when John, who frequently went from one bank of the river Jordan to the other, was found in his territory in Perea, had him arrested and, as Josephus relates, brought to Machærus, a castle on the east side of the Dead Sea, in the southern part of Perea, where he, therefore, was himself probably residing at the time ; at least, the Baptist must, according to the narratives of Matthew and Mark, have been kept imprisoned in the immediate neighborhood of Herod ; and it is rendered the more probable that he was confined near the place of Herod's residence at the time by the fact that Antipas had a palace in the neighborhood (Jos. *Bell. Jud.* 2. 4. 2.) ; not, however, as some think, because war was being waged at that time between Herod and Aretas, king of Arabia,—the former residing as near as possible to the boundaries of his territory on the side towards Arabia, in order that he might arrange and direct all things connected with the war the more readily in his own proper person,—for this war did not break out till after the execution of the Baptist.

The confinement of John could not have possibly been very rigid, since Herod had been induced to decide upon it contrary to his own better inclination, and, according to the testimony of Mark (v. 20.) took pleasure in conversing with him himself; and also, perhaps, on account of the people, who perchance would not have quietly endured a cruel incarceration of the honored Baptist, and whom Herod feared so much that he did not venture of his own will to complete his execution. Without question, therefore, we are at liberty to conclude that John still had free intercourse with his disciples, many of whom must indeed have followed him in his imprisonment.*

* According to Josephus (*Antiq.* 18. 5. 2.) the Baptist was imprisoned by Herod because he feared that John might excite an insurrection. Part of the account given by the Jewish historian will be found on p. 111: the rest is as follows: "And the others flocking around him,—for they were much delighted in listening to his words,—Herod, fearing lest by his great influence among the people, he might excite an insurrection,—for they seemed ready to do anything at his advice,—thinks it much better to prevent him from creating any disturbance, by removing him before-hand out of the way, rather than to have to repent when he has fallen into difficulties on account of a revolt. Having, therefore, been made a prisoner on account of the suspicion of Herod, John, being sent to Machærus, the castle before mentioned, is there put to death." The reason assigned by Josephus for the imprisonment of the Baptist, was, it would seem, something more than "a pretext;" and Von Rohden is wrong, probably, in supposing it to be only "the nominal ground" of his arrest, (p. 231.): it was, it is likely, the *general ground*, or state reason, of the imprisonment; while the reason assigned by the Evangelists was its *immediate cause*. The two accounts are perfectly harmonious. See Prof. Gams, *Joh. d. T. im Gefangnisse*, pp. 40–45.

CHAPTER II.

The Baptist's Doubts in Prison, and his Mission of Inquiry to Jesus.

How did this occurrence work upon the feelings of the Baptist, unto whom, as a free son of the desert, imprisonment must have been particularly hateful? This question leads us to take a glance at the previous mental formation of the Baptist's character. Initiated early into the Old Testament prophecies, in reflection upon the contrariety which existed between the idea and the actuality of the kingdom of God, he attained to the lively conviction that a Messiah must shortly appear. Many single circumstances in his education and occurring in general in the time of his youth, confirmed him yet more in this conviction, and induced him to make still deeper researches into the divine prophecies, whose sense he, supported and enlightened by the Holy Spirit, understood better and knew how to estimate better than the greater part of his acquaintances, nay, better than all his associates, and even better than the most enlightened and pious worthies among his people. Since he could not, until the prophecies had been fulfilled, fully comprehend their meaning, nor explain what he found to be seemingly contradictory in these Old Testament predictions, there must have arisen within him many an obscure conception and much that was heterogeneous and arbitrary in his Messianic expectations; in particular, must his ideas respecting a suffering and a reigning Messiah have been brought with difficulty to conform to the nature of his hopes;

and we may well suppose that, although he sought to explain to himself and to realize that the Messiah must, in accordance with his designs of bringing salvation to men, pass through sufferings (whether he conceived also that he must undergo the pains of death, must, as we have previously remarked, remain undecided), in order to gain a complete victory over all his enemies and to attain to perfect glory ; yet must he most frequently and with most delight have pictured to himself the image of a mighty monarch enthroned in royalty and splendor ; but still, whenever his mind reverted to the quiet and humble appearance of the Son of Man, those other less pleasing remembrances of the suffering servant of God must have been renewed within his soul.

Since, therefore, he held fast to both opinions, that, on the one hand, the kingdom of the Messiah was to be in reality a spiritual dominion which would bring forgiveness to repentant sinners, and yet that, on the other, it would reveal itself in earthly might and glory,—which latter revelation is promised to us only in connection with the second coming of the Lord, but which John could not conceive of as separate from the first advent,—there was formed within the mind of the Baptist the firm expectation that the Messiah would begin his ministry by some outward earthly act, and would then speedily attain, after a brief contest, to royalty and to earthly power and dignity ; and this expectation reflected itself, as we have seen, in all his connected utterances. He had been called by God to preach repentance, to announce the coming Messiah, and to bear witness of him when he had come ; and this office he performed with the greatest conscientiousness and humility The Messiah is revealed to him ; he puts confidence in the revelation, and testifies aloud and freely that this Jesus is he that was to come: so long as God does not call him away, and he receives no intimation to discontinue his ministry, he labors on joyfully, preparing still the way for the Messiah, and pointing others to him; he is gladdened, therefore, in observing the constantly increasing number of the adherents of Jesus, and his hope grows strong that now without delay the decisive step will be taken by the Lord which will represent him publicly to the people as the promised son of David and the Messiah, and will summon around him all who believe in his dignity, the Baptist himself as well as the rest, in order to begin in common the struggle against the opposing power of sin and of the world. But, alas, for his expectations in the midst of the blooming of his hopes, in the midst of his eager longings and strong convictions, he is suddenly arrested by Herod, that servant of sin, and cast into prison.

John's first feeling on being imprisoned must have been yet more indignant anger against those sinners whom he had so courageously reproved, and who now, as if in anticipation of the approaching struggle, sought to render powerless the most valiant champion of the simple truth. The next thought, without doubt, was this:—the kingdom of the Lord will now without delay break in upon the world, and after a short struggle with the powers of sin will come forth from victory in yet greater effulgence; and all the just will rule in joy and honor with their Lord: my imprisonment can only be short and transitory, for the Messiah will now hasten to establish his kingdom in order to free his faithful witness and confessor. But just here was his hope doomed to destruction; here was to begin the hard trial which God had resolved to bring upon him in order to lead him to perfection. Hitherto all had gone in accordance with his wish; all his expectations had been answered; the Messiah whom he had announced, had appeared, had been revealed unto him, and had already begun to collect numerous adherents around his person. What, therefore, could be more clear than that he would now speedily declare himself to be the theocratic king? The frequent opportunities which he had enjoyed of seeing the divine person of the Redeemer, could not have failed to have increased still more his confidence in him; while the consequences of his own ministry, and the divine inspiration which was manifested in and attended upon his public labors had hitherto elevated John, so to speak, above himself. Now, however, all these props were to fall away, and in their stead opposition and trouble were to assail him from every side; in order that, as he had been, so far, the mere organ of the divine will, an instrument in the hand of God, so now he might by internal struggles in his own heart, purify and complete himself, might work out from within himself, by his own reflection and by his sufferings, a firm belief in God and in his ambassador, who had up to this time been pressed upon his attention solely by means and by events from without; and might with humility and entire resignation to God be led to acknowledge that his ways are not as our ways, and that as high as the heaven is above the earth so high are his thoughts above our thoughts. The Scriptures afford us a glimpse of this serious and hard struggle within the breast of John: we see in the mournful picture of the imprisonment of the Baptist which is unrolled before our eyes, no longer as heretofore the divinely inspired prophet John, but only the weak man John, who must struggle, despair, contend, as every other sorrowful and desponding human heart.

Since now the imprisonment of the Baptist, which, as we

have seen, was brought about by the promptings of private passion, could not have been very rigid, he had opportunity of inquiring from his disciples what was happening in the outer world, and, in particular, how stood matters with Jesus. With what anxious desire must he have longed, each time he made the inquiry, to hear the reply : " He has at length openly announced himself as the Messianic king, and has entered publicly upon the struggle ; the day of his victory and of thy reception into his kingdom, is at hand." But a day, a week, one month after another, passed away, and yet he heard nothing of the kind ; on the contrary, he received reports only of discourses and teaching on the part of Jesus, of miracles of healing and of raising from the dead ; so that the Baptist was at last compelled to come to the conclusion that Christ had in truth no intention of creating a political party, but sought rather the contrary, even opposing himself to every attempt of the kind on the part of others. One of two things, therefore, must John surrender—he must resign either the hope of an earthly Messianic reign, which appeared to him so firmly grounded on the promises of the Old Testament, or his recognition of Jesus as the Messiah, which was on its side not less powerfully accredited by the divine testimony which had been given at his baptism. How must his soul have wavered, and how frequently must his mind have been carried now in this, now in that, direction ! Strive as he might to prevent it, the harassing doubt would still keep rising in his mind, until at last the testimony of the Old Testament appeared more trustworthy and more credible than that single divine witness given to himself, which might after all have been based upon an illusion. Every circumstance, therefore, however insignificant, which could in any possible manner throw doubt upon the divine origin of that testimony, was sought out and unconsciously magnified in his mind, until at length his decision partook of the coloring of his wishes, and doubt in the Messianic dignity of Jesus gained the preponderance in his soul. It may also be supposed that his disciples, who from the first had much more fleshly conceptions of the Messiah than himself, attacked now more vigorously than ever the wavering mind of their master, asserting that Jesus could not possibly be the Messiah; while his own desire to become liberated from the mournful condition which, pressing upon him with its whole weight, now burdened his troubled soul, at last fully turned for a time the scale of his opinion, and he came to the conclusion that he was mistaken in Jesus.

Notwithstanding all this, however, he did not turn completely hopeless away from him, as might easily and would probably have taken place in the case of another person; but a reaction speedily occurred in his mind in favor of the Messiah, when he began again to reflect upon the divine testimony which he had received respecting him; so that John came finally to the determination to inquire of Jesus himself what opinion he must hold with regard to his dignity, and what he must expect as the result of his labors. It is not surprising that he adopted this resolution; for there yet was present to his soul in all its clearness the image of Jesus as that of a man who was pure and spotless in word and deed, such as he had himself been conscious at an earlier period that Jesus was (whence his touching refusal to baptize him), and such as he had afterwards acknowledged him to be in the hearing of his disciples; and he was convinced that Jesus would tell him nothing but the simple truth in reply to his questionings. This was the only means which he could adopt to remove his hesitation and doubt. When, therefore, the Lord had probably come from Nain, where he had raised a young man from the dead (cp. Luke 7 : 11–17.), into the neighborhood of Bethany (Bethabara) on the other side of the Jordan, and was consequently not far distant from the castle Machærus ;* since the conviction that Jesus did not purpose to found a political kingdom had now been made almost a certainty in the Baptist's mind by the information which his disciples brought to him respecting Christ's ministry, and in particular, perhaps, by the sending out of the Apostles into the cities in order to teach, but not to excite the people, nor to produce political commotions (Matt. 10.),—John sent two of his disciples to Christ with the question, "*Art thou he that should [is to] come*" (ὁ ἐρχόμενος), —an expression by the use of which John shows clearly that he expected to recognize the Messiah by some earthly act, for only in such an expectation could Christ be spoken of as one that was yet to come,—"*or do we [shall we] look for another ?*" (Matt. 11 : 3., Luke 7 : 20.)—The whole occurrence is narrated in Matt. 11 : 2–19, and Luke 7 : 18–35.

This struggle in the soul of John and this public expression of it are in truth so natural and so easily explained, that one cannot help being surprised to discover that they have given to some grounds for cavil and objection against the historical truth of the narrative. Let one only revert in thought to the greatest heroes in the faith, as well of more ancient as of recent times, and he will perceive that they, after having publicly testified and preached with the utmost willingness and distinctness of the Redeemer, of his doctrine and his work, and

* The weight of evidence drawn from the connection of the New Testament narratives of this transaction, is rather in favor of our Lord's being at this time in the vicinity of Capernaum, in Galilee.

after they have experienced in their own hearts unnumbered times the conviction of the truth and of the wonderful power of the doctrines which they proclaimed, have notwithstanding fallen at other times into doubts and mental struggles respecting Christ, and have had to betake themselves in prayer to God for the enlightenment and confirmation of their faith. Let every believer examine himself, and see whether similar doubts have never risen within his own soul, with which he has had to struggle hard and long. Beyond a question every one will discover in his own history many such occasions when his faith has wavered and needed strengthening from on high.*—In estimating the character of such great witnesses and mediators of the truth, one is often led into error by viewing them only in the light of their public life, in which are represented only the power and confidence of the faith which they have attained by such internal struggles, but not the history of these struggles themselves. And with regard to biblical characters, in particular, have we been accustomed to conceive of them only in their purity and to estimate them

* Matthesius relates the following anecdotes of Luther, which illustrate very forcibly this melancholy truth. We translate from Von Rohden's treatise: "On a certain occasion a woman complained to him that she could no longer have faith. 'Do you no longer remember,' inquired the Doctor, 'the creed of your childhood?' When she had recited this correctly and with an air of devotion, the Doctor asked, 'Do you consider this true?' The woman replied in the affirmative. 'Truly, my good woman,' responded the Doctor, 'your belief is stronger than mine: I must pray daily for the increase of my faith.' On receiving this reply the woman thanked him, and departed in peace to her home.—Antonius Musa, minister in Rochlitz, said to me that he once lamented to the Doctor that he could not believe himself what he preached to others. 'God be praised and thanked,' answered the Doctor, 'that this is also the case with others; I thought it was true of myself alone.' This consolation I could never forget my whole life long."

only by their shining qualities : we cite them before all others as models of piety and of confiding, joyous faith, and this, in truth, they are ; but there is not one among them, respecting whom we have received more particular and circumstantial information, on whom we cannot discover some stain ; and for this reason it is that the most striking and magnificent descriptions which we have of pious and pure conduct refer us at the end to him on whom alone there was neither spot nor wrinkle, who alone could say, "Who can convict me of sin ?"

Our own internal Christian experience will give us the best explanation of the rise and operation of these doubts upon the mind of John the Baptist. "In the life of every believer," says Olshausen,* "are to be found moments of temptation in which even the most firm conviction will be shaken to its foundation : nothing is more natural than to conceive such moments or periods of internal darkness and abandonment by the Spirit of God, even in the life of John. . . . . In his gloomy prison at Machærus, a dark hour, no doubt, surprised the man of God, an hour in which he was struck with the quiet unobtrusive ministry of Christ, and wherein he fell into internal conflict concerning the experiences he had heretofore had. This is clearly pointed out in the words of Jesus : 'Blessed is he whosoever shall not be offended in me',—words which contain at the same time censure and consolation. For truly it would have been a sad thing for the poor captive, had he not stood firm in the hour of temptation, had he really taken offence ; but in this case, he was merely tempted to it ; and blessed is the man that endureth temptation (Jas. 1 : 12.). But inasmuch as there is no victory for sinful man without a

* *Bib. Comment. on the Gospels*, Eng. transl. Edinburgh edit. 1847, vol II., pp. 53, 54

struggle, hence was likewise the Baptist destined to pass through this struggle. But that he endured this struggle, and vanquished, is manifest from the very circumstance of his inquiring of Jesus himself. That he inquired of him *in this manner* shows his state of temptation ; but that he, in his state of temptation, inquires of no one but *himself* [Jesus], manifests his faith in him ; especially inasmuch as the free life of the Redeemer, so very different from his own, must have appeared something very astonishing in the sight of this most austere preacher of repentance (cp. Matt. 11 : 19.).—The question of John is nothing but another : 'Lord, I believe, help thou my unbelief ;' and this prayer was granted by our gracious Lord. Whosoever asks of God, whether he be God ; whosoever asks of the Saviour, whether he be the Saviour, is in the right path to overcome every temptation ; it is only thus that he can ascertain it with certainty. Hence it is that the words of Jesus concerning John which follow (v. 7. ff.) form no contradiction to the supposition that he sent the messengers to Jesus in an hour of severe temptation. Even thereby did he prove that he was no reed to be shaken by a breath of wind, but that he was firm as the foundation of the earth in his faith, and that he withstood the effects of every tempest. But if there be no tempest, how can firmness prove its strength ? It was therefore in the time of his greatness, when the fullness of the Spirit dwelt in him, that God made use of the Baptist for *his* purposes to serve humanity ; in the time of his littleness or poverty, and when forsaken, it was then that God perfected him within himself."*

* The translation of Olshausen's Gospels here quoted from was made by *Dr. Sergius Loewe*, himself a German. The version is upon the whole a good one ; but it bears everywhere upon its face proof of its being the production of

Comparing the question put by John (Matt. 11 : 2.) with the answer returned by Christ (v. 6.) we cannot, without doing violence to the evangelical narrative, do otherwise than conclude that John really entertained for a time doubts respecting the Messiahship of Jesus ; though, of course, these doubts never reached so far as the positive conviction that he was not in truth the expected theocratic king. This doubt was the product of feelings and reflections which have already been described. The only difficulty in the matter is, how to reconcile the existence of such a doubt, even though a momentary one, with John's previous testimony of Jesus as the Messiah and even recognition of him as a suffering Messiah. This difficulty, however, has also been already met and a solution offered.*

That our narrative, then, intends to represent the Baptist as actually in doubt respecting the claims of Jesus as the

a foreigner. In not a few places it is obscure ; and in many it does not give the meaning of the original German. In the extract above quoted, for example, not to mention many instances of improper choice of words, there are several inaccuracies in the rendering. For instance, "*himself*," should be *him himself* (*ihn selbst*): as it stands, it refers to John,—the *Jesus* in brackets being added by our hand. The phrase beginning "but that he was firm as the foundation" and ending with the words "every tempest," is an exaggeration of the German, which is simply, *but that he stood immovable in his faith amid all tempests* (*sondern unerschutterlich im Glauben stand in allen sturmen*). In the next sentence, "*its strength*," should be either *itself* or *its existence* (*sich bewahren*). So, too, in the next sentence, "*his* purposes to serve" should read *his purposes respecting* (*seine zwecke in*).

NOTE TO THE FIFTH EDITION.—Since the above was written Sheldon & Company have published a carefully corrected re-print of the English Translation of Olshausen on the New Testament, in six octavo volumes, under the supervision of Rev. Dr. Kendrick.

* Recent critical Biblical commentators generally agree in attributing to the Baptist such a doubt as has been described. So do Meyer, De Wette, Olshausen, Neander (*Life of Jesus*, § 41. 3.), etc.

Messiah, no one who is unprejudiced can hesitate to admit. We must, therefore, reject that supposition as arbitrary and as opposed to the New Testament representation,—which, however, is among one class of theologians the most widely received (by Calvin, Beza, Grotius, and, after them, by Hammond, Doddridge, Bloomfield, etc.),—according to which John did not send to inquire for his own sake but on account of his disciples, in order that he might by this mission and question remove the doubts of those who did not admit the dignity of Jesus, and convict them of their error. But, even if we do not lay any stress upon the fact that not the slightest indication of such a relation is found in our narrative, but that, on the contrary, all that is said and done is represented as proceeding from or as referring to John in person, of what advantage, we may ask, could such an embassy have been? Would the disciples of John have trusted to the witness of a man in favor of himself, against whom they had previously taken offence and of whose purity and truthfulness they could not have been as firmly convinced as was John himself, as much and even more than they trusted in the testimony of their master? It is altogether improbable. Would not John have rather confirmed them in their doubts, if he sent them to Jesus instead of himself opposing their error with his whole power and authority?

There is another supposition, however, which is not so inconsistent with the narrative: it is that of those (Lightfoot, Kuinoel, Hasse, Leopold, Alford, etc.), who think that John intended by this question to induce Jesus to hasten the establishment of his kingdom. If he indeed still cherished the hope that Jesus would found an earthly kingdom, and this hope could not as yet have altogether departed from him, this was, no doubt, a secondary intention of the mission; but its chief object must still have been the longing which he felt to obtain peace and quiet from the mournful distraction which reigned within his soul. Nothing, however, is gained by such a supposition; for it is by no means probable that John, if his faith had remained unshaken, should have desired Jesus to adopt any other mode of procedure in his Messianic ministry than that which he himself pleased to put into operation. Discontentment and doubt must have lain at the very foundation of such a wish on the part of the Baptist.

The two ambassadors of John found Christ engaged in works of healing and in benevolent actions of every kind: the sick and the diseased had, as was their custom, crowded around him from every side, in order to obtain from him relief from their infirmities (Luke 7: 21.). Jesus, without allowing the messengers to interrupt him in his employment, without entering into any express defence or explanation of his Messianic dignity, contents himself with merely pointing them to what they saw performed before their eyes, to his wonder-working and bliss-bestowing ministry. Of this they were to carry back intelligence unto John; for it was in truth the most convincing and the most palpable proof that he was the expected Messiah, the Son of God. "Go your way", said he, "and tell John what things ye have seen and heard; how that the blind see, the lame walk, the lepers are cleansed, the deaf hear, the dead are raised, to the poor the gospel is preached"; and by this answer, cited almost in the words of Is. 35: 5. 6, and 61: 2., he afforded to John a new proof that in him the Messianic prophecies of the Old Testament had been actually accomplished. The latter part of it was intended by Jesus to give to the messengers a glance at the inward spiritual work which he performed upon the hearts of men, while his miracles placed before their eyes the external power which he was wont to call to his aid.

Objection has been made by some to the expression "*the dead are raised*", since, as it is alleged, these disciples of John had not themselves seen this miracle, and because in general the assertion sounds somewhat hyperbolical, since only one resurrection, that of the son of the widow of Nain, had as yet occurred. It must be remembered, however, that the narrative does not oblige us to suppose that all the miracles mentioned were wrought in the actual presence of John's messengers; and, besides this, that Christ did not intend to limit himself to these single proofs of his power, but purposed to call their attention in a general way to his superhuman endowments, of which they saw particular instances in the single actions which they then witnessed him perform. And it must be recollected, furthermore, that he did not mean to restrict the application of these words to the mere healing of external imperfections, but to refer them also,—a reference, however, which, it must be confessed, must have been difficult at that time for the disciples of John to understand,—to the healing of internal infirmities, of inward spiritual dumbness and blindness, of spiritual leprosy, etc.; and that, therefore, he purposed, by using the expression "the dead are raised",—which, if literally and outwardly applied, does not, it must be admitted, seem altogether suitable,—to lead them to search out in these words for some deeper meaning than appeared upon their face, viz., the resurrection of those that were spiritually dead; and to this application of the words,—since he could not suppose that they would without some hint comprehend their meaning,—he directed their special attention by subjoining, "and to the poor the gospel is preached",—an expression which refers here, as it does often and naturally elsewhere, not merely to the poor in worldly goods, but in a far higher sense, to the spiritually poor.

A word or two more Jesus adds, adapted especially to the mournful condition of the Baptist, and intended to give to him, for his consolation and for a warning, a direction as to the ideas which he was for the future to entertain of the Messiah, and as to what was to be the relation which John should sustain towards him: "And blessed is he, whosoever shall not be offended in me." In this he indicates to the Baptist how immeasurably higher his career was to be than that which was expected of him by John and all his contemporaries; that John, therefore, should look on quietly and patiently, and see whither he directed his course; and that, if his conduct seemed to come into conflict with human expectations and conceptions, he should not on that account be offended, but must wait quietly and humbly, and look for the end.

Returning this answer, which contains not a word too much and not one too little, Jesus dismissed the ambassadors, that they might return to John. He himself, however, turns to the people that were standing around him, who might take offence at this implied doubt on the part of the Baptist whom they had hitherto honored as a prophet; becomes his mediator and advocate, and exhibits him in all his worth and significance to their view. He inquires of them what ideas they entertained relative to John, when, at an earlier period, they went forth so zealously to him in the wilderness; whether they had esteemed him a trembling reed, easily shaken by the wind, so that surrendering himself readily to every impression, he would at one time testify what at another time he doubted.

according to his varying circumstances; a man who would adapt himself to the caprices of the people and perform the work of his ministry according to their changeful wishes. Such an impression the conduct and character of the Baptist could not have made upon them, since he by no means allowed himself to be made the plaything of the people's caprices. To amuse themselves with him in this manner, therefore, could not, when they went to him, have been their expectation.—Why, then, had they gone?—Just as little could it have been with the hope of delighting themselves with viewing the pomp and splendor with which he was surrounded; for pomp and luxury they could not have expected to find in one who was an inhabitant of the desert; to behold such an exhibition, it was needful to go to the palaces of kings. They must, consequently, have been excited to their conduct by something else.—They went out, says Jesus, speaking the mind of the Jews, to see a prophet; for such they esteemed the Baptist. They had, then, gone out with reason to behold and to hear him; for he is indeed a prophet, and even more than a prophet: he is the messenger of the Lord, the forerunner of the Messiah who has been announced by Malachi, and, consequently, the greatest of all mortals who stand without the heavenly kingdom which has been introduced by Christ. This divine kingdom has now in truth appeared and been founded, the way having been first prepared by John; so that since his time all men have diligently sought it and endeavor with an eagerness allied to violence (cp. Luke 16: 16.) to make it theirs; and he who zealously seeks after it and spares nothing, who allows himself to be terrified from his purpose by nothing, who presses eagerly forward in spite of all hindrances, he actually makes it his own by means of living faith in Christ

John, then, who has prepared the way for and hastened the introduction of the kingdom of heaven, is in a certain sense the prophet Elias, of whom it has been said that he shall make ready the way and introduce the reign of the Messiah ; but notwithstanding this he stands yet without the heavenly kingdom, and is, notwithstanding his high dignity and honor, less than the least (or, more correctly, since the comparative is used in the original, the relatively small) of those who are actually citizens of this divine kingdom, which is elevated high above every phase of Judaism and above all human institutions. He as yet neither knew the full divinity, the living power and spiritual operation of the new kingdom, nor had he yet experienced himself the blessings which he had been instrumental in bringing to others ; though he stood nearer to the kingdom than any other man, and had in person beheld in close proximity what all the members of the old covenant had hoped for and expected only from afar.

To this explanation of Christ's respecting the relative position of the Baptist, " he that is least [comparatively *little*] in the kingdom of God, is greater than he," as we find it in Matt. 11 : 11., Luke makes an addition (7 : 29, 30.) in which reproach is cast upon the Pharisees and lawyers because they, —that is, the majority of them, for individuals among them had acted differently,—had not in their proud self-righteousness received the baptism of John, whilst the people and the publicans, on the contrary, had given honor to God, confessed their sins, and submitted to the ordinance. This reproachful language is subjoined to the representation which Christ gives of the high dignity of John, and forms a very excellent connection with what precedes : one is, therefore, doubtful which words stand as in the original discourse when delivered by

Christ, those of Matthew or those of Luke. It is probable, however, judging from the style of the narration given by Matthew, who generally states events in connection rather according to the nature of their subject-matter than according to their chronological relations to each other, that Luke has preserved here the original form; and, besides this, the connection with what follows is easier in Luke than in Matthew

Christ proceeds in Matt. 11 : 16. ff. and Luke 7 : 31. ff with the reproof which he had already begun in Luke against that degenerate race. The connection of this part of Matthew's narrative with what goes before, must be conceived somehow in this way: although the dignity of the Baptist is so great, although he can in a certain sense be called Elias, yet had the greater number of the people continued indifferent to him or even opposed him, because all had not gone in accordance with their wishes; but, on the contrary, he that prepared the way as well as he that founded the kingdom of heaven had showed himself to be different and had acted differently from what they had expected. Just as little children playing with their companions in the market become vexed with them, if they do not copy after what they have set before them for imitation, so had they regarded John and Jesus as such little children, looked upon them as their equals, and as persons who should dance to their music, who should be serious and mournful whenever they wished them to be so, but joyful and gay whenever their minds should be thus inclined. When, therefore, John came, he was too rigid and strict to suit their wishes; when Christ himself appeared, they thought that his mode of life was not sufficiently severe, and found fault at his going into the company of publicans and sinners. Instead of recognizing the wisdom of these persons who had been inspired by God, they had hoped and expected to find their own folly reflected back in them, and had called their wisdom foolishness; "but," adds Jesus, by way of consolation to the weak, but of warning to the haughty and foolish, "Wisdom is justified of her children", —by those who have surrendered themselves to her to be led by her as she will, and who wisely follow the paths in which she treads.

This discourse of Jesus which has just been examined (Matt. 11 : 7–19, and Luke 7 : 24–35.) is highly important as to its bearing upon the question, what relation did John the Baptist sustain to Christianity; and by implication, upon the still more important question, what is the relation of the Old Testament to the New Testament dispensation. Indeed, both these points may be considered as determined, either directly or inferentially, by the representation which we have just examined. In what way they are determined, Neander (*Life of Jesus*, § 135.) gives us a lucid exhibition. With regard to the relation of John to Christianity he says: "He was behind Christianity, because he was yet prejudiced by his conception of the theocracy as external; because he did not clearly know that the Messiah was to found his kingdom by *sufferings*, and not by miraculously triumphing over his foes; because he did not conceive that this kingdom was to show itself from the first, not in visible appearing, but as a divine power, to develop itself spiritually from within outward, and thus gradually to overcome and take possession of the world. The least among those who understand the nature and process of development of the divine kingdom, in connection with Christ's redemption, is in this respect greater than the Baptist, who stood upon the dividing line of the two spiritual eras. But John was above the prophets (and Christ so declared), because he conceived of the Messiah and his kingdom in a higher and more spiritual sense than they had done, and because he directly pointed men to Christ, and recognized him as the manifested Messiah."

Not less satisfactorily does the same vigorous writer portray the relation here represented, inferentially, as existing between the Old Testament dispensation in general and Christianity: "The fact that Christ places the Baptist *above* the prophets, who were the very culminating-point of the Old Covenant, and yet so far *below* the members of the new development of the kingdom, exhibits in the most striking way possible his view of the distance between the Old preparatory Testament and the New. The authority of Christ himself, therefore, is contradicted by those who expect to find the truth revealed by *him*, already developed in the Old Testament. If in *John* we are to distinguish the fundamental truth which he held, and which pointed to the New Testament, from the limited and sensuous form in which he held it, much more, according to *Christ's* words are we bound to do this in the Old Testament generally, and in its Messianic elements especially. Following this intimation, we must in studying the prophets, discriminate the historical from the ideal sense, the conscious from the unconscious prophecies."

CHAPTER III.

John's Death.—Glance at his Character and his Importance for the Development of the Kingdom of God.

What now was the impression which the answer of Christ made upon the imprisoned Baptist? If he put full confidence in the reply of the Redeemer, he could not help discovering that he was not called to comprehend, and perhaps was not capable of understanding him altogether; and the words "blessed is he, whosoever shall not be offended in me" must have induced him to resign himself fully to the incomprehensible way of God, and to determine to wait quietly until he saw the issue of what was then occurring. And, besides this, the reference which Christ had made to his miraculous works and to the preaching of the gospel, and the comparison of these events with the Messianic prophecies made by John himself, must have convinced the Baptist that Jesus was really conducting his ministry in accordance with the Old Testament announcements, that he must of necessity be the Messiah, and that, therefore, the prophecies of the Old Testament, which represent him as appearing in the character of a royal earthly monarch, must have some other sense, must be understood in some other way than he had hitherto been accustomed to suppose. In this way his belief in Christ was confirmed and reëstablished; and, difficult as it must have been at this time for him to resign his old expectations, which had become rooted in his mind from having attended him during all his life, we have yet reason to believe respecting him, the enlightened prophet and messenger of God, that his humility and submission to the divine will enabled him here, as in general before, to struggle out from his difficulties and doubts, and to arrive at the conception of the truth as it is in Jesus. Had his life been prolonged, and had he again obtained his liberty, he would probably have become an attendant scholar and disciple of Christ, and have entered himself into the kingdom of God; but God required not this highest act of self-denial at his hands. He was called as an Old Testament prophet; and was to afford a distinctive image of such in his whole life and character, a whole complete and perfect in himself: on this account was he called away from the world just as the conviction had become established in his mind that the Messianic kingdom must be something different in its nature from that which he had hitherto expected and imagined. His death, then, as well as his imprisonment was a kindness conferred upon him, a trial which came to an end just at the proper time.

We have already, in speaking of the imprisonment of the Baptist, exhibited the relation of the two narratives of Matthew and Mark to each other. Only these same two evangelists relate to us the history of his execution: Luke refers to the matter as to something known (9 : 9.), whilst in 3 : 19. 20. he merely speaks of the imprisonment. Mark gives a fuller account of the death of John than Matthew, as he does also of the imprisonment; but the latter evangelist entirely agrees with the former in the leading outlines of his narrative (cp. Matt. 14 : 6. ff., Mark 6 : 21. ff.).

Herodias, who thirsted to put the hated Baptist to death, sought out a good opportunity for inducing her husband, who, both on account of the people and because his feelings were at times opposed to the step, still hesitated to use harsher measures towards John, to give the order for his execution. She instructed Salome, her daughter by her first marriage with Philip, how to captivate the heart of her step-father by means of immodest and wanton dancing assisted by the power of her youth and beauty, in order that she might make use of her as a means for procuring the death of John ; and, accordingly, at a great feast which the prince gave on his birth-day to the nobles of his kingdom, she caused her daughter, practised in all the arts of the wanton and shameless dance by which the lustful passions of men may be aroused, to entertain and to delight the king and his guests with her performances. She succeeded in attaining her object. Inflamed by passion, Antipas was induced to make a promise of which he was soon, but too late, to repent : he swore to Salome to give to her whatever she should request of him, should it even be the half of his kingdom. She on her part, instructed it is probable by her mother, hastened to her to receive her further commands. Filled with joy at this successful issue of her plans, Herodias directed her to demand the head of John the Baptist : immediately, therefore, Salome preferred this petition to the king, and he, not wishing to appear false to his oath before his guests, yielded to her request, and gave the order for his execution. Thus fell by the hands of the executioner this last distinguished prophet of the old covenant, after having engaged in his public ministry scarcely the space of one year and having been confined in prison a few months, a sacrifice to his candor and determined love of right, through the revengeful hate of a sensual and ambitious woman. The weak-minded prince, in order to cover over and to make some atonement for his crime, permitted the disciples of the Baptist to confer an honorable burial upon the corpse of their master; but he could no more recall the dead to life, though, perhaps, he would afterwards have cheerfully done so, had he been able.

Such was the end of him who according to the testimony of Christ was the greatest of all those who belonged to the old covenant. Even if this expression of our Lord's refers immediately to the office of the Baptist and to his position in close proximity to the kingdom of God which had now made its appearance in the world, yet it can nevertheless be also said of him with entire truthfulness, that he was one of the greatest of the pious worthies of the Old Testament in respect to his character and his conduct. We find, indeed, in the Old Testament not many examples of such purity of mind, of such faithfulness in the fulfillment of a calling, of such firmness in opposing the hostile spirit of the times, and of such humility and such consciousness of a subordinate rank as we have displayed in John the Baptist. We have seen that he practised from his earliest youth the greatest self-denial, and this he exhibited, in accordance with the Old Testament stand-point, in the most rigid ascetic practices. For this purpose he fled into the wilderness away from the sinful converse of the world; he renounced all that is accustomed to entice men and to lead them away into sinful indulgence; he sought to control the temptation of the flesh by the most rigid abstinence, by ascetic practices and mortifications of every kind. To live only in God and with God, and to perform his commands with the utmost diligence and faithfulness, were the objects of his earnest strivings.

And yet, notwithstanding all this, John was very far from esteeming himself perfect; he did not, as was the case among the Pharisees, and ever has been among most men who have striven to attain to a pure moral conduct, estimate his virtues so highly as to suppose that he was now pure in the sight of God, and to imagine that he needed nothing more in order to make him a partaker of eternal life. Here it was that he showed his true greatness ; for, notwithstanding all his purity, he ever kept alive within him a sense of his unworthiness and of his sinfulness, so that he could utter from his heart the words, "I have need to be baptized of thee, and comest thou to me ?", and could feel himself so far inferior in dignity to his great successor as to declare publicly that he was not worthy to undo the latchet of his sandals. This honest, upright sense of his unworthiness, this humility worthy of all admiration, he carried along with him throughout his whole life ; he, the Baptist, who stood so high in the estimation of the people as to be supposed by them to be the Messiah, to whom it would have been an easy matter to place himself at the head of a great party and to strive for worldly honor, or to announce himself as the theocratic king who was called to reëstablish the Jewish nation in its former splendor and dominions, he who was continually urged by his own disciples to vindicate the superiority of his rank to that of him who first received testimony in his favor from John himself, and had been accredited by him in the office which he assumed, declared nevertheless with calm firmness and confidence, "I am not the Christ . . . . I must decrease, but he must increase"; and not for a single moment do we see him varying from his proper position respecting the manner in which, in spite of all the temptations offered by his disciples and the people to the contrary, he was conscious that it behooved him to conduct himself for the correct discharge and fulfillment of his heavenly calling.—This humility has appeared to some so improbable that they have on this very account objected to the credibility of our narrative; and there is no doubt that a self-seeking disposition, if it had existed in John, could not have exhibited such entire freedom from ambition and assumption of every kind. We must, therefore, only feel the more rejoiced that we are able to point out in biblical history, and we might even say in the history of Christianity an example of modesty so distinguished, and so worthy to be cited and imitated in every age.

"It was an excellent sweetness of religion," says one of the most pious, and perhaps the most eloquent, of English divines,* "that had entirely possessed the soul of the Baptist, that in so great a reputation of sanctity, so mighty concourse of people, such great multitudes of disciples and confidents, and such throngs of admirers, he was humble without mixture of vanity, and confirmed in his temper and piety against the strength of the most impetuous temptation. And he was tried to some purpose: for when he was tempted to confess himself to be the Christ, he refused it; or to be Elias, or to be accounted 'that prophet', he refused all such great appellations, and confessed himself only to be a *voice*, the lowest of entities, whose being depends upon the speaker, just as himself did upon the pleasure of God; receiving form, and publication, and employment, wholly by the will of his Lord, in order to the manifestation of the Word Eternal."—Humility was the prominent trait in the character of the stern and rigid Baptist. Though exalted in privileges and in position far above the prophets of the Old Testament, he forgot not, at any time, that he was subordinate to the Messiah and that he was commissioned only

* Jeremy Taylor, *Life of Christ* (written in 1648), Sect. viii. 9.; a work which contains many rich thoughts, warmly and eloquently expressed.

"to prepare the way" for the entrance of that kingdom which "the Christ" was to establish upon the earth. Thus, without wavering in his humility, he fulfilled his mission as the Forerunner of the Anointed of the Lord.

As the Baptist conducted himself modestly and discreetly with regard to his own personal conduct, so he opposed with determination and with firmness the corruption of his times. There was no person, however high and mighty, there was no prejudice, however universal and firmly strengthened, that he hesitated to attack, when necessary, with the severest reprobation; and this regardless of the consequences to himself. The fear of man he knew not. Herod as well as the Pharisees felt alike the sharpness of his reproof; here did he prove himself another Elias indeed, opposing himself, in the power of his word, and with the conciousness of the approval and assistance of God, to the transgression of the king, and announcing to him the divine punishment that was due to his crime. The more rigid he was towards himself, the less contradiction were the people able to discover between his conduct and his preaching, and with the more propriety could he require from those who flocked to him the most scrupulous repentance. He had experienced in his own person what a man is able to do, if he only strive in earnest, and therefore he was not contented with hearing the stale remark, that what he preached was easier said than done.—He knew well, moreover, how to discriminate between the different capacities and necessities of the people; and his wisdom is evinced in particular by the fact that he did not enjoin upon all ascetic practices similar to those to which he himself had conformed; that he did not require of them to renounce as he had done, all intercourse with the world; but showed unto each individual, according to his peculiar business or profession, the point from which he must commence undertaking a change in himself, in order to proceed working from that point until he had produced an alteration in his disposition, and, without renouncing his previous relations, his condition, or his employment, to exhibit unto all men, in these very relations of life and in these his appropriate circumstances, the proof of a mind and heart truly repentant.

So lived and so labored the man who was called to display before the eyes of a corrupt people and before the world, once more in all its purity and clearness, the brilliancy of the Old Testament dispensation, and to give proof in his own person of the divine power of the law and of the blessings produced by a reliance on the divine promises ; but at the same time to show the inadequateness of the Old Testament dispensation to afford a true contentment of heart which shall still all uneasiness and all desire, and assure to us peace and joy in life and in death.—The Forerunner was indeed "a burning and a shining light"; and among all the Old Testament worthies who had hitherto existed, there had not, according to the testimony of Christ, "risen a greater prophet than John the Baptist." And yet, according to the same infallible witness, "he that is least in the kingdom of heaven is greater than he." The "kingdom of heaven" here spoken of, is not, of course, the state of future and eternal felicity; for to this, no doubt, the Baptist is as much entitled as any personal disciple of the Saviour's, and will enjoy it in as full fruition as any one who, after his day, became a follower of the meek and lowly Jesus. No other Old Testament prophet was superior to John in outward holiness ; no other was more free from internal tendencies to sin ; no other kept himself more "unspotted from the world"; none had a clearer insight into the fundamental principles of the Messianic dispensation; while none had so immediate an agency as he in ushering in the light of the Gospel upon a benighted and ignorant world. He was the last and the highest of the Old Testament prophets; and his reward in the future world will be at least as glorious and as sure as theirs for all eternity.

Yet, in one sense, John was not, any more than Isaiah or Daniel, a member of "the kingdom of heaven"; that is, of the "kingdom" in its *earthly* manifestation,—the outward and visible Church of Christ. Before that kingdom had been completely established, John had been executed in prison, and, though it was indeed *founded* before his death, the Baptist had never been personally called into its membership. Some of his disciples had; but he himself still stood without, fulfilling his appropriate mission. Before the glorious work of redemption had been finished by the atonement, and before our Lord by his death, resurrection and ascension, and by the gift of the Holy Spirit, had perfected his Church, and established it in its full grandeur, the Baptist had gone to his everlasting reward.

Personally, therefore, the Forerunner was not a member of the new spiritual community, the earthly "kingdom of heaven", founded by Christ. In some particulars, then, he who spoke so authoritatively to the people, and promised to them, on repentance, forgiveness of their sins, himself needed elements essential to the Christian character in its completeness; needed to partake of the baptism of the Holy Spirit; and, in some respects, to receive enlightenment from the God of all wisdom. It was not consistent with his character and office, that he should be more perfect. It was his duty to point others to the door of "the kingdom of God"; not, however, to enter himself, and partake of its earthly blessings. He had been sent to prepare the way; to lead the bridegroom to the bride, to introduce the Saviour to his Church; and this responsible calling he fulfilled with a faithfulness worthy of all admiration.

Other prophets of the Old Testament dispensation had seen the day of Christ "afar off", and were glad; the Baptist saw it close "at hand", and prepared the people for its introduction. He had himself, as well as his Master, the Messiah, been made the subject of prophetic prediction, some four hundred years before his appearance; his birth was announced to his father by a special messenger from heaven; his mother was related by ties of blood to the mother of the Messiah: he prepared the way for the introduction into the world of "the kingdom of heaven", and made ready a people anxious for its reception: he baptized those who believed his message, and professed themselves repentant of their sins; he baptized the Son of God himself, separating him as holy from the world, and consecrating him to his theocratic reign; and then, bore witness to him as the Messiah announced by the Prophets. Such distinctions no other Old Testament worthy enjoyed; and well was John entitled to be called by his father in his song of praise, "*the prophet of the Highest.*"

The labors of the Forerunner were of the highest importance to the proper introduction and reception among the people of "the kingdom of God." The Jewish nation needed to be prepared for its appearance and establishment among them and in the world. They entertained very erroneous notions of the character and object of the "heavenly kingdom" which was about to be founded upon earth; and these had to be corrected, in whole or in part, before the reign of heaven could commence. To correct these errors, and "to make ready a people prepared for the Lord," not in profession merely but in heart, was the intent of the mission of John, the son of Zacharias and Elisabeth.—"As the Baptist, while he was in the wilderness", says Bishop Taylor (*Life of Christ*, § 8. 4.), "became the pattern of solitary and contemplative life, a school of virtue and example of sanctity and singular austerity; so at his emigration from the places of his retirement, he seemed, what indeed he was, a rare and excellent personage: and the wonders which were great at his birth, the prediction of his conception by an angel, which never had before happened but in the persons of Isaac and Samson; the contempt of the world which he bore about him; his mortified countenance and deportment; his austere and eremitical life; his vehement spirit and excellent zeal in preaching, created so great opinions of him among the people that 'all held him for a prophet' in his office, for a heavenly person in his own particular, and a rare example of sanctity and holy life to all others: and all this being made solemn and ceremonious by his baptism, he prevailed so, that he made excellent and apt preparations for the Lord's appearing; for there went out to him Jerusalem, and all Judea, and all the region round about Jordan, and were baptized of him, confessing their sins."

Had it not been for the great excitement which John produced among the nation by his powerful and effective preaching, the Son of God, whose habit it was to work quietly and in stillness, would not have secured at the beginning of his ministry so great a concourse of attendants from among the people, which, uncertain and vacillating though it certainly was, contributed essentially to the furtherance of the grand design of his labors. Had it not been for the repeated monitions of the Baptist, respecting repentance, had it not been for the explanation which he gave that only he whose heart was just could possibly find entrance into the kingdom of heaven, Christ would have had to combat yet more violent prejudices than he actually encountered in favor of the mere externality of the reign of the Messiah. Without his pointed testimony in favor of Jesus, without his express reference of his disciples to his person and dignity, such true and susceptible hearts would not so readily have surrendered themselves without reserve to Christ, and they would not have been prepared from the commencement to conceive and understand the true worth of the Redeemer, and to form themselves, by the proper employment of his society, his example and his words, to be the pillars of his Church. To those who looked for the Messiah he was a leader and a guiding star which pointed them to the longed-for Saviour; to the self-righteous and the confident, he was a sword which severed the slender cable of their self-righteousness and confidence; the sleeping he awoke and the inactive he aroused from their listlessness, summoning them to a life in accordance with the will of the Lord and to a line of conduct suited to an expectation of the speedy appearance of the Messiah; to the haughty and obdurate he was a hammer and a stone which cast them down with crushing violence from their high estate and hurled them to the earth. Thus did he prepare the way of the Lord, and thus make all things ready, that he might lead him to a union with his Church, while he, the friend of the bridegroom, stood apart without, and found a sufficient reward in the pleasure which he experienced in the joy of the bridegroom.

www.ingramcontent.com/pod-product-compliance
Lightning Source LLC
LaVergne TN
LVHW010243110826
845151LV00004B/1377

* 9 7 8 1 4 2 5 5 2 4 0 3 6 *